NEIL HEGARTY is the author of *Story of Ireland*, a history of Ireland that accompanied the BBC series, and *Dublin: A View from the Ground*. His short fiction, essays and journalism have been published widely; and he has written radio documentaries on the Irish diaspora in Argentina and Newfoundland.

BRIAN HILL is an award-winning director of both drama and documentary. His films have been shown by all major UK broadcasters and in many other countries around the world. He has been nominated seven times for BAFTA awards and won three of them. For the last twenty years he has been managing director of Century Films, one of the UK's leading independent production companies.

JOSEPH BULLMAN is a documentary writer and director. His films include the Bafta nominated *The Man Who Bought Mustique*, the Bafta nominated, Grierson winning *The Seven Sins of England*. He co-created and directed two episodes of *The Secret History of Our Streets*, nominated for seven television awards, and winner the Royal Television Society Best History Series Award.

The Secret History of Our Streets

A STORY OF LONDON

JOSEPH BULLMAN,
NEIL HEGARTY AND BRIAN HILL

BBC
BOOKS

First published in 2012 to accompany the television series entitled *The Secret History of Our Streets*, produced by Century Films Ltd and Halcyons Heart Films Ltd and first broadcast on BBC2 in 2012. This paperback edition published 2013.

Executive Producer: Simon Ford
Series Producer: Katie Bailiff
Commissioning Executive for the BBC: Emma Willis

1 3 5 7 9 10 8 6 4 2

Published in 2013 by BBC Books, an imprint of Ebury Publishing.
A Random House Group Company.

Main text by Joseph Bullman, Neil Hegarty and Brian Hill

The Random House Group Limited Reg. No. 954009

Addresses for companies within the Random House Group can be found at
www.randomhouse.co.uk

A CIP catalogue record for this book is available from the British Library.

ISBN: 978 1 849 90451 3

The Random House Group Limited supports the Forest Stewardship Council® (FSC®), the leading international forest-certification organisation. Our books carrying the FSC label are printed on FSC®-certified paper. FSC is the only forest-certification scheme supported by the leading environmental organisations, including Greenpeace. Our paper procurement policy can be found at www.randomhouse.co.uk/environment

Commissioning editor: Albert DePetrillo
Project editors: Caroline McArthur and Joe Cottington
Copy editor: Don Murray
Designer: Seagull Design
Production: Phil Spencer

Printed and bound by CPI Group (UK) Ltd, Croydon, CR0 4YY

To buy books by your favourite authors and register for offers visit www.randomhouse.co.uk

CONTENTS

Introduction
THE STREETS
OF LONDON

Nearly forty years of age, tall, abnormally thin, garments hanging as if on pegs, the complexion of a consumptive girl, and the slight stoop of the sedentary worker, a prominent aquiline nose, with moustache and pointed beard barely hiding a noticeable Adam's apple, the whole countenance dominated by a finely-moulded brow and large, observant grey eyes [...] an attractive but distinctly queer figure of a man.

So ran a description, penned in 1880, of a wealthy English industrialist named Charles Booth who would presently set out on an extraordinary 17-year quest. His singularly ambitious objectives were to chart, record and understand the true nature of London – at this point, the largest and most economically and culturally powerful city in the world – and to inquire into the nature of the lives and occupations of its inhabitants. The result of these labours would be Booth's extremely influential 17-volume *Life and Labour of the People in London*, published between 1889 and 1903.

The labours of Booth were characterized by a vast sense of scale and by an ambition to understand and map the world around him. They were of a piece with Victorian culture in general: as reflective of the *Zeitgeist* as Isambard Kingdom Brunel's spectacular railway and maritime works and Joseph Bazalgette's civil engineering projects. Britain in the 1880s was at the pinnacle of its global power and reach: its empire was approaching its zenith and the world's financial system turned on decisions made in London. Politicians and colonial administrators had created a global commodities market centred on Britain too: the raw materials of the world flowed into British ports to be turned into manufactured goods and exported out to the world. The nation was rich – and London, as its commercial and political heartbeat, was richest of all. And yet not all was well – for, even at this time of wealth and power, a sense of foreboding was developing.

This was in part the result of the changing nature of this ostensibly munificent world. For one thing, the structures that had been established to service the country's economic and military supremacy were being threatened increasingly by the growing economic might of Germany and the United States. In addition, in the 1870s Britain had suffered a harsh recession:

agricultural labourers left the fields and crowded into the cities, where there were fewer and fewer jobs available; immigration from Ireland and further afield had increased markedly – and again, the industrial cities were a favourite destination for these newcomers. The orthodoxy of *laissez-faire* economics, which had seemed to serve Britain so well for so long, began to be examined as never before.

On a philosophical level, the country's prosperity – or rather, the ways in which it had generated its wealth and the means by which it was being sustained – was also being questioned by elements within the very social class which had benefitted most from it. Liberal, middle-class Britain paused and took stock of its world. There had always been voices, of course, which dissented from this culture's image of itself: novelists such as Charles Dickens and Elizabeth Gaskell had had much to say, in decades past, of the social underbelly; artists such as Luke Fildes painted vivid scenes of deprivation and poverty for the education of the Victorian middle classes; and the existence of such journals as the *Graphic* and the *Pall Mall Gazette* demonstrated that there was a consistent appetite for tough, hard-hitting descriptions of contemporary society. The lives of London's poorest residents formed a particular focus of attention – although these same lives tended to be observed from a discreet distance. And there were dangers implicit in such reportage, not least in the tendency of such journalists to describe the London working class as one homogeneous group, and in terms which stripped its members of any apparent control or ability to alter their dire living and economic situations.

Commentary, however, also began to assume a tone of sharp, overt protest. This took a variety of forms: socialist writers and artists such as William Morris took umbrage at what he perceived to be the desecration of the cities and countryside alike in the name of industrial gain, and at the fouling of workers' lives and dignity in the name of progress. Trade union membership swelled and labour strikes became more frequent, more prolonged and more violent. A sense of insurrection in the country – or in quarters of it – entered the political mainstream, as factions in both the Liberal and Conservative parties groped towards a more interventionist economic model, one that contained the seeds of a future welfare state. A measure of local government was encouraged, state money was spent on education and on welfare, the franchise was extended and extended again.

The framework of a future democracy was being installed, in other words – but a sense of social distress was in place too, and it could not be easily swept away. And there was no consensus on the road that must now be taken: for every radical Liberal activist or One Nation Tory who could envisage a cautious expansion of welfare and of government spending, any number of others saw the road to hell opening up in this idea of greater state intervention. And yet others saw the world in overtly moral terms: they considered that the face of the country itself had become grimed, besmirched by years of excessive profits coupled with inattention to the physical needs – and to the souls, indeed – of the people as a whole.

* * *

Charles Booth was born in Liverpool in 1840, into a Liberal, nonconformist family. His parents were representative of the independent-minded, canny, prosperous and commercial caste who dominated the economic life of the industrial cities of northern England – and Booth soon demonstrated the same acumen: in the 1860s, he established with his brother a shipping company, plying the trade routes between Britain and North America; soon, the Booth brothers became extremely rich. In 1872 – a year after his marriage to Mary Macauley, a niece of the eminent Liberal historian Thomas Babington Macaulcy – Booth suffered a breakdown from overwork: as well as running a business, he had thrown himself into a range of social causes. It was simply too much. Booth pulled back for some years, watching politics from the sidelines. Early in the 1880s, however, he removed to London – and here he witnessed the world in its entirety: wealth, careful respectability and terrifying poverty. For this was, as he saw it, a metropolis consisting of several cities meshed tightly together, yet for the most part ignorant of one another. The squares and boulevards of Mayfair and St James's had as little in common with the terraces of comfortable Victorian middle-class housing that had sprouted north and south of the city in the course of the nineteenth century as they did with the slums of Shoreditch in east London and Notting Dale on the city's western skirts. To an inquiring mind, this was a conundrum – and Booth set out to educate himself on the absorbing and horrifying matter of London, its worlds, its classes and its myriad lives.

'Fascinating', wrote Mary Booth's cousin (and Booth's own assistant) Beatrice Potter years later, 'was his unself-conscious manner and eager curiosity to know what you thought and why you thought it; what you know and how you had learnt it.' Booth sought to listen to the ferment of London: to the socialist and radical thinkers who had taken as their cause the frightful poverty that existed in the East End and the city's docklands; and to more moderate figures who believed in a gradual education of the working classes into an alleviation of their situation. This exercise was in spite of his own firmly un-socialist views; and in spite too of his conviction that neither socialism nor social philanthropy held the key to social improvement. Most of all, Booth simply disbelieved the papers he read, the people with whom he spoke, the journals which painted such vividly bleak portraits of life in contemporary London. He could not accept the claims made about the degree of social deprivation that prevailed in London – and in particular, the startling statement made by M. H. Hyndman, chairman of the Marxist Socialist Democratic Federation, that 25% of all Londoners lived in poverty. There was nothing else for it but to begin his own investigation: to see for himself the nature of life in London; to measure the breadth and depth of the poverty that existed – and to suggest the ways in which it might be banished.

There was only one way to draw up such a report: coolly and scientifically, using the latest statistical methods – and undertaken by pounding the streets. Booth was convinced that such a survey would demonstrate that the poverty of London was in fact less vast than had been generally supposed. He could not know that his inquiries, beginning in the spring of 1886, would expose the fact that human need and deprivation were even greater and more firmly rooted than he could have imagined.

* * *

Booth at first had difficulty in designing and consolidating his method. It proved difficult, for one thing, to recruit and then to retain assistants – who tended to step back once the daunting scale of the survey was revealed to them. Then, a chance examination of the School Board records provided the entry he needed into London's statistical underbelly. The school board's representatives, Booth discovered, visited the households of London to gather information on future pupils: most of them 'have been working in the same district for several years, and thus have an extensive knowledge of the people'. This was exactly what Booth needed too – and these records, together with extant Poor Law statistics and police files, came to provide the foundation for his own survey. Of course, many individuals and families lay beyond the reach of school inspectors; here, the survey would be obliged to extrapolate. Booth himself devised the famous system that sorted London households into groups or Classes, each signalled by an individual colour. Black (A) signified the worst slum properties, inhabited by the 'vicious and semi-criminal' lowest class; dark blue (B) signified the very poor – and so on through light blue, purple, pink and red to yellow (H), signifying the wealthy servant-keeping upper classes. A second system classified the occupations of the individuals encountered by Booth and his assistants: it now became theoretically possible to plot each of these individuals on a graph according to their wage, job and apparent standard of living. A definition of what exactly constituted 'poverty' was his next job – and he decided that it lay within his bands C and D, the members of which could make shift to live, if they spent wisely, husbanded their resources well and had the added benefit of 'a good wife and a thrifty one' to help keep up appearances. Bands A and B were, therefore, below the poverty line: the members of these social groups could not hope ever to make ends meet. With his facts and methodology now clear, the process of information-gathering could begin.

Over the next three years, Booth and his team pored over the various records of the East End, and visited in person over 3,000 streets – and in 1889 the first volume of *Life and Labour* appeared. Booth's habitual discretion and delicacy – his assistants were forbidden from prying too closely into the lives they were investigating, forbidden from asking searching questions – was reflected in its pages: pseudonyms were given to individuals and streets alike. The research was written and phrased – or so Booth asserted – in such a way that it could not be accused of flights of fancy: he would not ascend the rhetorical heights of passion scaled by the journalists and socialists who had opened up the misery of the East End to the world. Rather, the simple facts could tell the story a good deal better – not to mention more honestly, as he told the Royal Statistical Society in 1888:

> I am indeed embarrassed by the mass of my material, and by my determination to make use of no fact to which I cannot give a quantitative value. The material for sensational stories lies plentifully in every book of our notes; but even if I had the skill to use my material in this way – that gift of my imagination which is called 'realistic' – I should not wish to use it here.

Yet it could not be said that Booth wrote his reports in a dusty, disinterested statistical style. Far from it: time and time again, his own opinions, conditioning and views of the world inform and direct his style. His moralizing anxieties about the poor, their deportment, their habits and failings are all clearly evident – and they undercut any sense of these 17 volumes as an exemplar of statistical analysis. His survey is therefore by no means authoritative – yet it is at the same time beguiling and highly attractive: a portrait of a city and a society at a particular phase in its development – and a reflection of that society's anxieties and issues, as filtered through a highly organized, highly intelligent and highly opinionated consciousness. Little wonder, then, that Booth's words have stood the test of time: for they consist of one man's compendium of a world, with its mores and its habits, that has vanished utterly.

The limitations of Booth's survey and methods, however, are readily apparent – not least in the form of his famous poverty maps, which have become instantly recognizable icons of *fin de siècle* British history. The maps encapsulate the extraordinary ambition of Booth's survey, setting out to impose a colour-coded visual order on a vast, seething city. But they stand too as emblems of a yawning gap between vision and reality – for Booth's statistical order could not be applied coolly to all of the neighbourhoods surveyed. The colour red inked onto a map of Deptford High Street meant, as we will see, something rather different from the colour red inked onto a map of Camberwell Grove: that is, his categories shifted confusingly in meaning according to context – a fact that in itself undercut the authority of his findings.

And there were other limitations and contradictions. For example, Booth may have cherished the ideal of statistical rigour – yet the behaviour of the people he and his assistants surveyed, including their look, their dress, their manner and the way in which they presented their homes, were deployed to ideological effect: again and again, the poor of London were portrayed in pathological terms, the reasons for their want and misery presented using the biological ideology fashionable – indeed, orthodox – at the time. The poor were poor because poverty literally ran with the blood in their veins: they made their environment dirty; and there was little or nothing to be done about such a situation than to clear such folk away, shift them from one part of London to another so that the cleared quarter of the city had a chance to cleanse and recover itself.

Yet Booth was more than capable of sensitive and penetrating engagement with the lives of these people – of descending from the rarified heights of physiognomic theory to explore the substance and material of human lives. This was especially the case in his earliest surveys, when he left his comfortable west London home at intervals to occupy lodgings in the East End – at first, the focus of his inquiries. This exchange was by no means disagreeable: he took pleasure in conversation and observation; in noting the street life and private lives to which he now had access; in admiring the household management skills of the average working-class married wife and mother; and in setting aside the fine dining of his home for the 'oatmeal porridge and thick bread and butter of his east London landladies'.

He was a *flâneur,* then, in the classic bourgeois style. Indeed, he was but one of a host of such *flâneurs* exploring late-Victorian London: George Gissing, for example, on his Grub Street; Robert Louis Stevenson, portraying a 'labyrinthine' city in thrall to Irish terrorists in his potboiler novel *The Dynamiter* (1885); and Henry James, who set *The Princess Casamassima* (1886) against a backdrop of anarchist violence in this 'huge, luxurious, wanton, wasteful city': each of these gentlemen took it upon themselves to pace the streets of what James called 'dreadfully delightful' London; and to absorb its manifold thrills and delicious horrors. And it is this force of observation – running alongside the wealth of empirical evidence presented in volume after volume and the visually arresting style of map after map – that help to account for the survey's lasting power. By setting out a version of London that might stimulate the eye and the imagination, Charles Booth sought to make sense of a city that at all times seemed to slip away from adequate comprehension.

As for his legacy: the significance of his survey could be measured within a matter of years of its conclusion in 1902–1903. Booth had not uncovered the *fact* of poverty in British society – but he had helped to define it, his notion of the 'poverty line' encapsulating in the public mind the shape and form of want and deprivation. While Booth was no social radical, then, his findings – the sheer volume and form of which could not possibly be ignored – provided a signal for change. The first of these reforms came in 1906, when the incoming Liberal administration of Henry Campbell-Bannerman began setting in place the changes – in the form of, among other measures, an expanded free education system, old-age pensions and national insurance – that laid the framework for the British welfare state. And so, while poverty and social distress did not vanish as a result of Booth's labours – not then and certainly not later – they became increasingly intolerable concepts to an increasing number of people. They became accepted as social evils and as collective issues – and Booth's survey can take some of the credit for this shift in public perception.

* * *

More than a century later, London is no longer the world's largest city – but it has retained its sense of enormity, with a further hundred years of narratives now compressed into its pounded streets and pavements. Much of the fabric of the city that Booth explored remains intact: or ostensibly intact, though changed by the accretions of war, prosperity, poverty, terrorism – by the endless accumulations of history. This book takes Booth's survey as its base note – but removes its vastness by settling on six streets, the histories of which in many ways represent the experience of London in the course of this intervening century.

Our streets are spread across inner London – from Camberwell, Holland Park and Islington to Shoreditch, Deptford and Bermondsey – and their dramatic histories have diverged widely. In west London, for example, the expensive pastel facades of Portland Road disguise a history of chronic poverty, disease and violence. Beneath the green, serene mound of Arnold Circus in east London lie the crushed remnants of one of the city's worst slums – while the elegant red-brick buildings surrounding the Circus represent a Victorian experiment in creating social perfection in the heart of the capital. The quiet, pretty nineteenth-century terraces of Reverdy Road in Bermondsey survived the wrecker's ball as a result of muscular local government intervention; while the character of working-class Deptford High Street was changed permanently – again as a result of local government policies. Airy Camberwell Grove has fought (not always successfully) to retain its almost rural tranquillity; but Caledonian Road – cut though it originally was through the green fields of nineteenth-century Islington – epitomises an inner-city thoroughfare, with its strengths and social and economic challenges. Taken together, they represent something of the diversity of London as well as a century of extraordinarily diverse social, economic and human history.

History has in the past too frequently been applied from the top down: a desiccated parade of political leaders, monarchs and administrators that, taken together, do little to expose the complex weave of real histories, real stories, real experiences. This book, by contrast, takes for granted that on a fundamental level Booth's method was correct: that history rises from street level, that it is composed of the experiences of a multitude of voices; and that it can only truly be experienced by listening to these voices and absorbing the stories they have to tell. The Deptford trader, for example, who remembers the devastating impact of the planning policies devised by 1960s' local government agencies: 'As I'm growing up, I can see what other kids feel when they want to fight. I wanted to fight the council, but you couldn't fight 'em.' The owner of a gracious Georgian property in Camberwell, who acknowledges that his house and its surroundings in fact own *him*: 'it has to take precedence over individualism'. And the resident of a slum house in the decrepit Notting Hill of the 1940s – 'half the floorboards were missing, because if my mum was short of a bit of firewood to start the fire, up a floorboard would go' – that is now worth over two million pounds.

It follows Booth in other ways too. He was fascinated by the domestic intricacies of life: of how people lived and where and by what means their businesses, their properties and their communities functioned – or failed to do so. This book asks these same questions by exploring these six contemporary streets, first surveyed by Booth a century ago; by colouring the context of the neighbourhoods within which they are positioned – and by bringing their stories up to the present day. The themes of life in London – gentrification, economic decline or revival, the influence of social class, the (in)ability of citizens and communities to control their destinies in the face of forces ranged against them, migration, whether voluntary or involuntary – all appear in certain guises in Booth's survey; they reappear throughout the history of twentieth-century London, and they dominate, in various and frequently startling forms, the histories of these six streets. It is a good deal easier to grasp the story of a street than of a city – of any city, much less a city like London. In exploring the history of six streets, this book seeks also to interpret the always evolving nature of London itself, and to frame it against its new, twenty-first-century world.

'The Belgravia of Bermondsey'

REVERDY ROAD

A feature of the district is the variety of its smells — jam, glue, leather, confectionery and poverty.

Charles Booth

In the heart of south Bermondsey, a small network of streets lies between Southwark Park Road and the Old Kent Road. These streets are Victorian in origin, and the presence of a fine Anglican church set on Thorburn Square at the heart of the grid seems to underscore the area's orderly beginnings. The houses are predominantly two-storey and neither large nor grand: their scale, like the streets themselves, is emphatically domestic. The Victorians, however, were fond of striking contradictory notes: in this corner of Bermondsey, the air of prim tidiness is leavened and lifted by arched windows that add graceful touches to many of the house fronts.

Naturally, time has altered this quiet corner of south London. Today, for example, the streets are tree-lined – this an addition of the early twentieth century. Some of the houses have been ambitiously extended; others have swapped their wooden window frames for plastic. On Reverdy Road, a row of six houses has vanished completely – to be replaced not by modern homes nor even by a small park, but by brambles, wild honeysuckle and sloes, by rough undergrowth, by an accidental refuge for wildlife. Other features remain: the church of St Anne on Thorburn Square, for example, is as stately as it ever was, though surrounded today not by the original elegant Victorian terraces (once the most aspirational houses in the neighbourhood) but by an eccentric box of 1960s-era flats. Today, the church deals with issues familiar to many London parishes: its congregations are in decline; and it must compete for attention with smaller churches based locally – many reaching out to the black population of south London, who travel to worship in Bermondsey from further afield. And at the corner of Reverdy Road and Southwark Park Road stands Church Cottage, a sign of potent continuity: since 1881, this has been the doctor's house, although today's doctor no longer works from the former dispensing rooms at the back. The area is changing. Venezuelan, New Zealand and American citizens now live on Reverdy Road and the surrounding streets; the Jubilee line extension has hooked Bermondsey more firmly into the commercial life of central London; and housing prices have risen. Estate agents can point to the desirable Victorian pedigree of this small corner of the borough of Southwark, to its relative lack of tower blocks, to the leafy quietness of its streets, to its status as a conservation area. At heart, however,

Reverdy Road and its neighbouring streets have remained predominantly white working class. There are many reasons why this is the case: as we will see, changes in policy and in land ownership, together with a vibrant local political culture have all been instrumental in forming the landscape of this corner of Bermondsey.

* * *

Bermondsey has seldom been glamorous. Wedged between the Thames and the Old Kent Road, it is a district surrounded by some of the capital's most recognisable sights and destinations; Tower Bridge provides a dramatic entry into (and a smooth exit from) Bermondsey; London Bridge station, with its mass of platforms and arches, its serpentine roads and its new, glittering Shard piercing the sky, lies just to the north-west; the bells of Southwark Cathedral chime the hours; the tourists flock to Borough Market and to the string of cultural landmarks – Tate Modern, the Globe theatre and the South Bank – just a short walk away; and the boats and expensive apartments of St Katharine's Dock lie just on the other side of the Thames. But none of these places belongs to Bermondsey itself: instead, like so many other districts of London, this is a place apart, with a sharply defined sense of itself.

The name, derived from Old English, first appears in the Domesday survey of 1086: *Beormund's Island* implies watery origins; and the tell-tale '*ey*' ending connects Bermondsey with any number of other water-bound places – Guernsey, Lundy, Bardsey, Jersey – on the margins of Britain. Not that Bermondsey was itself ever an island. Instead, it was something more mundane – an unpromising stretch of marshy ground, low-lying and prone to flooding from the tidal Thames. As a result, the Romans skirted the district: Watling Street – now the Old Kent Road – avoided the wetness and mud of what became Bermondsey, so that travellers and legions could remain dry-shod on their way from Dover and Canterbury up to London and on to Chester. The terrain of the district, together with its location on the wrong side of the Thames from Roman and Saxon London, meant that Bermondsey would remain obscure and undeveloped until comparatively late.

It took the Church – one of the very few institutions with the necessary clout, power and money in medieval England – to begin the long, expensive process of shoring up the banks of the river against the floods, building dikes and drainage channels, and eventually making the land profitable. Soon, the usual patchwork of fields and hedges appeared; the area gained a name for its orchards and fruit trees; and the Thames was pressed increasingly into service as a conduit of trade and influence. By the seventeenth century, Samuel Pepys could write of a languorous riverine Bermondsey as the home of delightful pleasure gardens – the so-called Cherry Gardens – by the river:

June 13, 1664. – Thence [from the Tower] having a galley down to Greenwich, and there saw the King's work, which are great, a-doing there, and so to the Cherry Garden, and so carried some cherries home.

June 15, 1664: – And so to the Cherry Garden, and then by water singing finely to the Bridge and there landed.

Such descriptions, however, are rare. Rather more common are the portraits of a district that is increasingly dense with houses, with labour, with industry. The Huguenot migration from France in the seventeenth century left its mark on Bermondsey, in the growth of weaving and other crafts. The development of the Thames docklands had a profound impact on the area: in J. M. W. Turner's *The Fighting Temeraire* (1839), the great ship is being tugged past the Bermondsey docks to be broken up. Later still, the district became associated with the trade in tanning and its noxious by-products; riverside districts in Bermondsey stank of urine and animal faeces. And as workers crowded in, living standards declined: in *Oliver Twist*, Charles Dickens could describe the mid-nineteenth-century horror of the notorious Jacob's Island slum on the Thames:

... crazy wooden galleries common to the backs of half a dozen houses, with holes from which to look upon the slime beneath, windows, broken and patched, with poles thrust out, on which to dry the linen that is never there; rooms so small, so filthy, so confined, that the air would seem to be too tainted even for the dirt and squalor which they shelter, wooden chambers thrusting themselves out above the mud and threatening to fall into it – as some have done; dirt-besmeared walls and decaying foundations, every repulsive lineament of poverty, every loathsome indication of filth, rot and garbage: all these ornament the banks of Jacob's Island.

Yet even in the early part of the nineteenth century, the southern part of Bermondsey remained relatively pastoral: the maps of the day still trace the old landscapes of fields, footpaths and hedgerows, the old Roman road replaced now by the Old Kent Road as the main thoroughfare striking south-east from London Bridge. By the end of the 1830s, however, the world began rapidly to change: railways were slicing through the flat fields on their way to Greenwich and further afield; and by 1836, a passenger terminus – the forerunner to London Bridge station – had been established in central Bermondsey. Indeed, the railway helped to mould the social order of the district: north of the line, the land stretched up to the river and its associated industries; south of the line, the residents could afford to cultivate a tentative gentility.

Bermondsey was famous for its biscuit and other food-processing factories, the chimneys of which sent sweet, malty aromas wafting across the area. This engraving, from the *Illustrated London News* of December 1874, introduces the reader to the world of Peek Frean biscuit manufacturing.

Since the 1700s, much of the land in south Bermondsey had been owned by the Steavens family. By the mid-nineteenth century, it had passed (by marriage and in the absence of any male Steavenses) to James West – and it was West's business ambitions that led to the development of this part of Bermond-sey. Another wave of new industries started up, mainly to do with food processing: most famous of these was the Peek Frean biscuit factory, the chimneys of which sent wafting over Bermondsey sweet, malty aromas to add to the medley of other scents and fumes already in the air. Later, Peek Frean would be joined by the Pink's and Hartley jam plants, Pearce Duff custard manufac-turers and by Crosse and Blackwell, purveyors of savoury relishes to the nation. This rapidly expanding sector needed labour – and ideally, this labour should reside close by: after all, if workers lived practically on the next street, they would have no excuse to be late for their shifts. West had a certain financial acumen, having served as Secretary to the Treasury: he soon realized the earning opportunities implicit in his banks of land in Bermond-sey – and he set about transforming the fields and marshes into streets of orderly terraced rows of workers' accommodation.

The process of systematic planning and development began as early as the 1850s, when local Anglican congregations started fundraising to establish a new parish and church in the area. Then, in 1868, the West estate began to grant long leaseholds to patches of land: the new leaseholder might build a house (as long

as it was the one specified by James West), agree a rent rate
(within a certain limit) and retain the land for 70 years. In return,
the West family would receive the ground rents; then, once the
leases expired, the property would revert to West ownership. And
so the streets of the West estate sprang up: Reverdy Road, Alma
Road, Balaclava Road – named, patriotically, for the famous
Crimean battle – and others; the socially ambitious villas of Thorburn Square lay in their midst; and the area rapidly became home
to a working class of skilled and semi-skilled workers. There was
an abundance of employment, and their families prospered – at
least in comparison to many in other parts of London.

This financial stability was relative. The censuses of 1891
and 1901 contain page after page of figures on Reverdy Road
and its adjoining streets and reveal that these homes were
seldom lived in by a single family. Instead, there was a density of
humanity packed into the modest terraces. Typically, one family
would be housed on the ground floor, another on the first floor;
for the sake of convenience, the oven stood on the landing
between the two households. Lavatories of any description were
far from being the rule in Victorian London – but the houses of
Reverdy Road could boast both an outside convenience, and an
outside tap, placed by the builders just at the back door. Even in
their crowded state, then, the houses on Reverdy Road were – in
subtle but important ways – a cut above the accommodation
available elsewhere in Bermondsey.

Not all of the residents made biscuits, custard, chutney and jam for a living. The 1891 census notes the presence of lift attendants, port watchmen, telegraphists and railway clerks, machinists, dyers, dressmakers and the occasional 'scholar'. In the 1901 equivalent, the Victorian mania for documentation and exploration seems a little on the wane – for now the denizens of Bermondsey are categorised rather more sweepingly: page after tart page of 'worker' is itemised. People from all over London – from Camberwell, Bethnal Green, Islington and Kennington, as well as neighbouring Walworth and Rotherhithe – had come to live in Bermondsey; and an occasional terse 'Scotland', 'Liverpool' and 'Ireland' indicates that others too gravitated here. Many of the listed individuals, however, were born and lived their entire lives in Bermondsey – and saw no reason to move elsewhere.

By the turn of the century the district had become established. St Anne's on Thorburn Square had been consecrated in 1879: a local vicar, Thornton Wilkinson, had taken to preaching in the streets and holding outdoor prayer services to raise both awareness of the need for a church and funds to pay for it; and by the 1890s, the church was obliged to add side aisles to cope with its swelling congregations. The area was decent and respectable: its houses were nicely maintained, its gardens spick, its doorsteps scrubbed; and the large houses on the square added a welcome gloss to the smaller surrounding properties.

'The people are no longer ists.'

In 1900, Charles Booth arrived on Reverdy Road. His report and colour-coded maps indicate the desirability of this street and its surroundings to a certain class of Londoner – he designated it pink, in sharp contrast to the blacks and dark blues that dominate his maps of Bermondsey, and his comments were, as usual, clear and concise:

> These are all 2 storied and comfortable streets. Yellow brick, built at the time of the Crimea [*sic*]. Some tenanted by one family as by salesmen and traveller but the majority by two: good gardens at the back: railwaymen, engine drivers, guard, police, live here: houses seldom empty and hard to get: small fronts with iron railings: fairly broad and clean streets.

Booth went on to sum up the nature of Bermondsey's social geography, its range of the very poor and the rather less poor, and the activities that kept some of the people of the district fed and warm:

> This round falls into the natural divisions i.e. the fairly comfortable who are found south of Southwark Park Road, and the poor who are north of it. The comfortable

are railway men and commercial salesmen and travellers
who come into their work from the South Bermondsey
Station. The poor are leather workers, glue makers, and
jam and sweet makers who inhabit round the spa road.

The very poorest streets, Booth noted, lay to the north and west,
as the streets narrowed in the direction of Southwark and
London Bridge. Yet – for all the delineations of class and rank
charted by Booth and held to tenuously in the minds of most
people – the range displayed by Bermondsey's society, its housing stock and its roads was not in the end so very great. 'There
is great sameness throughout Bermondsey,' he wrote. 'In this
division there is street after street built exactly alike.' It was a
vital point, underscoring the fact – doubtless an unwelcome one
to some of the residents – that the hard-won respectability of
Reverdy Road was at best fragile: its families were seldom more
than a few weeks' wages away from destitution.

And while the jobs were abundant and welcome, they were
harsh and potentially dangerous. Booth himself was well aware
of the fact: he discussed at length the conditions faced by female
workers in particular, who laboured under circumstances consis-
tently inferior to those of their male counterparts: their hours
more intermittent, their pay considerably less, their work skills
less honed. The women who worked in the confectionery factories, for example, tended to be thrown out of their jobs as soon

as the weather warmed: hot sun meant melting chocolate and
factories mothballed until the onset of autumn. In the weeks
after Christmas, sales of sweets dropped sharply; and female
workers were once more, at a moment's notice, out of a job. The
women employed to bottle quantities of boiling preserves in
Bermondsey's jam plants endured burns and scalds as an occu-
pational hazard; and those who worked in mineral water plants
lived with the threat of glass bottles exploding in their faces.

And the world was changing. Capital was highly mobile,
migrating rapidly to where wages and overheads were cheaper.
Newly formed trade unions could help a little, but they provided
no panacea: the employers continued to hold the cards.
Bermondsey's lucrative leather trades, for example, had begun
to leave the area by the end of the nineteenth century, moving to
the north of England in search of more favourable conditions:
'[T]he trade was going from Bermondsey', complained a former
official with the Amalgamated Leather Trade Union. 'Leeds was
the chief competitor taking heavy + light work; Warrington took
the light work only.'

Not that these circumstances always led to political radicalism. London's population was of course alive to the political
ideas of the day, and the city's militant edge had been sharp-
ened in the course of the nineteenth century by Chartism and
other forms of political agitation. The dockers' strikes of 1892
on the Thames opposite Bermondsey had electrified that sector

of the city's proletariat, and set the stage for more waves of industrial action in the years to come. But the poor of London often had more pressing material problems with which to contend; and Booth – though conscious of the sometimes fero-cious conditions prevalent at the time in the East End and in districts of Bermondsey – acknowledged this fact. His opinion – and it was aired frequently – was that London's working poor were rather more prone to a sort of lamentable social, political and moral lassitude. 'The general attitude is indifference,' he noted, 'and the people are more indifferent than they were. One result is that there is not so much opposition. They think "it will all end the same, it does not matter a bit" whether they have a Christian or worldly life.'

Booth's interviews with the local worthies – most but not all connected with the Christian churches – demonstrate that he had every reason to be concerned about his subjects' moral torpor. He learned from a Mr J. Lelliott of 14 Thorburn Square – 'a grizzled veteran of 50 to 55 but bright of eye and active as a young man' and a London City Missionary, whose patch covered much of south Bermondsey – that moral standards were in decline. Lelliott's interview created a vivid portrait of the district in the final months of Victoria's reign. He was himself portrayed as an enthusiastic gentleman, with a wide range of interests:

Mr Lelliott is a thoughtful and strong personality, stronger than the ordinary type of [London City Missionaries]. Very thorough in all that he does and enthusiastic in his work. He goes in for microscopy in his leisure moments. A microscope was standing on the dresser – the interview took place in the kitchen as the fire was burning there and as I was coming away he said 'Oh, I have something to show you'. He then put some waterweed from a glass jar into a small tank (homemade) and placing it under the microscope showed me some specimens of vorticella which he was culti- vating, and remarkably good and active specimens they were. This is characteristic of the man.

Lelliott seemed strongly inclined towards optimism: the district was 'poorer but cleaner', especially since some of the more noxious tanneries had left the area; the downside was that the well-paid tanners had left too, replaced by poorly paid casual labouring jobs. Housing was slowly improving; and the horrify- ing plagues of vermin that formerly characterized Bermondsey's streets were less noticeable. The children of the district tended to be christened; they liked to cluster around him on the streets when he convened open-air prayer meetings; and they even appeared from time to time at Sunday School and at the regular Band of Hope meetings on Wednesday nights. Charity funds were in reasonable shape and the district was also home to the genteel poor, including a number of 'respectable widows, they live here because plenty of work is to be had in sack and bag making, accoutrement making'. And although there had been an influx of people from east London – not necessarily good news in a district already short of housing and decent employment – Lelliott was able to detect potential advantages even in this situation: among the new immigrants were Italian ice cream sellers to add to the cheer of the neighbourhood.

On the other hand, Lelliott could not deny that fewer and fewer families were attending church together; that more and more unmarried couples were living together; that Sunday observance was on the decline; and that irresponsible publicans were organising weekend workers' excursions into the countryside for the purpose of drinking alcohol to excess. Booth concluded on a distinctly ambiguous note:

Of the results of his work Mr. Lelliott had not much to say. The visitation brings them into close contact with the people and they find that we (e.g., the missionaries) are friendly. This gives them a power with them. As an illustration of this he told how in visiting a factory that morning he had met a seaman just off to Africa, paying a visit to his mates before starting. This man was using foul language and Lelliott was able to rebuke him kindly with the approval of the 10 or 11 other men present, although he

added some of these men would have used similar language
if he were not present.

Booth's conversation with a Mr J. Humphreys Hall of 37
Reverdy Road – Secretary to the trustees of the United
Methodist Free Church on Upper Grange Road – turned even
more on these mingled issues of politics and morality. The
Methodists maintained a network of contacts across south
London; they could be expected, therefore, to offer a fair assessment of the state of society in the area. The Methodist chapel in
this corner of Bermondsey had been founded in 1861 and Hall
– 'a vigorous little man looking 45 but probably turned 50', with
'keen deeply set eyes beneath a shaggy brow and sharp features
[...] a shrewd and sensible fellow' – had much to say about
public morality in Bermondsey. One gains the sense that Booth
approved of Hall, not least because he bore a strong resemblance
to Sidney Webb (who married Beatrice Potter and in partner-
ship with her founded the London School of Economics), 'except
that he is rather sturdier and fair'.

Hall's comments displayed a touching loyalty to Bermondsey.
The area's public health system was quite good ('Have an active
sanitary officer,' Booth noted, 'a man who cannot be bought');
it also boasted a good police force ('you always know where to
find a policeman') – and the rates of crime were nothing out of
the ordinary. Brothels were not a problem, though there were

certainly a good many prostitutes to be seen 'along the South-wark Park Road and until recently in the wider roads to the south'; Hall had even seen women plying their trade on respectable Reverdy Road itself. But municipal modernization was having an impact: 'Now the lighting has been improved and they are driven to the narrow ways by the railway. This is a new thing comparatively and he wonders whether it is the result of the closing of houses in St. George's. The women are young and respectably dressed.'

In sharp contrast with Lelliott's comments on the alcohol-drinking proletariat, Hall did not worry unduly about local alcohol consumption: drink 'he does not think is worse than elsewhere'; and such problems as existed he ascribed to poverty, for '[I]t is not to be wondered that men and women seek the brightness and warmth in the pub that they cannot get at home.' The local Methodists had opposed publican licenses, though never to much effect, and Hall:

Thinks they have too many small publicans and the vestry has tried to reduce the number. Has opposed the licenses on the ground that they were not needed, basing their argu-ment on the fact that the keepers of these houses could not make them pay. Has carried the day with the licensing magistrates but the decisions have always been reversed at quarterly session, where the brewery interest is very strong.

Hall's own local organization appeared, on first sight, to be in rude health. His chapel – its patch covering the grid of streets surrounding Thorburn Square, including Reverdy Road – had a lot of pastoral work: the underlying poverty of Bermondsey was all around; and indeed, Hall expressed relief that some of the borough's worst slums had been lately torn down to make way for an extension to the railway. Still, there remained want enough: 'The people are literally labouring class. I have not 5 persons who could give a sovereign and have another in their pockets. Railway men, men employed in the tanneries and a few shopkeepers.' Booth offered this summary:

> For charity they have the poor fund. Small, not quite £10 a year. Minister has power to relieve needy cases. In the church, little need for relief exists, only a few old people. *Other Religious Agencies* St. Luke's do a considerable amount of visitation. Abbey St. and Rouel Road Chapels each had a sister at work. Thinks the Wesleyans are the most active.
>
> The range of Methodist activity is impressive: a score of Sunday School teachers, two Sunday services and a wide variety of clubs, guilds, bands and societies for old and young alike.

Yet Hall admitted to a certain gloom: Methodist attendance in the area was in decline. Some of the responsibility for this, he thought, might be laid at the door of the Church authorities, which were failing to make the distinctive Methodist message clear to the people – and here Booth inserted himself into the discussion, telling Hall that 'I was not surprised as my experience was that nine out of ten did not know the peculiar tenets of the sect or were not influenced by them in deciding about Church membership'.

Hall's fundamental reasoning, however, chimed with that of Booth: while the Church might suffer many structural problems, the underlying reasons for its decline were not organizational but cultural: the people of south London were simply 'not "ists"'; that is, they were reluctant – and in the case of those obliged to work on the Sabbath, unable – to commit to the exercise of a particular tenet or creed. This was especially the case with the men:

> ... Mr. Hall said it was no use blinking the fact that the bulk of our congregations were boys and women. You cannot get the men to church. If you get the men and talk quietly to them you find there is a strong religious sentiment with them but also a sort of feeling 'we don't believe in this call and parade of piety'. They are to be won but require a man of a type to do it.

Hall's underlying gloom was shared by other Bermondsey churchmen. Booth interviewed the Anglican incumbent at St

Anne's, the Rev. J. F. Benson Walsh and his wife at the vicarage on Thorburn Square – and here too the tale was not altogether one of Christian sweetness and light. Arriving late at the vicarage shortly after New Year, 1900, he found the vicar from home – but his wife (Booth does not give her full name) fairly bursting with angry and frustrated conversation. Mrs. Walsh was 'a lady of middle age, vivacious, out-spoken, chagrined. Her opinions must, like her facts, be taken *cum grano* (with a grain of salt). All alike were rapped out with the utmost frankness, and have the merit of giving us, in some respects, a new point of view.' She clearly held much of the power in the household, and was not shy of demonstrating the fact: 'Curates have sometimes been revealed to us in the course of our inquiries; the ladies of the clerical households rarely, although, doubtlessly, they are often the power behind the throne. At St Anne's it stands out more plainly than the Vicar himself ...' Mrs Walsh emerges as a loyal wife, an anxious mother, and a beady-eyed observer of Church politics – but more than anything else, as a frustrated, fretful resident of a corner of London – 'the desert of Bermondsey' – in which she would rather not live at all.

The Rev. Walsh, Booth discovered, had been running the parish of St Anne's more or less single-handed for over three years – and this at a time when the population of the parish was swelling considerably. Mrs Walsh's commentary betrayed the reason why Methodism struggled in Bermondsey: 'My husband has worked hard at the parish; has got the church in order, and the parish out of the rut of Dissent [i.e. Method-ism], in which it practically was when we came'. But all to no avail: 'He is getting not the slightest recognition for what he has done. It is hard on him, for he is over 50, and is not as strong as he used to be. The Bishop comes and tells us that he will try and arrange something and sympathizes – and does nothing. He never will. His suffragan is worth a hundred of him'. Much of Mrs Walsh's conversation was composed of bitter complaint at her husband's ill usage at the hands of the Church of England authorities, who blocked access to almost all vital funds. It pained the Rev. Walsh, who was not an extremist, but simply a hard-working churchman. 'The living is in the gift of trustees, and these will neither move Mr. Walsh nor help him to get an exchange. The latter arrangement they dislike, because they are afraid of having a man not of their colour in the parish. They are a narrow set, and include the Rector, Mr. Lewis, "a man of no weight".'

Having thus disposed of the local hierarchy, Mrs Walsh moved on to the folk of Bermondsey. The people of her parish had nothing to recommend them, consisting predominantly of the 'semigenteel', spiced with a little true poverty and squalor; and everyone drank too much, especially in the course of 'those terrible Bank Holidays'. (This last complaint would have found favour with Booth, who had railed bitterly against this relatively

new institution: 'very rarely does one hear a good word for the
Bank Holidays. The more common view is that they are a curse,
and [...] the mischievous results from a sexual point of view due
to a general abandonment of restraint, are frequently noted in
our evidence.') The women of Bermondsey, she thought, had
even more social pretensions than the men:

> [T]hat is the word that expresses it best — *lydies*; it is terri-
> ble. What do they do? – well, it is very difficult to say. No,
> they are not railway employees to any extent, and not in the
> leather trades. They are very difficult to classify, and are a
> very mixed set; most work outside the parish.

Mothers' meetings were of little use: 'I think they are played out'.
And the conditions of Bermondsey society were difficult for the
younger Walshes, who were socially isolated as 'except for the
local clergy, there is no one to know. And given these we can't
know round here – Mr Stobart is a snob, and Mr Ainsworth a
cad, and as for the wife of the latter! She is an obnoxious person,
impossible. On Mr Lewis we did not call.'

Congregations, Mrs Walsh admitted, might be increasing –
but she too condemned Bermondsey's apparent moral and religious sluggishness. Neither the work of the Church of England,
nor that of 'the Baptists, unitarians nor Salvation Army
Barracks' seemed to make any appreciable difference:

There is no religious life in South London; nothing but
absolute indifference. The children sent to the Sunday
School: that is their religion. But our attendances seem to
be as good as anywhere in Bermondsey. My husband went
to preach for Mr. Wallace one morning, and had a congregation of four! We have no early celebration now; what is
the use if no one would come? And nevertheless the bishop
wants it started again. It is useless. My husband himself
detests evening communion, but he is obliged to have it.

The Rev. Walsh appeared and Booth was more sympathetic to
the husband – 'baldish; grey; side whiskers and moustache; well
chiselled features; a tired look and a kindly manner' – than the
wife. The vicar said there was little squalid poverty, and revealed
his parish was sometimes referred to as the 'Belgravia of
Bermondsey'. Several of his fellow vicars had married money,
which was a situation both Walshes clearly found trying. As for
his parishioners, these were:

… friendly, but unapproachable, and Mr. W. described how
at the house of one of his best workers he had been that
morning kept on the doorstep. That is characteristic of the
class and of their attitude. But there is nothing 'awry' in the
parish, and Mrs. Walsh chimed in as to the affection in
which her husband was held. 'They don't like anyone else to

preach, and if he is not there they don't go and they don't give'. But the Vicar's absences are very rare: 'I have only been away two Sundays during the past two years'. One explanation of this was clearly the cost of finding a substitute, and, doubtless, straightened means have a good deal to do with explaining the exclusiveness of the family, as described by Mrs. Walsh. The Vicar said that he had no private means […] I saw no sign of a servant, Mrs. Walsh herself letting me in, and the room in which we talked was a little bare. It is easy to understand that the lady in any case would not find it easy to be intimate with her two well-to-do clerical neighbours, on both of whom she is inclined to look down. For she is as proud as she is poor.

It is a painful description: the vicar doing his best to make ends meet, the vicar's wife keeping up appearances and both maintaining the distinctions of class, in spite of their evident psychological isolation. Both husband and wife, it was clear, would sooner fall back on their own slender resources than consort with undesirables: for, as Mrs Walsh pointed out, it was no longer possible to assume that even a clergyman was a gentleman. And it was equally clear that the want in the parish would not attract wealthy benefactors to charity funds: Walsh's parishioners, while not comfortably off, were not quite poor enough either; the talk returned once more to the Bishop, who was not sufficiently thrusting to make up the difference; and the diocese was drifting. The Walshes longed for a change in regime: in the meantime, they had to make the best of things. This might have been the *de facto* motto of much of the population of Bermondsey at the time of Booth's survey of the borough.

'Where There's Life, There's Soap.'

The Rev. Walsh eventually left St Anne's in 1910, to be replaced by John Stansfeld, the founder of the Oxford and Bermondsey Medical Missions. These organizations were a precursor to the National Health Service, teaching the working class about Christianity in exchange for healthcare. In *The Doctor*, a biography of Stansfeld written by Barclay Baron in 1952, the area was described in familiar terms:

> St. Anne's Parish lies within the Borough of Bermondsey but belongs to a different world from the clamour of industry and traffic round about Abbey Street or the old-time squalor of Dockhead. Thorburn Square in which the church and vicarage stand, comes in the house-agents category of 'residential'. It is a small place singularly with-drawn disturbed only by the voices of gossiping neighbours and playing children. In the short street which connects it with

one of the busiest arteries of Bermondsey, reticent little houses face one another, each with a privet hedge and four feet of 'garden' between the iron gate and the front door. [...] Houses as like as peas. Most of them were proud of a lace curtain in the front window and of the room behind it, which they strove to maintain as the 'best parlour'.

Baron went on to remind the reader, however, that: 'human nature and human need are not altered by lace curtains and a "good address", that love is as warm, hope as high, loneliness as bitter, sin as besetting in Thorburn Square as in the tenements by the Tower Bridge.'

St Anne's, Thorburn Square, was consecrated in 1879 – the dignified heart of the West Estate. It belonged 'to a different world from the clamour of industry and traffic'. In the 1960s, the handsome Victorian houses surrounding it were demolished and replaced with modern flats and maisonettes.

The clean lace curtains and starched back parlours of Reverdy Road symbolize a developing theme in the story of Bermondsey. For the Victorians, cleanliness was second only to Godliness – but in the opening decades of the twentieth century, cleanliness took centre stage, becoming a social good and a moral imperative in its own right. This was hardly odd: late Victorian society had been fissured with doubts as to the existence of a Deity: the appearance in 1859 of Charles Darwin's *The Origins of Species* had been greeted with doubts and alarm; Sir Charles Lyell's *The Principles of Geology* (1830–33) had already provoked doubt about the origins of the world; and all over Britain, ordinary Victorian men and women had taken to spending their weekends equipped with hammer and magnifying glass, scouring the country's beaches for evidence of fossils embedded in chalk and limestone cliffs.

It was natural enough, therefore, that God should be bundled off the stage and replaced with an issue that was, in the eyes of many, rather more pressing. This developing discussion of hygiene was one aspect of a wider and more radical change. European modernism was on the rise and, with it, an emphasis on new issues: public housing, public health, public welfare, the prevention of disease as opposed to its mere treatment, the greater good of the people as a whole – these were all ideals circulating across Europe in the opening decades of the century.

Bermondsey, exposed by living conditions and local industries to a host of diseases, was a case in point. On 22 November 1902, the *British Medical Journal* recorded that 'Between October 12th, 1901, and September 6th, 1902, there were 297 cases of small-pox in Bermondsey', with vaccination providing only partial protection. The *BMJ* mourned the continual threat of cross-infection in London – for quarantine was impossible:

> Each borough is not self-contained, but has innumerable intercommunications with other parts of London, and in this way, notwithstanding every effort at co-operation between different medical officers of health, investigation is hampered and thwarted [...] Many people, mistaking a mild attack with perhaps one or two spots, for a 'chill' or 'influenza', or some other every-day complaint, have continued during the attack to go about in trams, buses, and other public conveyances, infecting others.

Bermondsey seemed particularly prey to such threats: there was a quarantine centre located on the riverfront and some feared that the disease might arise like a foul miasma from the building to contaminate the entire neighbourhood. The *BMJ* dismissed the possibility that the smallpox bacterium could be spread in this way: a primary school directly opposite the holding centre had had no more incidences of the disease than any other part of Bermondsey. Instead, the chief threat came from the continual coming and going from the London docks. Bermondsey was also racking up some startling statistics: in the fourth quarter of 1902, the borough recorded some of the highest rates of childbirth and of death in the whole of London; the highest incidences of death from both measles and diarrhoea; and one of the highest rates of infant mortality in the city. Small wonder, then, that public health should become an increasing fixation in Bermondsey.

The medical inhabitants of Church Cottage – the doctor's house-cum-dispensary at the corner of Reverdy Road and Southwark Park Road – played prominent roles in this developing discourse. Since 1881, the doctor at Church Cottage had been Dr George Cooper: the census of that year lists Cooper as resident in the house, together with his wife, eight children and a domestic servant. Cooper's life was bound up with the ideal of public service. Cooper qualified as a doctor in 1867, and spent the greater part of his professional life steeped in Bermondsey society: as general practitioner; and as member of the London County Council (LCC) from its inauguration in 1889, until 1906, when he was elected as Liberal Member of Parliament for Bermondsey. The house, then, witnessed a good deal of medical action, from dockers' injuries to lanced boils and minor procedures carried out on the premises.

In the course of a long career, Cooper focused attention on issues such as the treatment of epilepsy and dysentery, and the state of the boarding houses of Bermondsey. Following his election to the Commons his focus widened to the national scene: he gave evidence, for example, to the Royal Commission which, from 1904–1908, considered the situation of the 'feeble-minded' in society – this at a time when theories of eugenics were highly fashionable – and he pushed for the regulation of anaesthetists in the country's hospitals. He was fortunate, perhaps, in serving in the Commons at a time when radical legislative reforms were being considered by the ruling Liberal government – yet unlucky too, for he became involved closely in the passage of the so-called 'People's Budget' through the Commons in the spring and summer of 1909. This bill was bitterly contested every step of the way, for it proposed a measured redistribution of the national wealth – to the horror of the Tory opposition, which also controlled the Lords. The budget was finally passed (with the help of Irish votes in the Commons), but Cooper would not live to see it: following yet another late and 'peculiarly trying' sitting at the Commons, he returned home to Church Cottage in the early hours, collapsed and died late on 7 October 1909, at the age of 65. In his obituary, the *BMJ* noted:

He was an ardent politician, but he never forgot that he was a doctor, and he continued to practise his profession to the end. He used to relate with much glee his encounter with an undertaker, who remonstrated with him on his endeavours to improve the public health. 'A good 18 per 1,000 is what we want,' said the philanthropic tradesman. How, in the midst of his multifarious public work, Dr. Cooper contrived to attend to his patients is one of those mysteries the solution of which is doubtless to be found in Wellington's saying that it is the busiest men who make time to do things for which less strenuous workers cannot find a moment. [...] He was a perfectly honest, straight-forward man.

After Cooper's death, the medical practice at the end of Reverdy Road was occupied by a Dr Ellis Goldie, aged 34 and single – but by 1920, the surgery had been taken over by Alfred Salter, who would become one of Bermondsey's most influential residents. Alfred Salter was a radical republican, and an ardent supporter of Irish Home Rule. Inspired by Quakerism he embraced passivism. None of these causes was easy to espouse. He also continued Cooper's potent combination of public health and politics: he had been pursuing just such an agenda ever since qualifying as a doctor in 1896. In 1900, he had married Ada Brown: the Salters would go on to assist in the establishment of health insurance schemes and health education programmes. In addition, Alfred offered free medical care to those who could not afford to pay – in a district like Bermondsey, a significant proportion of the population.

In his survey of Bermondsey in 1900, Charles Booth had interviewed Alfred Salter in his role as a London City Missionary. The resulting notes of their conversation portray vividly the state of the very poorest residents of Bermondsey, including the families 'packed as close as the authorities like [sic] allow them to be, indeed tighter, for there is much more crowding at night than the inspections get to know of'; the Thames-side prostitutes and their pimps who 'lived with them and on them'; the dreadful dependency of much of the population on moneylenders; and the children who, should they not get a free meal as a result of charity, subsisted chiefly on a diet of bread and jam:

As with the other L. C. M.s , Mr. Salter's chief task is visitation: he visits about 450 families out of 750, and almost everywhere is welcomed; but there are few with whom it is possible to have any spiritual talk: 'as soon as you mention their souls they get uncomfortable and want you to move on'.

Mr. Salter visits most of the prostitutes: many of them come from more respectable, even from well-to-do homes and 'have been piously bought up': nearly all would be glad to learn the life, but this will not stand the restrictions of Homes, and insure work among them is almost hopeless.

Alfred Salter (1873-1945) shared with his wife Ada a keen sense of moral purpose – and as a general practitioner and Labour Party politician, he also possessed the tools to turn his vision into reality. From his base at the surgery on Reverdy Road, Salter helped to transform Bermondsey's public health regime.

The portrait of social despair and absence of religious feeling is rather more starkly and powerfully drawn than that allowed by Booth's other interviewees of the period. It permits, too, a useful glimpse of Alfred Salter at an early but pivotal point in his career; and it enables an understanding of the brand of politics – muscular, interventionist and founded on principles that were both Christian and ultimately socialist – that in the years to come would define Bermondsey culture in general and the

Salters' careers in particular. Booth gives a bracing assessment of Alfred in these early years:

> Mr. Salter is above the average of the L. C. M.s, a cheery, pleasant fellow whose visits are likely to be welcome and who is likely to be much more tactful than many of his brother missionaries in approaching the spiritual side of his task.

Alfred later occupied seats on Bermondsey borough council (replacing Cooper) and on the LCC, before standing for parliament in several elections. In the course of the 1918 election, *The Times* noted coolly that 'nobody has a word to say about him, but his views are of a very extreme kind'. Alfred was eventually elected as a Labour candidate in 1922, when he made a name for himself by complaining about the frequent drunkenness of his fellow MPs; he held the seat, with one brief interruption, until his retirement in 1945. Ada, meanwhile, won a seat on Bermondsey council in 1919; and in 1923, she was elected mayor of the borough. Their commitment to the district was exemplified by the medical practice run from Church Cottage – but it came at devastating personal cost: in 1910, an outbreak of scarlet fever in Bermondsey claimed their only child Joyce.

The Salters both drove and reflected a thriving political culture in Bermondsey in those first decades of the twentieth century, one that found expression in the area of public health in particular. In the years after the Great War, local government in the area was governed by the Labour Party and the new council at once set about creating a new Bermondsey, with a programme of public works including the construction of thousands of new homes; and policies to eliminate diseases such as tuberculosis. One of the first gestures of the Labour Council in 1923 was to remove the Union flag from the town hall and replace it with a new borough standard – for which the colour red was specifically chosen.

Speaking in the Commons, Alfred Salter spelled out Bermondsey council's distinctive social policies in the 1920s:

> In my own borough […] we are steadily buying up the whole
> of the house property. When a house comes on the market it
> is purchased by the municipality. It is then reconditioned or
> rebuilt, and, as the greater part of our area is practically one
> huge slum, we intend for the next 15 or 20 years steadily
> and systematically to purchase the whole of the house prop-
> erty and rebuild the borough from end to end.

The council's intention was to recreate a new Bermondsey: one that was clean, green and considerably less dense. Victorian housing stock would be replaced by a Garden Suburb in look and culture: houses would have green spaces, residents would have air and light. The council created a network of clean, free and modern public conveniences; and bandstands and a lido were constructed to cultivate an air of public gaiety. At the same time, Ada Salter chaired the borough's Beautification Committee: this had more than cosmetic window-dressing in mind, for it ordered the planting of some ten thousand trees – London plane, birch, hornbeam and poplar, including the avenues that to this day line Reverdy Road and its surroundings streets – and the creation of new parks and public spaces.

But the council's ambitions were blunted by central government: neighbouring councils objected to the housing plans, fearing that displaced Bermondsey residents would strain their own housing capacities; only limited rebuilding work was ultimately realised. And Ada's wish to have free window boxes delivered to the residents of the borough was deemed too expensive by the Town Clerk – though free plants and compost were permitted. Bermondsey would not become another Hampstead or Letchworth Garden City; and the council's wish that 'the drab sordidness of Old Bermondsey will have gone forever, and the district will be illuminated with touches of colour and beauty never known before' could not fully be realized.

In the area of public health, however, the local authorities went much further – and some of their measures were eye-catching. In the course of the Great War, Alfred Salter had acquired Fairby Grange, a manor house set in 20 acres of land outside

Dartford in Kent, as a shelter for conscientious objectors. After the war, the property (complete with pleasure grounds, pond, nuttery and extensive orchards) was used by Bermondsey as a recuperation home for convalescing mothers; at the same time, the council dispatched tuberculosis sufferers to sanatoria in the Swiss Alps. These were far from mainstream measures in the Britain of the 1920s, and show a council intent on pursuing a policy of paternalist interventionism.

The obituary of Donald Connan, a 'son of the manse' and chief medical officer for Bermondsey for almost 30 years from 1927, brings together many distinctive elements of the period: the will which propelled the borough's health policies in these years; the religious principles which underlay its policies – for Connan, like Alfred Salter, was originally a London City Missionary; and the tools that were used to gain its objectives. 'It was mainly through Dr. Connan's efforts,' declared the *BMJ*, 'that in the twenties Bermondsey led the country in public health matters. Posters, propaganda vans, and health exhibitions brought the elements of hygiene to the multitudes'. Connan himself was a significant reformer and innovator, who:

> [T]ook up this post with great zeal and the determination to
> improve living standards and to encourage the people to take
> a pride in the public health services which were provided. His
> interest in people made him deeply concerned with health

education, and he was convinced that there was a great need
for propaganda to educate the public in health and hygiene.
In this field he did some brilliant pioneer work ...

It is unusual today to refer in such breezy fashion to works of
'propaganda' – but this was indeed the intention of Bermondsey's public health films. These were novel innovations and they
helped to air subjects that had seldom been adequately described
or explained. The films were shown in the borough's new
libraries and gleaming marble-lined public baths; and open-air
film shows became a feature of life in the spring and autumn –
in July and August it was too light in the evenings for the films
to be properly viewed – in the process attracting large audiences
into the parks and streets.

Some 30 such films were produced between 1923 and the
end of the Second World War, on subjects as varied as the symp-
toms of tuberculosis, the means of meat production and the arts
of chiropody. *Where There's Life, There's Soap,* was the title of
a film on personal hygiene, aimed at the children of Bermondsey. They were never overly technical: in an interview of 1926,
Connan explained that:

The success of the films depends upon the plot which must
be devised in such a way as to ensure a simple continuity of
ideas throughout. The principle followed in preparing the

pictures has been to make them self-explanatory, so that
something should be learned from seeing them even if there
is no printed matter. To enforce the lesson the greatest care
has been given to subtitles. These must be simple and
accurate, and while conveying a considerable amount of
information, they must be concise and pointed.

And while they were manifestly directive and educational, they
were seldom critical in tone: in only one case, that of a film entitled '*Oppin* (1930), did council officials actively seek to dissuade
the viewer from participating (as was common in southeast
London) in the Kentish hop harvest, by emphasizing the difficulty of the work and the generally exploitative conditions that
prevailed in the industry.

The council took its message into schools; lectures were given
from municipal vans that set up shop on street corners; and the
borough established publicly funded health centres – this, a
decade and more in advance the creation of the NHS. And
crucially, all this activity was *local*, in every possible way. The
films featured council employees, the scenes were always set in
and around Bermondsey; the production companies were
contracted by the council – and the audiences were drawn from
the council's classes, clinics and hospitals.

All this activity, as well as having practical applications, was
also ideological – it championed the concept of the supremacy

of local authorities over national government. It set the scene for repeated clashes between Bermondsey council and successive governments at Westminster, which – although state policy in general was also moving decisively towards the principle of intervention – nevertheless disliked intensely the political independence pursued in this corner of south London. For Bermondsey council, with figures such as Connan and the Salters at the heart of it, was set on carving out a kind of social democratic autonomy, in which the local would always trump central government, the medical establishment and the conservative-minded local charities that for much of the Victorian era had provided relief and succour to the poor.

It is difficult to judge the consequences of the council's efforts: the incidence of tuberculosis did indeed fall precipitously in the years following the Great War, but this was at least in part due to the steep fall in the population of Bermondsey itself – from an estimated 123,000 in 1924 to approximately 60,000 in 1953 when the municipal lectures and films ceased. The increasingly interventionist policies of central government – for example, the Maternity and Child Welfare Act passed as early as 1918 – also played a part in the general improvement in public health; and the creation of the NHS immediately after the Second World War removed much of the *raison d'être* of Bermondsey's emphatically local health policies. Perhaps the greatest achievement of the Salters and others who worked for the municipal government of

Bermondsey in the inter-war years was to create among borough residents a keen idea of identity and belonging: a sense of collectivity and of purposeful and pleasurable possession of their own streets and communal spaces that was in itself a public good.

'*A place of homes as well as houses*'

In 1935, yet another medical resident moved into Church Cottage on Reverdy Road. Wilfred Bardwell Mumford differed from his predecessors: he hailed from a wealthy landed background; and his family had built their wealth on the milling of

German air raids on London's economically vital docklands left deep scars in Bermondsey. In this iconic image (1940) of the city at war, Tower Bridge stands starkly against a horrifying inferno.

flour, counting among their clients the Royal Family. Mumford studied medicine at Cambridge before moving to Bermondsey to work for the Cambridge University Mission, at the same time completing his training at St George's Hospital in Tooting. Mumford had intended to work in the foreign missions, but '[A]fter I had been in Bermondsey for two years, I felt very much that perhaps this wasn't the call after all. [...] I felt increasingly that I wanted to be as good a Christian doctor as I could be in that area, in the sense an ordinary Christian doctor working among ordinary people.' (Mumford's comfortable origins asserted themselves, however, early in his tenure: he installed an art deco fireplace on the house on Reverdy Road.)

A royal walkabout: King George VI and Queen Elizabeth in wartime London. But sandbags could not always save lives: in October 1940, for example, over 100 civilians died in an air attack on Druid Street railway arches, Bermondsey.

Mumford spent the first part of World War Two working in and around the Bermondsey docks – and he witnessed the conflagration that engulfed the timber yards of the Surrey quays on 7 September 1940 – the first night of the London Blitz. On that evening, German bombs ignited a firestorm that eventually covered 100 hectares of land along the Thames, the intense heat shattering windows and melting paint miles away: photographs taken that night show Tower Bridge framed terribly against a blazing sky. It was said to have been the greatest inferno seen in London since the Great Fire of 1666, and over 400 Londoners died in this first attack of the war. The conflict brought death and destruction on a shocking scale in Bermondsey: the borough, with its docks, maritime and railway infrastructure and dense industrial network, was close to the centre of London's most affected region and thus a repeated target of German bombardment.

The six vanished houses on Reverdy Road date from aerial attacks in these first months of the Blitz. Mary Ripper – now a resident of Reverdy Road – lived on nearby Alderminster Road: 'I was just 18, pregnant, husband away fighting and the bombs dropping every night. It was exciting though. My mother-in-law used to get in the Anderson shelter but I liked to stand outside and watch the guns trying to shoot them down. Well, I couldn't keep on doing that and we started going down to London Bridge to shelter under the arches there. [...] One night I was sitting there and I could feel the baby starting to come. People said there was no ambulance available because they were all out because of the bombing. So a woman said I'd be having my baby there under the arches. […] In the end, St John Ambulance took me to St Olave's. It's only a mile away from London Bridge but it took us an hour to get there because of having to dodge all of the bombs.' Later that night, a bomb fell on the hospital itself: '[T]he nurse just dived under the bed and shouted out, "I'm sorry, missus, it's everyone for themselves". Then she got out from under the bed but instead of looking after me she ran off, leaving me in labour on my own.' Ripper gave birth safely; later in the war, she worked in a plant which manufactured fake Japanese bank notes with the intention of flooding and destroying the enemy's economy.

A War Office memo outlines the effect of German bombing on London over three months in the autumn of 1940 – and the bald statistics, though phrased coolly, are frightful:

> The durable effect of the London raids has been the killing of some 13,000 persons, the wounding of some 50,000, the destruction of some 20,000 dwelling houses, and a proportionate number of other buildings, and the serious damage to some five times that number.

The report goes on to note that nearly all the damage done to railways was 'reparable and most of it was repaired before the end of the year. Only one power station was out of action for several weeks. Many warehouses have been destroyed, mostly by fire. No important factory has been destroyed, and in only a few of them has production seriously diminished. Chaotic passenger and goods traffic was probably more effective, as a retarding factor, than direct damage in the early weeks.'

Certain residents of Bermondsey might not have agreed with this relatively upbeat assessment – particularly those caught in a German bombardment of Druid Street on 25 October 1940. It was commonplace for Londoners to sit out periods of bombing in the deepest Tube stations and under the stout Victorian railway arches that criss-crossed the capital. On this particular evening, a 50-kilogram bomb exploded close to the Druid Street arches: the structure withstood the blast but the explosion killed more than 100 civilians and injured many more. Such disasters, if not quite everyday, were relatively commonplace: and although under-reported by the media of the day, they nevertheless took their toll on wartime civilian morale. Wilfred Mumford – who remained in Bermondsey until called up for naval service in 1941, returning to Reverdy Road at the end of the war – recalls that:

> Whole streets were completely empty, and rows and rows of little houses, which had been cockney homes, were damaged and perhaps beyond repair [...] the people who had been left behind for various reasons, all went to live permanently as sort of troglodytes in the underground shelters [...] only coming up in day time between raids.

In the aftermath of war, the borough was in need of massive investment and rebuilding – not to mention repopulation. In a speech delivered in 1947, the then Archbishop of Canterbury, Geoffrey Fisher, promised that:

> The new Bermondsey that will arise from the ashes of the old may be a place of homes as well as houses, of neighbours as well as door numbers, a place of civic pride and common service.

At first, this new Bermondsey would take the form of high-rise blocks of flats erected to house a gradually rising population – but the impact of such new living arrangements was not always beneficial. High-rise flats, Mumford wrote, 'were hailed at the time as the answer to the housing problem, but many of us now know only too well what social and psychological problems are created amongst those who have the misfortune to live in them'. The old housing stock epitomised by Reverdy Road and its sister streets might well have been pulled down at this time, to make way for just such blocks of flats. And some *did* vanish: the elegant Victorian homes which lined Thorburn Square were demolished in 1963 and the present four lines of flats and maisonettes erected in their place. The remainder of the neighbourhood, however, was saved as the result of a sudden, transformative development. In 1960, the West estate (which still retained ownership of these houses) put its entire housing stock up for auction – and the council, acting secretly through a front man, bought the lot – 787 houses, 37 shops, 16 sites, 2 garages, 6 factories, the estate office, a Territorial Army drill hall and the Bermondsey Telephone Exchange – for a grand total of £375,000. It was one of Bermondsey council's last grand acts before it was subsumed into a larger Southwark council five years later. The houses, then, remained in public ownership – but the rules of the game changed fundamentally. No longer could a property (or a storey of it) be sublet informally: suddenly, this was all done through the council; and an informal housing allocation system that had worked through word of mouth and family members for decades was now decided instead by local council officers, who were duty-bound to consider one's stake in the street and local community as part of a housing application.

It was a more modern system, to be sure, but it was not welcomed by all. Reverdy Road was administered from one such council office on nearby Lynton Road, staffed by an interviewer in the front room and an allocations officer in the back room. The office held the keys to all the houses. The council also had a duty to bring the houses – some war-damaged, many still featuring toilets in the back garden – up to modern standards. As a result, the streets were renovated, property by property – and in due course became much sought-after. Houses could be allocated in a casual manner that would be unimaginable today; equally the local council officials could, on occasion, be corrupted – as Terry Sullivan, resident of the area, recalls:

When the council bought up the street, they moved people
out temporarily so they could re-decorate the houses and
do them up a bit. I noticed this house. [...] It was opposite
where I lived at 150 Fort Road, which was about to be
redecorated [...] so I went along to the council and they
offered me temporary accomodation at 113 Fort Road, and
I said I'd like 143 Fort Road if possible. Well, the woman
dealing with me looked in a drawer for some keys and
found them and said: 'well, here you are; you can move in'.
She gave me a tenancy agreement as well. So we just moved
in. A couple of days later a man came from the council and
he said he needed to see our tenancy agreement. He just
took it and said we had to move out because he's already let
the house to someone else. I asked him and he wouldn't tell
me. I reckon money had changed hands ...

Sullivan managed to retain the house, but more dramatic changes
were underway which would begin to alter fundamentally the
nature of Bermondsey society. In 1979, Margaret Thatcher's
incoming Conservative government passed the Housing Act,
conferring on council tenants the right to buy their homes. In an
area such as Bermondsey, renting property had been for decades
woven into the fabric of everyday life; now, however, council
tenants could buy their house with as much as a 70 per cent
discount. This was an important practical measure – but it was
ideological too, and this was understood clearly in Bermondsey.

The Conservatives wanted to create a nation of homeowners –
but for those on the Left, such a policy would eventually lead to
the filleting of the nation's stock of public housing. On and
around Reverdy Road, some residents took the chance to buy
their homes: Terry Sullivan and his family bought 143 Fort Road
in 1984 for £11,000.

These were profoundly divisive times in Bermondsey. In
1983, a by-election pushed the area into the national headlines
and exposed the deep divisions within the once all-powerful
local Labour organisation. Bermondsey had once been an
impregnable bastion of Labour power – but at the close of a
disastrous campaign for the party, the seat was lost to the
Liberals on a massive 44 per cent swing. The campaign was
marked by openly expressed homophobia and bitter personal
invective – the Labour candidate, Peter Tatchell, was gay – but
it also crystallized in local terms the ideological strife that characterized the national political culture in the 1980s.

On Reverdy Road, a pattern began to unfold – one that
would soon become familiar up and down the land: every few
houses, the older tenants would exercise their right to buy; and
today, a third of the houses are occupied by people who moved
in during the 1970s. These would be the last generations of
their families that could afford to live in Bermondsey – and the
impact of this change would ripple in the years to come. In the
late 1980s and early 1990s, the local housing departments
were centralized into large single processing offices: the office

that covered Reverdy Road and the surrounding streets, for example, was located in Peckham. How could an official working from Peckham know whether or not it was appropriate to house a given individual or family on Reverdy Road? In addition, the new housing policies were guided by the principle of need, with priority given to those who *needed* most over those who on paper deserved it most. As a result, a son or daughter of someone who lived on Reverdy Road could not compete with other, more needy, applicants – and would inevitably end up moving out to London's suburban fringe. The only way one could hope of getting a house around Bermondsey was, as one resident noted, to lie: 'I told the council my mum was chucking me out because I was sleeping with a black man.' She was rehoused rapidly.

The present shape of Reverdy Road owes much to the vagaries of history: to the development by the West Estate of a batch of sturdy houses on a group of tidy streets a century and a half ago; to the twentieth-century evolution of a socialist culture in Bermondsey; and to a final intervention of a soon-to-be-extinct Bermondsey council in the housing market of the 1960s. The area might have been cleared and the community dispersed to tower blocks, or to outer London and Kent – but instead, the streets remained essentially intact. Today, the third who exercised their 'right to buy' remain living on what was the West estate. Another third of the houses are still council owned: however, now when a council house comes available, the council is more likely to sell, or often auction, it off; recently, for example, 62 Reverdy Road was auctioned by the local council for over £300,000. Others who bought their homes in and around Reverdy Road have since moved out or passed away; and their children's new lives in outer London and Kent won't be exchanged for a return to Bermondsey. With these social changes, and the council continuing to sell off homes, the face of the community in this part of the district is likely to alter in the years to come. While the residents might be different, however, the impulse remains the same today as back in 1951, when the *Picture Post* noted:

Nobody ever loved the whole of London, but there are people who would die for a side street in Bermondsey or a corner of the Old Kent Road.

Things Fall Apart

DEPTFORD HIGH STREET

The whole of the working classes of Deptford are impregnated with free thought. Not because they really believe the Bible is untrue but because they would like to think it is. This leads to great indifference to spiritual things.

Charles Booth

In July 1899, Charles Booth arrived on Deptford High Street to survey the area and incorporate it into his social map of the city. The street was at that time the Oxford Street of southeast London: a thriving thoroughfare thronged with shops and market stalls, a community in which traders lived over their shops and prospered. And the shops, it seemed, could cater to every commercial need: fishmongers, china shops and coffee houses, butchers and bakeries, hosieries, greengrocers, jewellers, confectioners and milliners – they were all represented on Deptford High Street. At weekends, the shops and stalls stayed open until ten o'clock – and the street was packed with shoppers. And, while these traders came from predominantly working-class stock, many households included at least one servant.

Booth duly zoned the High Street as red – well-to-do and prosperous; and something of a surprising conclusion in a district rarely visited by 'respectable' folk. This red zone, however, ran north–south through one of London's poorest districts – for, while the people of Deptford might have dressed with the respectability that was the code of the time, there was no wealthy customer base in the area. Instead, a working-class community sustained the High Street's wealth; the streets that ran off east and west were light blue, dark blue and black – inhabited by, in Booth's coding, by the poor, very poor and vicious and semi-criminal. This was an old, tightly-knit community – and in the century to come, the history of the High Street would be bound up with the history of these people and this network of streets.

More than a century on from Booth's survey, Deptford High Street still runs from New Cross north towards the Thames. The street layout with which Booth became familiar remains identifiable: on either side of the main thoroughfare a host of other streets still branch to east and west – Douglas Way, Albury Street, Reginald Road, Giffin Street, Frankham Street, Edward Street. At its mid-point, the High Street is sliced in two by the viaduct carrying the railway line from London Bridge down to Greenwich: north of this line (the first commuter railway in the world) the life of the High Street is quieter, more subdued; south of the line lies a more dense cluster of shops and cafes. As with Bermondsey, the architectural character of Deptford High Street was fixed in the nineteenth century – and this Georgian and Victorian legacy survives above the modern shop fronts, in handsome facades, confident decoration and brickwork laid to stand the test of time.

At street level, the shops themselves are modern now: convenience stores, pawnbrokers and bookmakers, bric-a-brac shops and a gleaming fishmonger jostle against a range of African churches and ethnic food stores; the life of Deptford's long-enduring street market still hums and bawls and jostles all around. Three times a week, a second-hand market meets on Douglas Way, selling everything from vinyl record collections to sofas and kitchen tables. A modern arts and community centre faces the second-hand market and it attracts other visitors: pre-school playgroups meet here; the local MP holds her surgeries here; market customers take their rest at the cafe. The commercial atmosphere is vibrant and lively – yet the proliferation of pound shops and heavily discounted goods betrays the deep-seated economic poverty of the area: they jar against the glinting towers of Canary Wharf on the other side of the Thames; and against the golden cube of the new primary school building – so strangely at odds with its surroundings – on nearby Giffin Street. On the quieter side streets, meanwhile, are further layers of history. Towards the Thames, Albury Street represents a more genteel Deptford: its handsome early Georgian terraces are being gentrified; and property prices mirror its changing fortunes. Further north, conversely, Reginald Road is a product of the 1960s, its old housing stock swept away and replaced by

Albury Street, noted Booth, had been 'built for middle class and formerly occupied by sea captains' – but in this scene, dated 1911, it has fallen on hard times. By the 1960s, it had become a slum.

modern council flats. Deptford is stamped indelibly with the evidence of its long past – but its High Street with its bustling market represents London at its most emphatically multi-ethnic, various and diverse.

This version of Deptford, however, is a relatively recent phenomenon. Until the 1960s, the High Street exemplified the Deptford that Booth surveyed and understood: a white, working-class society that lived amid challenging economic circumstances. The businesses that filled the street – the public houses, the market traders – had their role to play, each catering to a specific section of a delicately balanced and intricately constructed community. How this Deptford came to evolve, and how it came to dissolve with startling rapidity, is the ongoing story of power and possession. For the question of who precisely owns Deptford, its spaces and its people has never been easily answered – and it continues to be posed today.

* * *

Deptford, even more than most riverside districts of London, owes its life to the water. The Thames flows to the north; the muddy Ravensbourne comes down through Beckenham and Lewisham to reach the Thames at Deptford's waterfront, by which point it is known (prosaically) as Deptford Creek or (affectionately) as the Quaggy; the heart of Deptford lies in the angle of the two rivers. The terraces and views and splendid symmetrical buildings at Greenwich lie just to the east; high-rise buildings gleam on the Isle of Dogs to the north; and the hilly terrain of Lewisham and Blackheath clip the district to the south. Deptford, however, is defined by its margins of water – and in a city of distinct neighbourhoods and local loyalties, its character is one of the most distinct and local of all.

The Romans found on this spot a suitable crossing of the Ravensbourne – and the name derives from this *deep ford*; but it was not until Tudor times that Deptford began to figure in larger national calculations. Henry VIII came to the throne in

1509 eager to rebuild the power and prestige that England had lost during decades of internal strife and foreign policy reversals; and anxious too to secure the still-doubtful Tudor hold on the throne. One result was the establishment of a naval dockyard on the Thames at Deptford, with the intention of establishing a powerful national fleet. The yard would function for the next 300 years; and the fortunes of it and the area in general gradually became intertwined. In 1581, Henry's daughter Elizabeth I – born in nearby Greenwich – visited the new dockyard to knight the adventurer and privateer Francis Drake; in 1593, the dramatist Christopher Marlowe was stabbed to death in a Deptford tavern; a century later, Peter the Great stayed for three months in Deptford to study the intricacies of shipbuilding and to plan the construction of a new Russian fleet.

The area began to profit from its associations with the New World: ships fitted out at the Deptford docks were mainstays in the Atlantic 'triangular' route, bringing slaves from Africa to the New World and sugar back to Europe; at Deptford, the Pett family of master shipbuilders built many of the ships that took part in this highly lucrative trade; and the interior of St Paul's church features a plaque acknowledging the economic prosperity their activities brought to the area. James Cook had his *Resolution* fitted out to ultra-modern standards at the dockyard too, before embarking on his second circumnavigation of the globe; and folk memory has it that Lord Nelson visited his mistress Emma Hamilton at her Albury Street home. Deptford was close to the centre of things: precious timbers were stored here; grain and other foodstuffs were landed and processed here before being despatched to feed the swelling population of London; strategic and commercial decisions were made here; and ships were repaired and fitted out here that would sail to secure Britain's control of the seas. And it was a sign of this rising prominence that the commercial life of the area began to shift from Church Street to the previously unprepossessing thoroughfare known as Butt Lane, where there was more space and larger premises to be had. In 1825, a polite notice appeared: 'THE PUBLICK', it stated, 'are respectfully informed, that by the general Consent of the Inhabitants, the NAME of the STREET hitherto called BUTT LANE is now altered to HIGH STREET, by which Appellation it will in future be designated.' By this stage, three public houses already operated on the newly designated High Street within 50 years, this number would rise to 12.

Deptford's significance was bolstered by the arrival of the railway. As early as February 1836, the London and Greenwich railway company ran a track from Bermondsey down to Deptford; later that same year, London Bridge station opened to a flood of commuters and pleasure trippers for whom Deptford and its environs were now mere minutes away. Twenty thousand passengers used the railway in its first month. The navvies built the Bermondsey–Deptford line across landscapes that were still open fields and orchards: fewer houses had to be pulled down to make way for the new line; and so the area was able to receive its first trains earlier than most.

And yet such signs of modernity also brought distress: London south of the Thames might have been less densely urban than the city north of the river – but in Deptford as elsewhere in south London, many people were displaced by the building of these new railways; and these people seldom had anywhere to go. The railway companies insisted that such unfortunates could move into the large new neighbourhoods that were opening up across the capital – but naturally, not everyone could afford such a move, any more than they could afford the price of a railway ticket; and one result was chronic overcrowding in the small streets that ran off Deptford High Street. In 1861, *The Times* noted that:

> The poor are displaced but they are not removed. They are shovelled out of one side of the parish, only to render more overcrowded the stifling apartments in the other part. [...] But the dock and wharf labourer, the porter and the coster-monger cannot remove. You may pull down their wretched homes; they must find others, and make their new dwellings more crowded and wretched than their old ones. The tailor, shoemaker and other workmen are in much the same position. It is a mockery to speak of the suburbs to them.

Nor did Deptford benefit from Britain's creation of a modern industrial economy. This became starkly evident as the Royal Navy expanded to adapt to the challenges of the new imperial century. It became clear that the Thames at Deptford was too confined and shallow to permit the construction of the larger modern vessels now needed by the Navy; gradually, work diminished, until the dockyard finally closed in 1869. Associated industries the victualling of the ships, the trade in timber and sails and the paraphernalia of maritime life – also began to fade away; the area struggled to match its past success and prominence. The writer Edgar Wallace – best known as the creator of King Kong – remembered his nineteenth-century south Deptford childhood against a backdrop of decline and dissolution:

> The houses are narrow fronted and of a set pattern. There are over hanging wooden canopies to each of the doors: in some one finds traces of oak panelling but usually the present day tenants have utilized such of the wood as they can detach for the purpose of lighting their fires. For what was once Deptford's glory is now Deptford's slum. The great houses ring with the shrill voices of innumerable children. Floor after floor is let out in tenements and in some cases a dozen families occupy the restricted space which in olden times barely sufficed to accommodate the progeny of opulent ship's chandlers.

Other economic activities moved in: in particular, the establishment of the Cattle Market in 1871 on a section of the former
docks provided a boost for the area. New laws enacted in 1869
stipulated that livestock imported from overseas must be segre-
gated and contained within specific areas – and so the docks at
Deptford came to be seen as a place apart, removed from the
public sphere. Significantly, they also provided employment now
for a partially *female* workforce, tasked with the slaughter of
sheep and cattle and the processing of their carcasses. It was a
vital local source of income – but it also confirmed a sense that
there was nothing picturesque about Deptford: this was a place
that got its hands dirty and in the process failed (spectacularly
in the case of the women and girls in the slaughterhouses) to
conform to the norms of Victorian society.

As a dockers' and naval community, however, Deptford had
always been beyond the pale. This was a hybrid world: a variety of Londoners mingled with people from across Britain, from
Ireland and the Low Countries; Jews from the Baltic, Poland and
Russia; descendants of Huguenots fleeing persecution in Europe
– and others busy with myriad trades. The traders on the High
Street itself, attracted by the commercial opportunities available
in Deptford, came from all over the world – from Germany,
Poland, the Caribbean, India and the United States; the fish and
chip shop was French-run. 'Many had thick Irish accents,' Terry
McCarthy wrote in his history of the Great Dock Strike of 1889.

'Many of the seamen and dockers were Lascars [i.e., Indian seamen], a name given to any man or woman who appeared to be of foreign origin or dark skinned. There were also migrant workers from Wiltshire who specialized in the timber trades in the Isle of Dogs and Deptford and Millwall, who still wore their traditional garb of no boots but feet swathed in cloth.'

Privacy was difficult to come by: houses and lodgings were too small, too unpleasant, too crowded to function as communal living spaces: the result was that lives tended to be lived in public – and specifically on the boisterous, rowdy, theatrical, hard-drinking High Street itself and in the warm interiors of its myriad public houses. It was impossible to categorize or control such a population, living in such a way – and the result was that Deptford began to occupy a specific place in the Victorian imagination: a focus of anxiety and of moralizing, agitated rhetoric. Commentators began to pronounce judgment on the area and its people. 'The courts and alleys round about the dock,' noted Henry Mayhew in his voluminous *London Labour and the London Poor*, 'swarm with low lodging houses; and are inhabited either by the dock labourers, sack makers, watermen or that peculiar class of the London poor who pick up a living by the water-tide.'

Mayhew noted too the urchin who scavenged the waterline of the Thames at low tide: a chilly, comfortless job at the best of times, but especially so when the urchin in question had no shoes and could not remember when last he possessed a pair. And there was more: Deptford folk drank too much, fought too much, sang and shouted too much; and domestic discord spilled indiscreetly over the doorsteps onto the High Street and its web of side-streets and alleys. The Wesleyan commentator Robert Sparrow described these scenes in terms that translated a rising anxiety of respectable folk: the mob of Deptford must be ruled and reduced to a state resembling submission – the alternative being a threat to the stability of society itself:

> Deptford High Street is not a desirable place to be in on a Saturday evening, *unless* you enjoy being jostled here and there, or pushed anywhere by a crowd. If you are out looking for quietness, whatever else you do, don't come into the vicinity of this street. Even before you leave New Cross Road you can hear the noise and the bustle, and once you enter the High Street you are immediately in the midst of 'Buy Buy Buy', 'Here you are, lady!', 'Pick where you like!', 'Four and a half a pound!', 'A penny a bunch!' etc., etc. What with shop assistants and curbstone merchants, the air is filled with all kinds of discordant noises. The clock has struck 11 p.m. but as yet there is very little evidence of the lateness of the hour. As you look at the crowds of people, and notice the signs of activity on every hand, it is easy to forget that it is rapidly approaching the midnight hour. [...]

It is not long however before you are faced with a most
lamentable fact. See the number of children who are, at this
late hour of the night, out on the streets, uncared for,
neglected and apparently for the time, forgotten.

To respectable Victorian opinion, it was too much to be borne.
On 8 June 1894, a public meeting was held in a church hall at
Brockley, south of Deptford High Street, to launch the Deptford Fund, aimed at alleviating the social and economic distress
in the neighbourhood. The Fund quickly gathered strength and
resources and established its own programme of providing
subsidized meals to the sick of the area: in 1895, the kitchen
served 5,427 meals; by 1910, this had risen to over 30,000. In
1898, the Prince of Wales laid the foundation stone for a permanent building for the Deptford Fund on Creek Road, at the
north end of the High Street; and in 1899, this new Albany
Institute was opened by the Duchess of Albany, daughter-in-law
of Queen Victoria. It was the beginning of an improbable but
sustained relationship between the British establishment and
the Deptford poor.

The reasons for this particular attention to Deptford lie in the
political and social context of the time. Victoria had marked her
Diamond Jubilee on 21 June 1897 with a vast celebration: some
three million people had gathered to witness a royal procession
through the streets of London, a service of thanksgiving at St

Paul's, and a march-past of some 50,000 troops gathered from all corners of the empire. There seemed every reason to be complacent about the future – and yet it was clear to the Victorians that not all was well. Britain's military and commercial might were under threat as never before, with Germany and the United States snapping at the country's heels. In Ireland, the Jubilee had been marked by a silent procession through the streets of Dublin, which culminated with an empty coffin, symbolizing the death of empire, being tipped into the river Liffey. In 1899, early reverses sustained in the Boer War seemed to underscore British vulnerabilities; and as that conflict progressed, tales of concentration camps and military massacres undermined what had been an abiding Victorian sense of moral rectitude.

Closer to home, the rise of socialism was also becoming difficult to ignore: the writings of Karl Marx were already several decades old; in the Jubilee year, the Scottish Labour activist James Kier Hardie dismissed Victoria and her large family as parasites; and waves of industrial unrest rippled across London's docklands. Deptford was particularly prone to extreme Godlessness and political passions: one contemporary commentator noted of the area that '[T]ens of thousands attend no place of worship. Atheism, Secularism, and Socialism, with their attendant lawlessness and immorality abound, and are publicly propagated. Intemperance and religious indifference, with the direst poverty, and the deepest degradation ...' Some observers of the scene were

Radical politics traditionally had deep roots in Deptford: anarchists, socialists and revolutionaries of every stripe found a secure home in the public houses that lined the High Street; and street confrontations – like this one in 1921 – with the authorities were woven into the culture of the district.

acutely aware of the plight of the workers, and railed at the harsh criticism levelled at the dockers. 'You only have to see the ghastly tenements, the cramped and crowded hovels, in which these men and their families live,' noted the Wesleyan minister J. Gregory Mantle, 'to know the rent they have to pay; to calculate the cost of coal and provisions when they are at their normal prices, and are of necessity bought in small quantities, to cease to wonder at the prevailing exasperation. [...] These men were on strike, because they felt that the time had come when they ought to make an effort to improve their condition...'

Such liberal notions would have cut no ice with the authorities responsible for keeping the peace at this volatile moment.
The Times of 11 February 1886 reported that:

10,000 men were on the march from Deptford to London,
destroying as they came the property of small traders. A
jeweller had informed Southwark police that he had seen
'roughs' gathering at Deptford. The police alerted shopkeepers and from there the panic spread throughout South
London [...] The shops closed and people stood at their
doors straining their eyes through the fog for the sounds of
the 10,000 men who were stated to be marching to the City.
[...] By mid afternoon the terror in South London was so
general that the schools were besieged by anxious parents
wanting to take their children home. [...] In Whitechapel a
mob was said to be marching down from the Commercial
Road, at Bethnal Green, the mob was said to be at Green
Street. [...] In the City and West End approaches were
guarded. Banks closed down and bridges were protected.
The gates of Downing Street shut [...] Troops were confined
to barracks in the company of magistrates who were to read
the riot act when the mob approached...

Eighteen months later, a joint socialist-Irish nationalist march
to Trafalgar Square ended in violent clashes between the

Charles Booth (1840–1916): his immensely influential *Life and Labour of the People in London* was the most comprehensive survey of the city ever attempted. The series eventually ran to seventeen volumes.

London County Council Election

THURSDAY, MARCH 5th, 1931.   *8 a.m. to 8 p.m.*

West Bermondsey Electoral Division

Mrs. F. M. LOWE, J.P.

Election Address of the

Labour Candidates

Mrs. A. SALTER

Your support is earnestly requested on behalf of

LOWE & SALTER
The Labour Candidates

Ada Salter (1866–1942) was committed to socialism, Christianity and female suffrage: 'her motive was religious but she soon added a social purpose to it'. She left a lasting legacy in Bermondsey in the shape of the thousands of trees – plane, birch, hornbeam and poplar – planted in the borough during her time as councillor.

Deptford High Street, always packed, always raucous, was in its commercial heyday the thriving Oxford Street of south-east London. In this image, dated 1913, the local version of the *passeggiata* is in full swing.

The shops on bustling Deptford High Street could cater to every commercial need: fishmongers, china shops and coffee houses, butchers and bakeries, hosieries, greengrocers, jewellers, confectioners and milliners – they were all represented.

Dorothy Tennant's *Street Arabs at Play* (1890) – painted as Booth's survey was gaining momentum – is a reminder of the innocence of childhood. Yet even here, the harsh realities of life in the city are evident: note how the smoking chimneys of London furnish a forbidding backdrop.

Celia and Simon Finkelstein: Jewish refugees who had fled religious persecution in Russia and settled in the East End. By 1896, they had prospered to such an extent that they could afford to rent a two-bedroom flat on Calvert Avenue – part of a thriving Jewish community on the Boundary estate.

By the 1960s, the ethnic and religious composition of the Boundary estate was shifting: the Jews of the East End were moving to other parts of London; and their places were being taken by a rapidly expanding Bengali community.

The Victorian Caledonian Road featured every form of shop under the sun: from butchers and bakers to coffin-making emporia and pie-and-mash shops; the streets were thronged with hawkers, barrows and flower and fruit sellers; and at night, the whole scene was lit brilliantly with gas lamps.

Elegant Keystone Crescent at the southern end of the Cally (1971). The Crescent – one of the area's prime architectural features – was threatened with destruction (along with much of the neighbourhood) by the proposed Channel Tunnel rail link: ultimately, the street was saved and is now listed.

The streetwise, cigarette-clutching youth of post-war Portland Road. There are still few indications of the wave of gentrification shortly to sweep much of the street.

This street scene captures the ramshackle nature of Portland Road in the 1940s and 1950s, when living conditions were frequently atrocious. But there is also a sense of safety and community in this image: these children – unlike those today – are actually playing on the street.

Camberwell Grove began life as a tree-lined avenue. It was most likely formed as a picturesque feature in the landscape; and to enable the residents of nearby Court House to stroll easily to the top of the hill, to take in the views over Surrey and distant London.

Camberwell Grove S. E.

The fortunate residents of Victorian Camberwell could avail of any number of local delights, including galleries, department stores, baths, libraries – and here, the Metropole Theatre and Opera.

marchers and the police on what became known as Bloody Sunday – the first of that name. Three demonstrators were killed; and a hundred more injured.

In the eyes of the authorities, however, there were even more alarming phenomena than socialism – notably the rise of an anarchist movement in London. In *Degeneration* (1892), the political theorist Max Nordau outlined his pessimistic vision of Europe's future and identified anarchists (with artists and authors) as members of a single, contaminated family responsible for engendering 'vertigo' in society – and such degeneracy had specific connections into Deptford itself. In April 1897 one Rollo Richards of Edward Street, Deptford appeared at the Old Bailey on charges of 'Feloniously causing an explosion by gunpowder on August 14th, 1894, likely to endanger life'. A prosecution witness, Michael Walsh, testified that:

[F]or some years I have attended meetings convened at Deptford Broadway, on Sunday evenings, by persons calling themselves Anarchists – I have seen the prisoner at them scores of times – on January 24th, 1897, at one of those meetings, in a discussion about the Barcelona Anarchists, the prisoner intervened – he said foreign Anarchists, as a rule, used nitro-glycerine in manufacturing bombs, especially for blowing up safes, and they throw rugs and carpets

over the safes to deaden the sound – subsequently he added
that was much easier than a bomb. [...] There are plenty of
Anarchists all over London, some foreigners...

Given the sustained impact of Irish terrorism also in evidence on
the streets of London at this time, this idea of an evolving strain
of homegrown political extremism racheted up levels of anxiety
yet further.

Personal connection helped to focus wider attention on Deptford's plight in a positive way. The district had received up to
then very little systematic Victorian charity: instead, the political spotlight had been turned onto other areas – resulting in new
housing and infrastructure for needy districts of the East End.
Efforts at charity and grassroots work in Deptford, by contrast,
had been undertaken principally by local agencies, to limited
effect. One such agency was the Women Workers for God, better
known as the Grey Ladies, an Anglican community which served
the sick and disadvantaged. The friendship between one of these
Ladies (a Miss Rice) – and a well-connected aristocrat (one
Viscount Templeton) lit the spark that led to the establishment
of the Deptford Fund. From such a random connection came an
enduring Deptford presence.

Victorian philanthropy and charity tended to come with
strings attached – in this case, pressure to circumscribe the unbe-
coming work undertaken by women and girls in the Deptford

slaughterhouses. The result was to deprive dozens of women and girls of their jobs. (Attempts were made on behalf of the Duchess of Albany to chivvy the girls into 'service' in nearby well-to-do areas of Brockley and Blackheath: the only problem was that work in the slaughterhouses was both better fun and better paid; and on one visit, the Duchess was booed for her pains.) It seemed appropriate that the building for the new Albany Institute – the overriding purpose of which was to instruct the unruly folk of Deptford in virtuous activity – should be faced in stone, sport turrets, slit windows and the thickest of walls, and stand like a fortress on the Thames. The message was clear: this was an institution built fundamentally to stem the tide of workers' militancy.

The day began at the Institute with hymns and prayers; classes followed in needlework, laundry, dressmaking and other aspects of domestic economy; there were regular improving lectures; each course lasted for five months. The usual array of Christian clubs, mothers' unions, Bands of Hope, Sunday School classes, temperance organisations and missionary activities were also housed in the building: the Albany became a positive hive of activity. From here, these organizations fanned out onto the High Street: missionaries worked the public houses and the crowds of street drinkers, attempting to coax converts into the way of respectability; temperance halls bribed new recruits with free food and house visits; and the Salvation Army marched up and down the High Street, deploying music to open the road to righteousness, political moderation and social respectability. Not every observer of this frenzied scene was pleased: in order for the Institute to raise funds, the situation in the neighbourhood was frequently portrayed as worse than it was. For the area's expanding working- and middle-class population, it was vexing to have their home portrayed continually as a nest of wickedness and vice.

The work undertaken in the Albany building was impelled by philanthropy, and the urgent need to address pressing social and economic issues. Yet it was something else too: an assertion of a philosophical vision, of a kind of ownership, a bid for power and influence. It staked a claim on the area's present and on its future, and it laid down a marker for the kind of society Deptford *ought* to become. Its fundamental paternalism established a theme of possession that would endure as the new century unfolded.

'These people are not like ordinary South Londoners'

This was Deptford High Street as Charles Booth found in July 1899, stepping out in the company of a variety of police officers to survey its streets. He met his first companion, an Inspector

Gummer, at Deptford Bridge, with its modern, prosperous shops, clock tower and Liberal Club ('red as map') – and the usual pen-and-ink descriptions were immediately flourished: his first companion, for example, 'is a smart well-dressed, portly man. Jacket suit and straw hat'. The diversity of the area at once became apparent: the zones ranging from red to purple to black and back again; the well-heeled drapers' shops, German bakeries and proliferation of other shops on the High Street giving way abruptly to bare-footed children and loitering men, to 'Irish streets' and the 'Italian colonies' living above a stables at the railway arches, to ponies and traps standing idle and vacant spaces where houses had lately been demolished. The area was chronically overcrowded: '[H]ardly a family in Giffin Street or Regent Street has more than one room. This overcrowding is a great drawback to visiting. Most difficult to get a chat with the men and women because the children overhear everything and are mischievously precocious.' In general, however, Booth could rely on his own observations in order to describe life on and around the High Street:

> Two men breaking up some gas fittings and putting the metal in a sack [...] Low class, some prostitutes, hawkers etc. Like streets in Notting Dale. [...] broken windows some street sellers. Two women talking in roadway as we entered. 'Well known prostitutes' said the Inspector. The women

moved off quickly, evidently recognizing him. [...] Candle factory at end of street, emitting very evil smells. A few Italians; some costers and prostitutes; shoeless children running about and frowsy women gaping at the doors.

Later, Booth made his way onto Reginald Road, where he found – significantly, given the later history of the road – good housing, all crisp curtains, flower gardens and trim neatness: the inmates, though crowded usually two families to a house, were 'comfortable working people'. These were 'nice little houses,' concluded Booth approvingly, 'only a few' looked otherwise. Moving north along the High Street to Albury Street, he found more to approve – even though the street had fallen visibly from its previously prosperous social position: 'Old 3 storey houses,' notes Booth, 'built for middle class and formerly occupied by sea captains etc. [...] PURPLE as map. [...] Mary Anne Buildings at east end is a small cottage, about 3 rooms ground floor only with large garden in front filled with vegetables, "new laid eggs for sale". Pink in character.' The two men continued their walk, however, and rapidly 'squalid poverty re-emerges once again'.

Police officers insisted that Deptford had improved – but they were evidently disbelieved: 'I have grave doubts as to the knowledge of the police of the social condition of the people. They measure the streets mainly by the proportion of offences against the law; and diminution of these is an improvement which they attribute to the improved social position.' And the following week, he discovered more than enough evidence to back this assessment – in crossing Evelyn Street and into the low-lying tangle of lanes and roads north, between the High Street and the Thames, he uncovered ample human deprivation:

> Watergate Street [...] Except a few shops on west all is poor [...] Faint fetid smell prevails, overpowered in places by disgusting stenches. Rough women; one with head band-aged; others with black eyes; one old harridan sitting on doorstep with a dirty clay pipe; shoeless children. Costers, street sellers, gut cleaners. 'Wherever there is a beer there they are and the more the better' was the sergeant's summing up of these people. Some of the houses have been good family residences: one now occupied as a tenement house has a fine carved overhanging porch with a fat cherub carved in full relief supporting the pediment on either side. Dark blue as map.

Booth's notes create a powerfully evocative image of Deptford High Street and its tributaries at the close of the century, frequently recording in microscopic detail the conditions of working-class existence in the area, the ills of a large proportion of the housing stock, the fragility of the economy and the sheer difficulty and stress of much of the available work – details

which, taken together, reveal the life of a High Street now utterly
lost. But they also indicate the rich texture of this life: for
although poverty, overcrowding and wretchedness are very
much present in Deptford, they by no means define it: commercial activity bustles; and pockets of relative affluence, even of
civic pride, can be discerned. The monochrome Deptford that
drove the work and ensured that funds were raised for the
Albany Institute was only part of the picture.

Booth's writings reveal his awareness of this larger and more
complex world, and even reasons for optimism. The work of a
variety of local authorities was having an impact of sorts, and
private money was also being invested: his notes record that the
stern-minded social philanthropist Octavia Hill had established
a promising presence in the area. And much of the poverty so
ubiquitous among Deptford families could be put down, not to
an absence of jobs, but to the simple fact that men were spending their wages in the beer shops before they even reached their
front doors. A thread running through Booth's work in Deptford, however, is the area's fragile economic conditions. In 1895,
as part of his previous survey of the area, Booth had described
– insightfully, though in testy tones – the work of the area's
slaughterhouses.

Slaughtermen work in gangs of from 3 to 10: the usual
number of a gang is 4 or 5; they are divided into dressers,

poundsmen and offal men. In a gang of four there will be one dresser, an upper and under poundsman and one offal man. The actual killing is usually done by the dresser – who is the head of the gang – but sometimes by the upper poundsman. They are paid 2/6 for each bullock and 6d for each sheep. The dresser has to finish off the carcass after it has been skinned and cleaned out. The poundsmen pound the bullock, skin it and prepare it for the dresser, the offal man cuts off the head and cleans out the offal. [...] Some men are able to carry out any part of the operation. [...] However as far as earnings go this does not seem to affect their position as the gang shares all money equally between them.

Both hours and wages available to the men were 'exceedingly irregular'; in addition, the men seldom had any guarantee of work in advance. The results were inevitable: average wages remained very low. Other interviews further highlighted this chronic irregularity of hours – and therefore of quality of life, in effect illuminating Deptford's difficulties in the face of modernization and regulation. The situation echoed that of Bermondsey: capital and industry that were mobile in nature, able to migrate rapidly from one place to another in search of optimum conditions. In addition, the advent of refrigeration was bringing to an end the live animal market – and the meat trade in the area, it seemed,

simply could not adapt nimbly enough to keep up with these seis-
mic changes. There had been a time when half of Europe was
sending its animals to Deptford – but this was no longer the case:
'Whereas they used to have 30,000 sheep a week, they now do not
have more than 5,000. The poverty of Deptford is due more to
their falling off of trade at the market than to anything else.' The
trade in animals was not only uneven and insecure – it was brutal-
izing and led its practitioners (in the company of publicans and,
curiously, fishmongers) along the road to an alcohol-fuelled hell.
'At Deptford especially,' Booth remarked, 'the drinking is fearful.
Many a man earns little in two days, and spends every penny of
it on drink in the two following days.' Nor were the police above
administering a few knocks themselves – considering that the men
who congregated around the market deserved nothing less. One
PC Divall said of the market that:

> Thousands of men were employed in this work, in addition
> to the seamen of various ships bringing the animals from
> America and other countries. The latter class of men
> consisted chiefly of the scum of New York and Chicago.
> [...] On their arrival at Deptford, these men often had to
> wait two or three weeks before they could find a ship to
> take them back. They spent their time hanging about this
> neighbourhood, and generally wound up by getting mad
> and drunk. Their great object was to attack the police, and

I have often seen our charge room at the station more like a slaughter-house than a place for human beings. [...] About one in the morning I was on night duty when I heard a lot of roughs singing and shouting in Stanhope Street. I moved them on with the exception of two men, who were in argumentative mood. One of them wouldn't budge, so, being aroused, I gave him a good smack on the side of the face. This he resented, and taking a running kick at me, which I dodged, he fell face downwards on the pavement. [...] That was the way we dealt with roughs in those days.

* * *

The clergymen of Deptford, as in Bermondsey, were highly opinionated observers of the local scene; and they provided a variety of insights into Deptford's alcohol and poverty-related social woes. Booth's first interview, in May 1900, was with Dr J. Hodson, the 'gloomy, dull and matter-of-fact' Anglican Rector of St Paul's – the better-off of the two Deptford parishes. Booth, however, was ready to indulge him, and as the conversation proceeded, he began to detect in the clergyman certain 'qualities of solidity and persistency, perhaps closely allied to obstinacy here, that inspired a feeling of respect. But Dr H cannot in any case be described as either an attractive or even an interesting man. He is a stick, with a keen sense of duty.' Hodson also had a keen sense of social geography and rapidly sketched the necessary contours of Deptford's landscape. It appeared that the High Street, as the main commercial thoroughfare, held most of the area's wealth: that in Deptford, the *shopkeepers* were the aristocracy; and that elsewhere, there was little or no material comfort to be had:

> Apart from the High Road [i.e., the High Street], and the small part lying to the south of this, all of the parish may be described as poor. Tradesman are his 'aristocracy'; clerks, earning as a rule, low salaries, perhaps not more than 30/- or 35/- a week on average, number perhaps 500. Then come artisans and mechanics, earning much the same amount of money; and last a labouring class, like those employed at the Victualling Yard, and earning about £1 per week.

Hodson considered that 'the slaughtermen are the most degraded class in the parish, although by no means the poorest, and of many the saying "a good drink and a woman" describes all that they ask for.' But he reserved his true disgust – in the genuine Victorian manner – for the remaining women and girls undertaking work in the slaughterhouses; and in the process he shone a light on the activities undertaken up at the Albany Institute. His description of the 'gut girls' – the remaining female workers in the local slaughterhouses – resonated with a sense of horror: the girls and women were degraded, 'perhaps more than men', by such work. The staff at the Albany, reported the clergyman, had reached out to these girls by forming clubs and a Home for Working Girls – 'one of the best things the Fund has done'.

As Hodson's interview wound on, Booth's description of him as lacking interest begins to sound unjust. The clergyman appeared, on the contrary, as one well able to deliver a good story:

> In many parts of the district, in classes other than those mentioned, there appears to be an exceptional amount of low-toned life. He mentioned the admission of a young fellow who had been caught *in flagrante delictu* 'in a drain' (an admission made to show how constant temptation was), that he could never pass a girl on the stairway of the factory where he worked without being caught in the privates.

Hodson proceeded to itemize the most immoral streets in Deptford: Baildon Street, off the south end of the High Street, was 'a thoroughly rough and bad street'; nearby Addey Street, 'where there is not a virtuous woman living'; Watergate Street leading up to the Thames, was a little less vice-plagued but 'only because it is not a cul-de-sac'; and to round things off, Irish and Roman Catholics clustered in undesirably large numbers. Hodson's parish, however, was in reasonably good shape: he was supported by three curates; and by the Nursing Sisters of

St John the Divine, who were in turn aided by four or five 'ladies'. The church had been lately renovated; the parish schools were well supported; services on the Sabbath attended by a respectable congregation; and charities and social agencies, though 'not very numerous or important', were active. 'Visiting,' noted Booth, 'is systematic throughout the parish,' and the Rector, 'like a dutiful stick, makes a point of going to every house at least once in the course of every three years'. As in Bermondsey, the clergy in Deptford seemed to spend their time either quarrelling with or ignoring each other: collections were withheld; and schisms all too frequent. Hodson emerges as an impressive surveyor of the local scene; and one with, moreover, a cheering sense of what might still be possible even in benighted Deptford. Times were harsh, and the population degraded by savage working conditions – when they had an occupation at all – and their own predisposition towards drink, gambling and fornication. However, all was not lost: such drinking and gambling must be curbed; and jobs found to replace those lost with the closing of the dockyard and decline of the animal trade – but in the end, '[T]he place has many resources, and ultimately he thinks that things are going to be much better than they are at present in Deptford'. The clergyman's vision was only moderately prescriptive and his words underscore a sense that the district's problems were economic in nature, rather than intrinsic to the people themselves.

The interview ended in startling fashion, even by Deptford standards: with a claim that the Rector was approached and offered a bribe not to oppose the establishment of a new music hall 'and Theatre of Varieties' just off the High Street. Hodson checked that he was in fact being bribed: or, was he simply being offered a 'new reredos, or even an organ, or something that the church or parish might be wanting'? Apparently not: he was being tempted with 'money I could have put in my own pocket'. Booth added, probably unnecessarily, that the Rector's credibility would have been destroyed had he accepted such a bribe – and commended Hodson's pluckiness.

Corruption was something of a Deptford theme. A month later, Booth conducted a second clerical interview: this time with the Reverend A. T. Wallis, curate of St Nicholas's, at the latter's home just off the High Street, on Albury Street. This parish, wedged into the angle between the Thames, the Creek and the railway line to Greenwich, was much the poorer and less reputable of the two local Anglican parishes – and although the London County Council (LCC) had recently made a stab at slum clearance and rebuilding, these attempts had been neither carefully executed nor effective. Efforts to obtain a public library had failed; and street lighting had not been provided either, since the electricity network lay in the hands of private companies with no interest in illuminating this poverty-stricken and unprofitable corner of London. The parish gave the impression of having been thoroughly abandoned by the authorities. 'The buildings were bare, cold and uninteresting, and the slum dwellers would not go where dirt and freedom were denied them,' noted Booth. 'It does not pay a builder to erect new houses here and now the LCC has a number of pieces of wasteland in the locality, which it would be glad to let to anyone at almost any price.'

To add to these woes, St Nicholas's seemed to attract degraded clergymen too. There was a very good reason why Booth was interviewing the curate at St Nicholas's, rather than the vicar of the church: the latter was a notorious drunkard who had been removed from his position for having run up impossible debts. Not only in Deptford, either: he was wanted by a Scarborough hotelier for having slipped away from his lodgings leaving a £200 bill unpaid. His predecessor was equally unruly, being frequently drunk in the pulpit. By contrast, Booth found the curate Wallis 'an excellent man. Not a bit clever or remarkable but a very frank, friendly, sincere man with a bright pleasant face and an engaging manner. When Mr W came church work was positively dead: the church was empty...'

Wallis rounded out Hodson's previous portrait of Deptford – though he occasionally contradicted it, especially in the matter of the piety, or lack thereof, demonstrated by the local people. His church struggled to drum up support, admitted Wallis – a fact hardly surprising, given the profile of the clergy, past and present – and it seemed that secularization was already making inroads. Yet the hard-pressed curate was – like his fellow minister up at St Paul's – able to take a rounded view of his flock. Far from being the feckless, rowdy crowd of Victorian legend, in need of curbing by higher authority, 'they are not vicious or criminal in any way. [...] They are very largely a settled population who have lived here for years and generations [...] and when you get to know them are exceedingly friendly and pleasant, and very far from hopeless to work among'.

And Wallis was also happy to note Deptford's distinctive culture, comparing the average resident of the area to that of his previous parish at the Elephant and Castle, who was 'the ordinary apathetic South Londoner who was incessantly shifting and it was almost impossible to get hold of them; these people are not like ordinary South Londoners'. But they certainly did, Wallis agreed, drink more alcohol ('it is the worst place I have ever known') than anywhere else in the city: 'The police are insufficient and can't or won't cope with drunken disorder and noise. It is almost impossible to sleep at night owing to the shouts and singing of drunken revellers.' The curate was a good informant: Deptford, he revealed, possessed fewer brothels than other parts of London; its people married early and with enthusiasm – and its stock of housing, though chronically overcrowded, was nevertheless in parts perfectly good.

There was also a regiment of active Baptists, Methodists, Congregationalists, Wesleyans and foot soldiers of the Salvation

Army in the area – and the local Anglican clergy looked askance at all of them. In general, these churches took a less optimistic line regarding the state of the local community. The radical element in Deptford was very strong, noted the Reverend David Honour, pastor of the Baptist chapel on Octavius Street – too strong for his tastes. "I am a thorough radical,' said Mr H, 'but I cannot go on with the wild socialist element'. However, the Reverend Sabine Read, Minister of the Congregational Church on the High Street, was more focused on the importance of an active ministry. Pastoral visitations were part and parcel of his job, it seemed – even when they were neither solicited nor appreciated ('One local woman at her wash tub exclaimed, "you are the fifth one who has come this morning".'). Such efforts had shaped the course of his own life: 'When I came here 25 years ago,' said he, 'I said to myself: 3 years of this is enough for any

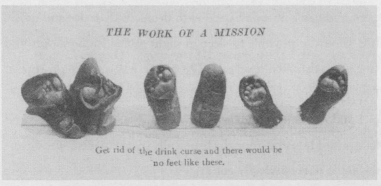

THE WORK OF A MISSION

Get rid of the drink curse and there would be
no feet like these.

Deptford's energetic, politicised and hard-drinking working-class culture drew the fretful gaze of many Christian charity workers, anxious to draw the populace back to the paths of righteousness. Here, the missionaries' concerns are only too apparent.

man – and here I am now. The officers have said, "if you go it will be a bad job for the place," and I have denied myself.' Read too understood the perils of excessive drinking:

> Some chronic want exists in the district and occasionally in a hard winter there is distress but it is well met. The real cause of the poverty, the real mischief is the drink. If you could do away with the drink – but you can't – you would change the aspect of the place. You see children with hardly anything to cover them with a great [tankard] of beer running in and out of the houses and at one o'clock on Sunday hanging like bees around the doors.

These various narratives share the same uneven note: Deptford was infected with alcoholism and violence, threatening political radicalism and urban deprivation – yet touched too by a note of community spirit and community cohesion. Perhaps the evidence of these members of the clergy can offer insights into the shape of contemporary Deptford culture: that this social intricacy was a paradox, existing both in spite and because of the area's relative economic deprivation. The note of contradiction is underscored by the account of the Reverend J. T. Chenhalls, resident at the Wesleyan church on the High Street: he seemed to suggest that Deptford was a place of uncommon depravity, where decent people could not exist for any length of time: 'In this quarter the earnest Christian's life is made unbearable and sooner or later they have to leave either for themselves or their children.' In the very next breath, however, Booth related a description of a class of Deptford people living a relatively comfortable and respectable life: they conscientiously salted money away in the savings bank; attended temperance concerts; and encouraged their drunken neighbours to do the same 'because they are raw material'.

This dichotomy remained when Booth broadened the scope of his inquiries to take in the educationalists and charity-workers of the district. The Deptford Ragged School had been established in 1844 at premises on Giffin Street, which was marked in uncompromising black on Booth's map. Mr E. Dodd was the Honourable Secretary of the School ('a brisk, business-like man in early middle life') and on 21 May 1900, he called 'by appointment' to meet Booth. Dodd had maintained a connection with the School for more than 20 years, and in that time had seen his share of Deptford's seamier side. The School was located just off the High Street in one of Deptford's more depressed corners: not only Giffin Street but its surrounding thoroughfares were 'of very low character'; the population was continually shifting; and drinking – as time went on, among women in particular – was endemic. Dodd described a population that could not be relied upon, that had learned to be wary of those intent on ministering to their needs:

'Although we do a lot of work we merely touch the people,' says Mr Dodd. The children are largely influenced and so are many of the women, but they cannot do much with the men [...] To get hold of the men involves such heavy expense, as there must be separate accommodation for them.' They will not come where the women are. Even in the few cases where a man and his wife attend a service, they separate at the entrance and come in at different doors. He does not know the reason for this but attributes it to the ordinary habits of these people. The men and their wives never go out together anywhere [...] He thinks a considerable number of the children remain under religious influence as they grow up, but, he added, 'it is very difficult to know when people are amenable to religious influence, there is so much hypocrisy and cadging about'.

Dodd's evidence supplies a compelling portrait of the harshness of life in this 'nest' of roads surrounding the High Street, especially for the most vulnerable. Here children crippled through poverty, brutality or neglect were fed and maintained not out of public funds but from private charity in the form of hampers supplied via Fleet Street. To this bleak example, Dodd added a plague of 'precocious' children; few or no resources for adults and children alike; and slum conditions prevailing in and around the High Street, with families crammed into homes that ought to have been condemned. The horror of alcohol abuse that ran like a vein through all of Booth's comments on Deptford was now discussed explicitly, in the official report of the Ragged School on Temperance:

> There is no human being in so pitiable a plight as the inebriate: despised by his fellows, loathed by himself, a mental wreck, a moral suicide, cast out from earth. Who does not feel like making an effort to save him?
>
> We hold that 'prevention is better than cure' and strive by our Band of Hope to save our children from the curse of intemperance. We have 186 members who are total abstainers, and know of many cases where they have been an influence for good. A meeting is held every Thursday evening to encourage and entertain them, as well as to lead them in prayer and praise Him who alone can keep them faithful to their pledge.

Mr W. J. Marriot of the London City Mission on Prince Street, added drily that the charitable ladies at the Albany Institute sent the local girls 'baskets of flowers, costly bibles etc. The girls however prefer dress: – pay 10/6 for ostrich feather.' He also mentioned 'a widow living in the only house left in Barnes Alley. Her husband fell down and broke his neck whilst in drink. This woman had signed [the pledge] again and again. She came to him one day and said "Mr M., I suppose it must be the booze to the bitter end."' Following this gloomy conversation, Booth and Marriot ventured out again into the streets of Deptford, discussing the evils of alcohol. 'My companion said they met with hardly any opposition anywhere and that they were good friends with the publicans. "The kind of man who is most likely to give trouble is a Roman Catholic drunk."'

Booth also met a Mrs Lambert, representative of the Deptford Fund itself and 'its moving spirit', whose emotional commitment to her cause was revealed occasionally in a 'tremor in her voice'. Lambert was a good example of the respectable class of people who helped the work of the Fund: she was a founder member and she continued to interest the aristocracy in its workings; she also had at her fingertips, it seems, every available statistic on how many charitable meals were prepared (10,000 per year), for whom they were prepared (expectant mothers and invalids given priority), on what days charity was available and who was responsible for what aspect of the Fund's organisation. The work of the Fund rose above most inter-Church squabbles: Anglicans and conformists alike partook of the Fund's philanthropy; although the Catholics (Booth was informed delicately) had elected to opt out of the whole affair.

Lambert's detailed analysis of the workings of the Fund was by no means an exception: in true Victorian style, its affairs were detailed exhaustively in a variety of reports.* The Fund could not be faulted for its streamlined ability to maintain itself, propagating its good works and disseminating its message and skills amid the Deptford populace. Nor can the impact of its work be denied: the image of 10,000 free meals a year speaks for itself. Materially, then, the work of the Albany Institute, of local churches and charities found its mark. The general tenor of the conversations recorded by Booth, however, is most striking for its sameness of tone: this was charity emphatically handed down from above – and handed down, moreover, in the company of a certain set of assumptions. The working-class people of Deptford were not consulted.

'Our time is now that we should all have clean homes'

The shaken confidence that characterized the final years of Victoria's reign seemed to be borne out as the twentieth century opened. Workers and suffrage agitators caused ripples at home; there was

---

* The Sixth Annual Report, on the year to 31 March 1900, reports that the total cost of these thousands of meals was £150, 'or practically 5½ d per dinner (consisting of chicken, rabbit or mutton with two vegetables, or fish with potatoes, beef tea, chicken broth or jelly).' The children's dinners were supplied from Lady Maitland's Children's Guild Fund, to which each child contributed a farthing: these farthings in turn were channelled towards maintaining a bed for Deptford children in a south-coast convalescence home.

strife in parliament; and disturbances in Ireland and further afield. The outbreak of the Great War in the summer of 1914 brought anti-German feeling, which had been on the rise for years, to fever pitch. The day after the declaration of war, the Aliens Restriction Act was rushed through parliament, along with a Trading with the Enemy Act, which obliged all German-owned commercial operations to be confiscated. German businesses had been trading on Deptford High Street for decades: Booth had noted the presence of at least eight German-owned shops, including bakeries, butchers and confectioners – all of which was in keeping with the area's broadly-based cultural flavour. In October 1914, a number of these German businesses on Deptford High Street were attacked, looted and burned and their owners forced out. 'Anti-German Mob Wreck Shops', screeched the *Daily Mirror*, reporting that: 'shop premises in the occupation of persons bearing German names in High-street, Deptford, Old Kent-road and Brixton were attacked. About 10.30 p.m. on Saturday a crowd of 6000 people in Deptford High Street and Evelyn Street attacked nine shops, and some of them were pillaged.' Germany had recently invaded Belgium – and it appeared that the sight of 800 Belgian evacuees recently arrived in the Deptford area was enough to ignite outraged passions in their defence:

It is said that the sight of these people, recalling the sufferings which they had undergone, was the cause of the riot.

The first shop to be attacked was that of Mr Peseti, pork butcher. Then the crowd wrecked the premises of another pork butcher named F. Riegler. The shop of F. Arold, beef and pork butcher, and that of J. Goebel, baker, were also wrecked. In the case of Arold's shop, cash register, meat and tools were seized and carried off. At Goebel's the mob reached the first floor, tore out the windows, flung into the street piano, bed and bedding, tables, chairs, china, clocks, and smashed everything they could lay their hands upon.

Later, the mob attacked the Prince Regent public house on the High Street, before moving on to pelt the police themselves with stones and bottles. The violence was indiscriminate – and ironically even some Belgians fell prey to the chaos: a German confectionery was looted, with its owner forced to lock his Belgian wife and their child in the bathroom for their own protection; meanwhile, it was reported that the German butcher had to flee to safety over the Deptford rooftops. The authorities were obliged eventually to call in the military to restore order. The paradox of this violent episode was that the owners of the affected premises were embedded in the community – either naturalized British citizens or fixtures for generations on the local Deptford scene.

Such violence did little to curb the tide of anti-German feeling. The following year, the new *Daily Mail* scandal sheet was running articles pointing out that interned German prisoners were 'coddled [...] to the disgust of all right-thinking women and men' – while the mass-market and notably jingoistic *John Bull* called in foaming terms for a 'vendetta against every German in Britain, whether 'naturalized' or not. [...] You cannot naturalize an unnatural beast – a human abortion – a hellish freak. But you *can* exterminate it. And now the time has come. [...] No German must be allowed to live in our land. No shop, no factory, no office, no trade, no profession must be open to him [...] the moral leprosy of the tribe to which he belongs must be emphasized by a boycott in every station of life.'

Such bursts of public disorder continued to be episodic features of life. The General Strike of 1926, for example, was observed scrupulously in the area, with virtually no incidents of local strikebreaking; the strike, however, was accompanied by clashes with police on Deptford Broadway, which was reported by the *Kentish Mercury* to be 'rendered almost impassable by a dense crowd'. More clashes were reported in the throes of the Great Depression, when police on Deptford Broadway ordered a group of people to desist from singing the 'Red Flag' – written by Jim Connell, Secretary of the Deptford Radical Club, which met in the Duke of Cambridge public house at 52 Deptford High Street. This was ignored – and they were baton charged, and six protestors arrested. The next day, unemployed workers in local training centres went on strike – and a crowd of 5,000 met in the

Broadway and defeated and scattered mounted police. Such incidents pointed not least to the economic travails that characterized the inter-war years – and that were felt keenly in already deprived areas such as Deptford.

To the outside observer – here, for example, Ellen Chase, housing activist and associate of Octavia Hill, in comments written at the end of the 1920s – life appeared to be rolling on in its usual raucous vein:

No matter how often one might run down the stairway of the South-Eastern and Greenwich Railroad at Deptford, he could not fail to be struck by the motley crowd of people jostling along the High Street. There were tottering, grey-headed old pensioners with gilt buttons to their reefers; pinched, careworn women in rusty, ragged black; over-dressed, boisterous girls amusing themselves by giggling and chafing with strangers; smart young red-coats swinging along in couples; and groups of rough hearty sailors from the cattle-steamers, shoving and rollicking along the crowded sidewalks, carrying all before them. And there were generally pedlars and beggars of one kind and another, women selling jumping-jacks from trays hanging about their necks; and in their season, men hawking primrose-roots from baskets, or rabbits dangling from the end of a stick. Here would be a vendor of whirligigs, there a mender of old umbrellas, or perhaps a blind bugler, or a couple of gaily kerchiefed Italian women with cages of fortune-telling canaries set above their rattling hand-organs. To add to the din, the noisy salesmen of the rival butchers' shops, 'touting' for customers, shout out at the top of their lungs: 'What'll you buy, buy, buy? What do you want, my dears? Lovely steak! Lovely chops! What'll you buy? What'll you buy, buy, buy?'

Beneath the colourful surface, however, there was drift and an absence of leadership. No charismatic local figures had appeared to match the Salters of Bermondsey and their discourse of social and medical improvement; little sense of municipal purpose to match that emanating from Bermondsey could be detected in the grand new Deptford Town Hall on New Cross Road; and it was left to small local organisations to try to cope with the array of social problems. Increasingly, the clubs and gymnasia of the Albany Institute – like the turreted building itself – seemed to belong to another era. By now the Institute's world of Victorian paternalist assumptions was gone: central government was beginning to take a more active role in the organization and running of local communities – and it would require another war to bring the organization back into vogue.

The Second World War impacted harshly on Deptford: the district's place at the heart of London's docklands made it, like

Bermondsey, a magnet for German bombers; and the civilian death toll was very high. Many civilians left the area for Kent and the safer countryside; for those who remained, death was a continuing possibility until the very last days of the war, as the Germans aimed the V1 and V2 flying bombs at southeastern England. In June 1944, a flying bomb killed 22 civilians on Reginald Square; in July, 13 died on Prince Street; and a further 15 were killed the following January on Adolphus Street. In November 1944, 168 civilians died as the result of a direct hit on the branch of Woolworth's in nearby New Cross: it was the worst single loss of life in Britain as a result of the flying bombs. The Albany came into its own again in these years, its associations with the Royal Family and its fortress-like design seeming to encapsulate the national will to survive the war: the Institute dedicated itself to wartime activity, sewing sandbags and operating as a relief centre for the local community.

The war caused a sharp drop in Deptford's population, and left its landscape pockmarked with ruined and derelict buildings. In 1947, the writer Dunstan Thompson took a train to New Cross. Turning into Deptford High Street he felt 'a deepening of the shadow, a darker greyness,' and 'caught the smell of over-ripe vegetables and rank fish [...] cheap greasy cooking from the open doors. The crowd became so great it was almost like being at the fair or circus, except here there were no high spirits and there was no fun'. Yet the crowds –

the defining characteristic of the street – remained as massed as ever. After the war, the LCC prepared a series of bomb damage maps, colour-coded to explain the extent of damage in each quarter of the city. Deptford High Street, however, was portrayed as curiously colourless – for it had, remarkably, escaped the war more or less unscathed.

Post-war prosperity began to rejuvenate the area once more – in ways that, given the area's later history, now seem startling: there were abundant jobs; and people began to invest in and even buy their homes in the streets surrounding the High Street. The old tenement system, the homes in multi-occupation, the chronic overcrowding: these blights of life now began to vanish, as Deptford shed the gloom of war and invested anew in itself and its environment. The old backyard washhouses, for example, were now converted into bathrooms, bringing houses up to modern specifications in ways that reflected the specific mores of place and of class: indoor toilets were frowned on as being intrinsically unpleasant concepts; it was considered better to keep modern sanitary zones separate from the house itself. 'You never had a toilet in the house,' recalls one former resident. 'There was no toilets in the house. They was all in the yard [...] a toilet in the house, oh terrible, you've got to have it in the yard.' Deptford had never had it so good: the area now began to move ahead of other parts of London that remained mired in poverty and deprivation.

In addition, the public houses of the High Street were now experiencing their heyday. The local pubs, as we have seen, had traditionally played a significant role in the life of the area: hives of hard, destructive drinking and of radical politics many of them certainly were – but they had, as well, been vital public spaces, not to mention refuges from overcrowded home conditions. The pubs also played their part in courtship and more general displays of fellowship and community attitudes. Saturday and Sunday nights on Deptford High Street witnessed the local equivalent of the Italian *passeggiata*: as one resident remembers: '[O]n Saturday and Sunday nights we'd get dressed up to walk up and down the High Street. It was *alive* with stalls. There weren't shutters, they had window displays so you'd walk up and down, have a look at what was in the windows and then go into a couple of pubs while you were at it, for a drink.' And each pub fulfilled a particular function: for example, the Duke of Cambridge on the High Street, was popular with courting couples; the pubs clustered at the north end of the street were for the dockers. Although these nights might end raucously and drunkenly, such rituals were a vital part of the fabric of everyday life in the High Street of the period.

Politicians and administrators, however, were oblivious to the radical changes taking place in Deptford. The County of London Plan of 1943 and the Greater London Plan a year later envisaged a new, modern, orderly capital city – and disorderly

Deptford, be it prosperous or not, had no place in this new future. A propaganda film (shot partly in Deptford) argued for the destruction of the old nineteenth-century London, with its 'pubs, schools, churches [...] all jumbled up together in a hopeless confusion. You can see,' the film's voiceover intoned, 'mean hideous slums of which any city ought to be ashamed, row upon row of dirty, dismal houses which ought to have been pulled down and done away with long ago. All these bad things must go; and the sooner the better.' Part of this plan – to the dismay of the traders on the High Street – involved the removal of Deptford's market, which was seen as an impediment to the free flow of traffic. A campaign was mounted to oppose this measure – and the proposal was defeated. Local businesses appeared to have the upper hand – although in the longer term, this would prove not to be the case.

Even before the outbreak of war, the local authorities had drawn up proposals to clear and rebuild large swathes of housing in the area – and now, in the aftermath of the conflict, these plans were renewed. The area of Giffin Street (branching from the High Street) had been slated for demolition as early as 1939; and compulsory purchase orders had already been issued. Forty years before, Booth had coloured the area uncompromisingly dark blue and black. ('Many of the houses at the east end are dilapidated and boarded up. Slatternly women standing about, some shoeless children.') Now as a resident's

archived letter makes clear, not all the locals baulked at the
prospect of clearance:

> 1939 November
>
> Dear Sir,
>
>   Cannot you do something for the poor people of Giffin
> Street the worst slum street of Deptford, poor children living
> in rat infested and black beetles on the table we are eating
> on, also sleeping and eating in the same rooms cannot get
> places because of having children, our time is now that we
> should all have clean homes, not to have to eat what rats are
> touching and running over the beds at night.
>
>   Hoping and trusting you will do some thing soon.
>
>   I remain
>
>   Yours sincerely
>
>   A resident.

With the war now at an end, Giffin Street was first in the council's sights. A memo of April 1953 sets out the plans for '64
houses covering approximately 1.4 acres [...] The severe disre-
pair in the majority of these houses is apparent in the bulged,
settled and fractured main walls, the defective main roofs and
the rotted and decayed woodwork of the window frames and
sashes.' Other correspondence provides a cost – some £200,000
– and the number of people displaced – 389 – as a result.

However, the available records indicate that, given the state of the housing on the street, nobody objected to the proposed demolition taking place. Instead, attention centred on a house included in the clearance area, at 100 Deptford High Street – the only home remaining on the street and inhabited at this time by the Brittons, a family of 15. The authorities, it seemed, were focused on how possible it would be to re-house them. The correspondence reveals the conditions – 'almost uninhabitable [...] damp, seriously dilapidated [...] verminous' and chronically overcrowded – in which some families were obliged to live.

The clearance of Giffin Street was part of a much greater scheme: the intention was to sweep away most of the existing housing of this part of southeast London and replace it with the modernist dream of cities in the sky: large tower blocks equipped with lifts and the latest modern conveniences which, together with an efficient infrastructure, would lift old cities like London from the ruins of war and into a bright future. One such 'city' was created in the heart of Deptford itself: the Pepys Estate – consisting of three monumental residential towers, flanked by a range of smaller units – was completed by 1966 on the site of the Navy's former Victualling Yard on the Thames. It became a truism that decent and respectable people could not possibly wish to live amid the decay of old Deptford: instead, they would naturally want to move into such modern towers – or alternatively relocate to outer suburbia.

Such an idea was perfectly understandable, given the trauma of war and destruction which the country had so recently experienced, and given too the belief that this was an opportunity to mould a new society in a new way. It did not, however, always take into account the needs of those who were to be rehoused and relocated; and the process took on a momentum that could not always be halted. These measures, though couched in language that emphasized modernity and progress, were as paternalistic in substance as the earlier charitable activities of the Victorians had been. This was planning from the top down: planning that granted itself ownership and possession of the process; planning that assumed the consent of the community – but made no attempt to seek it out. The political and administrative elite did not ask the people what they wanted: '[T]hey didn't talk to anybody in Deptford about it,' says Nicholas Taylor, later a local councillor and chair of the planning committee on Lewisham council. 'They talked amongst themselves.'

Take the example of Reginald Road, running east from the High Street in the direction of the Creek. By the 1960s, most of the properties on this street were no longer rented; instead, they were owned and had been improved by the Price and Ovenell families, both long-established presences on the Deptford social and commercial scene. The Ovenells were descended from Huguenot stock; and they and the Prices had made their home mere yards from the High Street. 'You see how easy it was,' says

In the 1960s and 1970s, many of the terraces of old Deptford were swept away and replaced by the modernist dream of cities in the sky — as here, in Deptford's Pepys Estate. All too often, these high-rise estates became the focus of social deprivation, crime and unemployment.

John Price, who today runs a pound shop on Deptford High Street. 'You used to fall out of bed, and go to work at the top of the High Street. [...] And one stall used to keep three families. It used to keep my father's family, my Uncle John and my Uncle Jack's family.' The street itself, once zoned indeterminate purple – neither poor nor well-to-do – on Booth's maps would now be zoned in pink: respectable, stable working-class. Archived correspondence demonstrates clearly that the housing stock on this road and on adjoining Reginald Square was – as in Booth's day – not comparable with that of Giffin Street nearby. Surveys were carried out by the council's environmental health inspectors: powerful figures with the authority to enter homes and to observe and report on lives lived and properties owned, despite having no background in either architecture or social science; to judge the futures of citizens whose destinies frequently depended on the statements issued. In this case, however, the inspectors in question recorded that the houses on Reginald Road were in good repair: only modest expenditure was needed to bring them up to scratch, and demolition need not be considered:

Maintenance is fair to good, there is evidence that the owners are maintaining these houses, few roofs actually leak and tenants state that this, that and the other was repaired recently. Quite a few tenants and the two or three owner occupiers have very well decorated internally and installed

sinks to upper floors, new fireplaces etc. [...] There is no
doubt in my mind that this whole street could be dealt with
by other action than clearance if the Borough Council
wanted to...

But the council did *not* want to. In November 1964, the properties on Reginald Road were condemned as unfit for human
habitation: John Price recalls that the owners were offered
£1600 as part of a compulsory purchase plan. By the late 1960s,
one side of Reginald Road had been cleared; on the other side,
houses were vacated and knocked down one by one, rapidly
rendering uninhabitable the remaining properties; water and
power mains were cut; water pooled in the road. Slums were
created where no slums had existed before. 'It happened to Aunt
Violet first,' remembers John Price. 'She lived down Hales
Street, and they pulled all down round her, and she lived in this
house in Hales Street on her own. Just rubble all around. It just
become wasteland. And the house was sitting in the middle. And
course, you know, you had – where they pulled down then
you've suddenly got vermin everywhere, haven't you. And
nobody wants to go down there of a night because all the lights
are out.' Some residents held out, either because they were
determined not to move or they were hoping for a better financial deal. But 'any idea of staying by then was absolutely
hopeless,' says Nicholas Taylor. 'It was a sort of long, drawn-out

war of attrition, the clearance of these areas: it didn't happen
overnight, it took years and years and years.' By 1971, all the
houses on Reginald Road had been torn down. In the same
period, other streets in the area were demolished in the name of
slum clearance: in some cases, of course, this was a perfectly
appropriate term, the housing being unfit for human habitation,
yet at times, perfectly good housing stock was swept away in
the name of progress.

And in all cases, the results were the filleting of the commercial life of the High Street – and in general the fraying and
eventual disintegration of a community, with inevitable consequences in psychological and social terms. 'Once they started
pulling everything down it went down,' says John Price. 'Nothing
at all is going in the till.' As early as the beginning of the 1960s,
the external pressure on the commercial life of the area was beginning to register in contemporary accounts of the High Street. In
The London Nobody Knows (1962), Geoffrey Fletcher's descriptions contain signs of incipient disintegration:

A stone's throw away is the market in Douglas Way, a
Hogarthian scene on Saturday. Vegetable stalls without
number appear, stalls full of disinfectant and toilet paper
and those selling lino and rugs. There are stalls selling pet
foods, especially strong in budgie-toys, stalls of tinned fruit,
wireless stalls. That almost obsolete form of transport, the

horse and cart, comes into its own in Douglas Way, and very nice these carts sometimes are, too, decorated with curvy flourishes, fat roses and carving, here and there. It is like the London of Phil May, less vigorous, perhaps, but the jokes still have the special London quality. At the end of the street are junk dealers' stalls – pitches only, many of them – a pile of miscellaneous goods laid out on the pavement, but the junk and marine store dealers appear to be decreasing in numbers. Although I have made one or two finds in this market, including a complete set of old kitchen jars for four shillings, straight off the pavement, the wares have a dreary look about them. Battered suitcases minus a lock or the handle are nearly always found [...] together with decrepit television sets, old clothes, ancestors with mutton-chop whiskers and other articles whose specific purpose, if they ever possessed such, can now only be guessed.

John Price remembers how his extended family moved from being concentrated in two or three streets in Deptford to being scattered across southeast London: '[W]e ended up in Charlton, Aunt Violet ended up in Greenwich, and Aunt Harriet ended up in Brockley, and Aunt Grace ended up in Woolwich, and Uncle John ended up in Brockley – and eventually it just breaks up, more and more.' In addition, it took time to adjust to living else-where – whether in a tower block nearby or a semi-detached house in Brockley or Eltham – after a lifetime spent in Dept-ford's densely woven streets: to be sure, many of the residents were happy to resettle amid new surroundings, but not everyone could readily make such a leap. One former resident described her former life in south London, consisting as it did of close family ties: 'My mum just lived across the road, and that. And even my old gran lived in the same house where I was born. There wasn't a day went past when I didn't see my mother. She either came over to me or I went over to her.' Another said of her new suburban life: 'I very often get bored. I mean, I will go out and smash things in temper, rather than have rows with my husband. Which I have done in the past. [...] I try not to [get upset]. He [i.e., her husband] has to work long hours and I try to be happy. But very often he's come home and found me crying and I can't explain why. It's just a fit of depression you get into.'

In financial terms the consequences are rather easier to meas-ure: for example, similar housing in nearby Greenwich – housing which was not torn down – commands premium prices in today's property market. Or take Albury Street, branching off the north end of the High Street, and by the early 1960s a slum to match the worst in all of Deptford: its houses too had been condemned and its residents evicted – but by a quirk of the plan-ning process, they were retained. Today, the terraced houses of Albury Street have been thoroughly gentrified – and they sell for

A quirk of the planning regulations led to Albury Street evading the wrecker's ball —
and today, the street is one of the best-heeled corners of Deptford, its gentrified
early-Georgian terraced houses fetching premium prices.

a small fortune. Albury Street reflects in miniature the situation on Reverdy Road several miles to the east – where the retention and ultimate conservation of housing rather than its clearance paid rich long-term social and economic dividends.

As Deptford's former community was scattered, another arrived to take its place. By the early 1970s, it was becoming clear that the high-rises of Deptford were not offering the new modern lives that had been promised: fewer and fewer people were willing to live there. Nicholas Taylor remembers 'a lot of my older council colleagues couldn't understand why people were so ungrateful. I remember one of them saying to me, "but they've got wonderful, lovely kitchens, lovely bathrooms – what are they complaining about? And why are these people so ungrateful when we've given them these wonderful places to live in?" Even though he was living in a big Victorian house up the hill.'

Lacking a supply of Deptford people willing to live in the sky, housing staff were obliged to track further and further down the waiting lists to secure tenants. These new Deptford residents were among the poorest and most disadvantaged in society; they included large numbers of immigrants – and soon, Deptford had become a distinctly multi-ethnic society. At the same time, it became evident that the new flats and tower blocks around Deptford were intrinsically flawed: there were limits to the improvements that could be made to their fabric – and limits, therefore, to their desirability. They remain plagued by poverty and crime – and they act as a lock on the future; a brake on the development of the area.

The social changes visited upon Deptford can best be measured by the decline of that once-vibrant pub culture. On Deptford High Street today, there are two pubs where once there were 12: the Deptford Arms is now a bookmaker's; the Mechanic's Arms and Royal Oak are African restaurants; the Pilot is a wholesale nail shop; the Windsor Castle is an outreach centre for problem teenagers; and the White Swan, which once doubled as the location both of inquests and trials – one of many Deptford pubs pressed into service as de facto courtrooms over the years, until the paraphernalia of a modern state made such occasions both undesirable and unnecessary – is now run principally as a Vietnamese restaurant and karaoke club. At least part of this decline is as the result of the social changes in Deptford: in particular, various ethnic groups perceive pubs as unfriendly places; and as the preserve of a diminishing white working-class population. Such a situation underlines the difficulties in establishing a new sense of community, when the spaces and places that previously helped to fulfil this function now barely exist.

Contemporary Deptford is the focus of sustained efforts at regeneration, with new transport links connecting the area to the City and the rest of London; a new rail station nearing completion; and a range of new resources for the community, in the form of libraries, artists' residencies and performance spaces, colleges and schools. The story of the Albany is instructive in this respect: having emerged from the war into a world of a new welfare state, it seemed even more than ever out of kilter, its purpose swept away by new ideologies and new ways of thinking. Its eventual response was to reinvent itself as a genuine campaigning organisation, its premises a radical shared space used by arts and community organizations. In 1978, the original building was badly damaged by fire – started, it has been claimed, by far-right activists – and was finally demolished in 1981: in the following year, the new building, which now overlooks the second-hand market on Douglas Way, was inaugurated (maintaining the connection with the Royal Family) by Princess Diana, who would become its new Patron. Today, the Laban contemporary dance centre operates from its new building on the newly-named Creekside – in itself an attempt to connect Deptford with its more economically fortunate neighbour at Greenwich; and the old Victualling Yard on the Thames is the focus of further sustained attempts at development, with plans to create a new residential quarter with up to 3,000 new homes. All these landscapes – new and putative – explicitly refer to the notion of mutuality: spaces are shared; are threaded with footpaths and cycleways; are accessible and open to all. Yet the stark truth is that there is a limit to the extent of development and gentrification that Deptford can ever expect to witness. The low-quality, low-cost housing inserted into Deptford High Street's tributary streets can never be significantly improved; and gentrification of such poor housing stock can never realistically be expected.

As for this concept of shared space: it has always characterized Deptford and its history. Such spaces have not always been genteel or fragrant or hushed: instead, the slaughter-houses, smoky public houses and tangled roads of the area have reverberated, often violently, with raucous noise and activity. Equally, the lives of those who lived here – members of a predominantly white working-class population – cannot easily be sentimentalized, for they were often harsh and subject to brutal economic circumstances. But as efforts are made to 'regenerate' Deptford, a fundamental lesson can be taken from the history of the High Street and its hinterland: that change and a new energy can indeed flow from social, financial and political intervention – but that this intervention will only work and pay long-term dividends by engaging with and seeking the consent of the community itself.

The Safe Area

ARNOLD CIRCUS

*For brutality within the circle of family life,
perhaps nothing in all London quite equalled the
Old Nichol Street neighbourhood. [...] It seemed to
offer a very good opportunity for rebuilding on some
entirely new plan, such as might provide light and air,
and possibilities of welfare and health for all.*

Charles Booth

Seen from the air, broad streets radiate off a central, circular green space, like spokes from the hub of a wheel – Calvert Avenue, Club Row, Rochelle Street. These spokes are edged in their turn by a square of containing roads: Boundary Street, Old Nichol Street, Virginia Street, Swanfield Street. Beyond this structured and measured area, lie some of London's most colourful thoroughfares: Columbia Road with its flower market; Brick Lane with its bagel emporia and mosque and south Asian restaurants. These surrounding dense landscapes of East End serve as a foil: against them, the neighbourhood of Calvert Avenue asserts a distinctively planned and contained modernity.

A prominent feature of this district is its silence. Turn away from the traffic and the buses of Shoreditch High Street and Hackney Road and onto Calvert Avenue – and the acoustic of London, its sheer volume, falls away into a sudden tranquillity that itself startles. This is a broad, handsome, tree-shaded road, less than 200 metres long: the good stonework and surrounding trees of the Anglican church of St Leonard lies to the left; and at the end of the road, is the green circular island space of Arnold Circus, with its careful planting and its Edwardian bandstand and its grove of magnificent London plane trees, rising prominently out of the urban landscape.

As one approaches the Circus, the neighbourhood coheres, and other, similar buildings appear in neighbouring streets, all five storeys tall, imposing, significant; the brickwork is ruddy red, striped with yellow and skilfully laid, a work of art in itself. And these tall buildings are replicated in all directions; the long windows of Virginia Road primary school look out onto the Circus and the bandstand; the Rochelle School lies just beyond. These are the buildings of the Boundary estate, created at the turn of the twentieth century as Britain's first public housing scheme – and as a world unto itself, with its own shops and businesses established to meet residents' needs. Calvert Avenue had its grocer, dairy, butcher and baker; today, these shops have been replaced by the fashionable and expensive emporia and designer outlets of the new Shoreditch; and the Rochelle, which predates the rest of the Boundary by several decades, has become a private gallery and art space.

Arnold Circus and the Boundary estate's wheel of surrounding streets are borderlands. They lie on the line between

Hackney and Tower Hamlets, between Shoreditch and Bethnal Green. In classical times, they lay just beyond the fortifications of Roman London; and later, just beyond its successor Saxon and medieval towns; today, they lie a mile beyond the City, the waxing influence of which is nevertheless to be felt all around. The East End begins here, at this seam in the capital's densely patterned fabric of buildings and arteries, where Bishopsgate comes up from the City and turns into Shoreditch High Street. And, as the area lies always just beyond the centre of things, so – as the marginal and the liminal always does – it exerts a telling influence over the culture of London.

* * *

The East End has for centuries been associated, not only with marginality, but with poverty and with filth and ordure: from medieval times, commentators have pointed, aghast, to the narrowness of the streets and the prevailing stench – literal and metaphorical – of human deprivation. This outsider status was only intensified in the years following the Great Fire: as so much of central and west London was laid out anew, with broad boulevards and airy terraces and villas, so the east of the city continued in its role as the labouring heart of London – and as time went on, these contrasts with the wealthy and leisured west grew sharper. The landscapes of the east – the narrowness of its streets, the meanness of its houses – came to be seen as true reflections of the people who used them and lived in them: the real sickness of the area, so the orthodoxy went, issued from the feckless, lazy, indigent people themselves.

As industrialization intensified in the later years of the eighteenth century, so the face of east London was transformed. The Thames became thronged with shipping; the docks ran for miles from the Tower east towards the estuary. And the filth and pollution of east London grew apace: glue factories and soap factories and match factories lent the very air a malodorous aspect, the water became filthy, tributaries of the Thames such as the Lea and Barking Creek ran with dirt. It was at this point in history that the area's long-established reputation for want and misery and dreadful living conditions became of a piece with something else: with a kind of depravity that, as the nineteenth century progressed, came to be seen as an indelible part of East End life. The area was infamous now for its crime and its dangers and its ambience of subhumanity: these features seemed soaked into the old bricks and rotting timbers of the buildings, as the smoke from the factories clung and hung in the air.

The area also became known as the refuge of swelling immigrant communities: over the course of centuries, layers of newcomers – Huguenots, Irish and Germans, Italians and Chinese, Flemings and Poles – had made their homes in the East End. In particular, a Jewish population of more than 10,000 had come to Britain in the latter half of the nineteenth century, fleeing religious persecution in Russia and eastern Europe. This Jewish community was concentrated in and around Shoreditch, Spitalfields and Whitechapel, to such an extent that the street signs in these neighbourhoods were written in Yiddish; the former Huguenot chapel on Brick Lane became a synagogue. These changing demographics had led to occasionally sharp responses like the anti-Catholic Gordon riots which convulsed London late in the eighteenth century as they swept through the Irish community.

The fact that immigrant ethnic groups tended to live in tight-knit communities, and that they took on some of the most unpleasant jobs made them even more objects of contempt and of fear. They came to be known as 'arabs' – taking into account, maybe, the eastern districts of London in which so many of them lived, and the vast, unknown cultural East out of which many of them were perceived to have come. Even the kindest representations of such communities were shot through with pain: in Dorothy Tennant's painting of *Street Arabs at Play* (1890), for example, the children in question swing on railings by a grey, glassy Thames: it is a charming picture, until one notices the shabby garb of the children, their shoeless feet, and the backdrop of a smoking, sullen London on the other side of the Thames.

The East End inspired another sort of fear: that of radicalism and extremism – and this originated in the waves of political fervour that spread through the area in the nineteenth century. We have already seen how nearby Bermondsey possessed a stout variety of socialism that left a lasting impression on the fabric of that area of south London; the East End was similarly marked, though in this case the political waves came thick and fast in the form of anarchism, communism, republicanism and a furious assertion of workers' rights in the face of desperate labour conditions. Chartist meetings demanding political reform and expansion of the franchise are recorded in the East End in 1816, 1826 and 1832; later, the Tolpuddle Martyrs were welcomed back from exile in Australia in this same area; trades' unions and Fenians met and organised here; and the teachings of Marx and Engels rippled out from here to affect the world.*

Scenes of urban deprivation had always attracted viewers. Late in the eighteenth century, the poet William Blake had 'wandered thro' each charter'd street, / near where the charter'd Thames does flow', noting the abiding atmosphere of fear, infection and oppression. A century later, Henry James, arriving in London from the United States, wrote of the city that 'it would be wrong to ignore her deformities' – and many took him at his word, arriving to see this depravity and deprivation for themselves. Some of these observers were doubtless mere

---

* The Tolpuddle Martyrs were a group of Dorset labourers who in 1832 organized in opposition to the gradual reduction of agricultural wages. As a result, they were sentenced to seven years' transportation. As a result of public disaffection with this sentence, they were released after two years.

tourists: glad to come, yet happier to go away again swiftly. Others, however, came to east London with more specific motivations: as statisticians and journalists, to note and to record; as social or religious missionaries, to bear witness and spread the word and perhaps, to channel in different directions the political radicalism that sprang from the sour London soil; and as philanthropists, to alleviate if they could – and the records of these years bear out their work.

These records took many forms – and were part of a more generalized cultural tendency towards fretful, moralizing concern as to the state of the nation. Henry Mayhew's *London Labours and the London Poor*, which appeared in four volumes between 1851 and 1861, was a sociological treatise in the classic mould; it was also a text with distinctly modern overtones, for it boasted illustrations of east London life in the form of daguerreotypes, the new photographic invention. Mayhew went to some lengths: now, plotting the streets of Bethnal Green and finding shacks set upon the earth without foundations, their inhabitants occupied in 'noxious trades like boiling tripe, melting tallow or preparing cat's meat ... '; now, ascending over the city in a hot-air balloon – but could detect little below except 'vice and avarice and low cunning'.

And in December 1869, a new weekly newspaper appeared on London's newsstands: the *Graphic*, founded and funded by William Luson Thomas, a wood carver and publisher with reformist tendencies. The *Graphic*'s pages included reports on the usual eclectic Victorian melange of science, literature, society garden parties and music – but its principal intention was to feed its readers potent and repeated doses of social realism. The journal published the work of such prominent artists as Luke Fildes and Frank Holl, whose paintings found favour with the Queen

Contemporary journals and magazines frequently treated the Victorian middle class to manifold images of the London poor. Child chimney sweeps were a favourite object of scrutiny, charity – and prurient concern.

herself. Their work did not focus overmuch on the filth and general cruelty of life among the London poor, instead telling a version of this story while reassuring the viewer that it had little to do with their own lives. The fact, however, that such artists were prepared to turn their gaze on such subject matter in the first place, and that their work found an audience in middle-class Victorian society, indicates this sense of anxiety.

It took the work of the French artist Gustave Dore to illuminate the true texture of life in the East End – and his book *London: A Pilgrimage* (1872), with an accompanying text by Blanchard Jerrold, reproduces graphically the world of Victorian London. Doré's images of the East End resonate with shocking detail. His subjects are recognisably human – yet grotesque too: their faces engraved with desperation and misery; their homes filthy and sooty from factory chimneys and from the smoke of trains that pass over clattering railway arches nearby; their futures and prospects as circumscribed as the tiny, damp yards in which they hang their clothes to dry in the dirty air. Some of Doré's images – *The Exercise Yard at Newgate*, *Over London by Rail* and *Dudley Street, Seven Dials* – have become enduring images of Victorian London. He was criticized by some for drawing the divisions between the classes and regions of London too sharply, and for portraying the East End as an urban hell. But he recorded and preserved the texture of London life at its most desperate – and in so doing provided an example for others to follow.

'We pretend that all have
equal chances and equal hopes'

In 1891, Charles Booth paid a visit to an area of the East End he called Summer Gardens – a district that would have appeared only too familiar to readers of Doré and Jerrold's book. This district was, according to his evolving colour-based lexicon, dark blue in character: close or very close to the bottom of the social heap. Neighbouring streets – for example, Baxter Street, 'the leading business street to which the other two in some sense pertain' – were filled with the clatter and noise of business, but of an unprepossessing nature: 'cheap cabinet-work, furniture, and chairs [...] men pass about with great bundles of chair backs or legs'. This bustling activity could not prevent Baxter Street from being coloured uncompromising black: indeed, the whole district was essentially black, a block of darkness standing out from Booth's map.

Summer Gardens itself, as Booth described it, was the epitome of the darkness of the East End: narrow and lightless, the streets snowy and the air freezing; the inhabitants supping on a little broth for their dinner – doled out from a local mission house into jugs borne by queuing residents – and nothing else. The streets were filled with grime and discarded litter and worse – the sights and sounds of casual death: 'In one street is the body of a dead dog and near by two dead cats, which lie as though they had slain each other. All three have been crushed flat by the traffic which has gone over them ... ' The streets featured a multitude of little shops, selling onions or dripping, bread and cheap sweets; barrows were piled with oranges, ready to be wheeled down to Liverpool Street for vending. But there was nothing here to cheer or refresh: the houses and the roadways and the inhabitants were dank; the wages from their miserable jobs were barely enough to eke out a living, and a wave of imports threatened to wipe away even such pitiful livelihoods. An old man, for example, scraped a living from making dolls: but cheap dolls from Europe were flooding the market; and 'he should be busy when the Germans were all dead'. A woman had been confined for the birth of her child, 'but the baby is dead'.

There was some industry and activity in the area – and this too was representative of the labouring East End, where money was to be made, and crimes and sins committed. At 14 Summer Gardens lived a Mrs Richards, for example, who kept a shop for 14 years and gradually, painstakingly saved enough money to enlarge it; her son went out to work, respectably, as an omnibus driver; her daughter was a saver too, and thrifty with it. Next door at number 12, 'the children want books'. Other inhabitants took in laundry, or made match-boxes, or worked as bricklayers and seemed 'decent' and 'very respectable'. But these – amid a throng of ruffians and idle good-for-nothing

layabouts, women with black eyes and men with ready fists –
were the exceptions.

Summer Gardens and its surroundings was that area on the
borders of Bethnal Green and Shoreditch where the Boundary
estate now stands – but an explorer of Victorian London would
search in vain for such a network of streets. In the report, the
names of the streets had been changed: 'Summer Gardens' was
in fact Half Nichol Street; 'Baxter Street' was Old Nichol Street.
At this time, the district was known as the Old Nichol, and later
Booth would note ('[I]t must be admitted') his pseudonymic
sleight of hand. His reasons for originally disguising the identity of these desperate streets lay in his basic intentions and
methodology: it was vital that his informants learned to trust
him and rely on his discretion.

And in this case, there were particular reasons why discretion
was needed: the Old Nichol was one of the most notorious areas
in the East End and a byword for criminality; even the surrounding inhabitants of deprived Shoreditch and Bethnal Green, it was
said, preferred to give the place and its dangerous population a
wide berth. Its origins dated back to the late-seventeenth century,
when John Nichol built a few houses in the district and leased a
section of land to be dug for bricks. Over the decades the neighbourhood expanded, until by the mid-nineteenth century, it
consisted of a dense pack of streets, several hundred houses,
some 6,000 inhabitants.

The streets were for the most part just sufficiently wide to allow a horse and cart access; the warren of alleys was so narrow that two could not walk abreast; and buildings were narrow too, and built cheek by jowl. Among the earliest inhabitants of the Nichol had been Huguenot silk weavers, which accounted for the long windows in many of the houses, created to maximise the levels of daylight within. The expansion of London's railways had had its effect on already grim conditions in the area: in the 1830s, the Eastern Counties Railway obtained permission to move its London terminus from relatively distant Mile End into Shoreditch; and the resulting railway line dispossessed family after family – which crowded in their turn into the Old Nichol.

By mid-century the conditions in parts of the estate were truly appalling: its alleys and streets were pocked with pools of 'night soil'; its housing was desperately overcrowded and had virtually no running water – to say nothing of other services. For those in work, the chief imperative was to gather enough money together to pay the rent – against such a background, family life was a secondary concern. 'My mother monopolized the table with the paste for the matchboxes,' noted one contributor to an oral history of the Nichol, 'if you wanted to eat she might give you a couple of slices of bread and you'd go outside and eat it on the doorstep – there was no room for you inside. [...] The predominant idea was paying the rent, cos you know how damned hard it was to find another room. So the rent came first ...'

'For brutality within the circle of family life, perhaps nothing in all London quite equalled the Old Nichol Street neighbourhood.' The Nichol was one of Victorian London's most appalling slums: Booth categorised the area as essentially black, a block of darkness standing out starkly on the poverty map.

The estate and its inmates became an object of fear and fascination among late-Victorian commentators. Indeed, a distinctive iconography of crime evolved within the area: a gallery of faces and figures and a lexicon of tales and notoriety. Gangs fought turf wars; rings of prostitutes were ruled by pimps who would stop at nothing to protect their patch. Infamous figures rose out of the throng: one such, in the final years of the Nichol, was Isaac Bogard – better known as 'Darky the Coon', a flamboyant Jewish gang leader and pimp who controlled large prostitution rackets from his base on Commercial Road. Bogard was known for his outlandish garb and behaviour: local legend says he strutted the streets of Spitalfields in cowboy uniform, complete with gun hanging from his belt, and acted as overseer of the numerous turf wars that blazed across the East End. Bogard later enlisted and fought in the Great War, before retiring to the East End.

Booth was greatly exercised by the social conditions that existed in such places: not only were they a social evil in and of themselves, but they also fostered still greater wickedness and vice in their inhabitants. This was the heart of that culture he labelled as 'vicious and semi-criminal', for vice was incubated in the very blood of its inhabitants; and from such a place no good could ever come:

> With sharpness instead of knowledge, cunning for wit, no fore-thought at all, but living entirely in and for the present, inheriting a thousand defects of blood and with no will or never power at all, who can wonder that such unhappy ones should succumb to the inevitable influence of their surround-ings, which go to make virtue and morality impossible?

This comment neatly sums up the imperative that drove Booth's work: such conditions could not be permitted to exist, for the sake not simply of the unfortunate inhabitants of the Old Nichol, but for their successors and of society as a whole.

Booth was not alone in his attention to this corner of east London, nor in his preoccupation with the root causes of the criminal predisposition of the Victorian poor. As some Georgians had invested in the study of physiognomy – the idea that the fundamental character of a person might be interpreted through their facial features and the shape of their skull – so some of their descendants took this notion further, by adopting the idea of the criminal tainting of the blood as a relatively uncontroversial theory. In fact, it was a central plank of contemporary moral philosophy – and it helped to bolster the Victorian class system too. It was an easy matter, after all, to conclude that certain tendencies – among immigrant communities or the indigenous poor – were simply aspects of their very being, as natural and unchanging as dark hair or green eyes. Environment could have nothing to do with it: the fact that one lived in the midst of a fearful slum could not be blamed for the subsequent course of one's life – and this attitude in itself helps to explain what is often taken to be the inflexible morality of many Victorians. It was of some comfort that these criminal classes would, in the working out of nature, inevitably become extinct: theirs was a social dead end.

There was no shortage of public figures willing to give their opinion on the state of Victorian society and how it might be bettered. Of all the figures who populate Booth's accounts of life and society in the Nichol, one in particular stands out: the

Reverend Osborne Jay, who arrived at the parish of Holy Trinity, Shoreditch, in December 1886. Booth described him as 'a
stout, plain coarse-looking fellow with all the appearance of a
fringe-fighter out of training.' Jay, irrespective of his features,
had practical nous: within 18 months, for example, he had
raised most of the funds needed to build a church for the parish
(until then, communicants had made do with a room above a
stable), together with a social club, gymnasium and lodging
house in Old Nichol Street. He also set about raising public
consciousness about the plight of his flock – ruffling Victorian
feathers in the process. Jay inspired – indeed, he still inspires –
strong reactions. Among some contemporary commentators, he
was a social radical in a world where radicalism was viewed
askance. A century later, he has been viewed by some as a
rampant self-publicist, misogynist and egomaniac, and by
others as a truly inspirational and electrifying figure in a down-
trodden corner of the East End. One fact, however, cannot be
disputed: he was a most original character, and his methods
were original too. During his tenure at Holy Trinity, for
instance, he managed to swell the paltry numbers attending
services tenfold by reaching out to the men of the district
through the establishment of a boxing club. The club met on
the ground floor of the church and through it Jay was able to
build pastoral relationships with its members. For many
respectable Victorians, this was a shocking move: these same

men after all carried the virus of criminality in their very blood-
stream, so it was morally unacceptable to indulge their tendency
towards violence by putting a boxing ring on consecrated
ground. In addition, the most enthusiastic boxers tended to be
those excluded from the very heart of the surrounding Old
Nichol; it was all, in other words, distinctly challenging to the
contemporary mainstream.

Jay would have none of it. He took to preaching sermons –
short sermons, for he said that the people of the Nichol would
never listen to long ones – at Holy Trinity with titles like 'May
a Christian Box?' The answer was a resounding yes: the sermon
was packed out; and Jay went on to laud the pursuit as both
rational and healthy – not to mention condoned by the Lord
Himself. Booth's opinion of the man was considered and
ambiguous: he praised Jay's 'genuine keenness for the district,
his ability not to be too straight-laced when brought face to face
with their peccadilloes or their crimes,' and noted the clergyman's 'touch of vulgarity, [all of which] have insured him his
remarkable position in Bethnal Green'. And he went on:

Behind the almost brutal exterior there must be a man of the
most sincere religious sentiment: no other motive seems
adequate to account for the extraordinary devotion displayed
in his life [...] one cannot but feel that he has been a civiliz-
ing and humanizing even if not a spiritual influence among

the criminals, semi-criminals and the degenerates whose confidence and intimacy he has won.

Still, the Bishop of London pleaded with Jay to maintain a lower profile, and to try to undertake pastoral work that erred on the orthodox side. Instead the Reverend went in quite the opposite direction – penning, for example, three books on the life and culture of Shoreditch and Bethnal Green. These were in part exercises in self-aggrandizement: they gave the quite false impression that there had been virtually no religious activity in and around the Nichol before his own arrival in the area. But they also helped to spread the word about conditions in the area among a curious public. Jay took this strategy a step further by inviting the writer and commentator Arthur Morrison to visit the area and witness its conditions for himself. Morrison had been born in nearby Poplar of working-class stock; his short stories had been collected in a volume entitled *Tales of Mean Streets*; in short, he could be expected to have a feeling for the mores of East End life.

Jay hoped that Morrison would commit his impressions to paper once more – and sure enough, the result was *A Child of the Jago*, a portrait of the life of Dicky Perott, 'a boy who, but for his environment would have become a good citizen' – but who instead is stabbed to death in a street brawl. Morrison barely fictionalised the area – even maps of the Jago, hand-drawn to accompany the book, bear a striking resemblance to the actual streets of the Nichol; and his heroic 'Father Sturt' was Jay himself in all but name. The book was a nightmare vision of deprivation, fear and darkness: its backdrop was instantly recognizable to anyone who had the smallest interest in the doings of the East End – and it caused a sensation. In one corner of what itself became a boxing ring of accusation and counter-accusation were those who claimed that Morrison – and by implication, therefore, Jay himself – had libelled the entire population of the area, who were not hopelessly corrupt and criminal at all but who had been carelessly and cruelly labelled thus in the course of the book. H. G. Wells noted in a review that 'neither ignorance, wrong moral suggestions, nor parasites are inherited. The Jago people are racially indistinguishable from the people who send their children to Oxford ...' Booth himself recorded the irritation of the authorities at the local Ragged School (the forerunner of the Rochelle), who were 'indignant with *The Child of the Jago* not only for exaggeration but because it ignored all other remedial agencies except Mr. Jay [...] When making his enquiries Mr. Morrison never came near the school "which has done more to humanize the district than all the parsons".'

From the other corner, a chorus of voices claimed that the novel had merely illuminated a fact that everyone knew to be true: the inhabitants of the estate *were* scum, and dangerous criminals who deserved their notoriety. Morrison's opinion, via the newspapers, was aired several weeks later, with a claim that while the inhabitants of the Old Nichol were indeed profoundly tainted:

> [...] the majority of Jago people are semi-criminal [...] Look at these long lists of families going back to the third or fourth generation and all criminals and lunatics [...] you never see a tall man among them, all the criminal classes are stunted [...] for my part, I believe as Father Jay does in penal settlements; it would be far cheaper than our present prison system. Why not confine them as lunatics are confined? Let the weed die out and then proceed to raise the raisable.

And Jay's own attitude remains controversial. He certainly subscribed in his writings and statements to the notion of a fundamental and natural tendency towards criminality: he wrote of his parishioners as a breed, a race apart; as doomed; morally and racially defective. He 'abhorred' them: they possessed, not knowledge and wit, but cunning and sharpness and iniquity. 'And all the time,' he noted astringently of the chorus of Victorian do-gooders who *would* see a future for such people, "we pretend that all have equal chances and equal hopes".' Such views were not extreme or even particularly unusual for the time.

Booth noted that Morrison's tales of the Jago had certainly exaggerated the sheer criminality of its inhabitants. 'To read *A Child of the Jago*,' he wrote, 'you might infer that murders were an everyday occurrence but in fact there has not been a murder in Mr Jay's parish since he set foot in it [...] There has only been one in the last 16 years.' Yet it is clear that he had a fundamental sympathy for the views held by Jay and many others: this is implied in the very classification system that he employed; how else to explain his categorization of whole streets and their inhabitants as 'vicious and semi-criminal'? But Booth was also what his near-contemporary George Eliot called a 'meliorist': he believed in the 'possible better' – and he believed too that general degeneracy might be arrested and even pushed back, if only environmental conditions could be swept away.

This might, however, mean sweeping away the inhabitants too: '[P]ersistent dispersion,' he observed, 'is the policy to be pursued by the State in its contest with them, for to scatter is necessarily to place them under better influences.' Nor was Booth alone in his theorizing: the sharp reaction that greeted Morrison's tales of the Jago indicated that a portion of the population did not subscribe to these despairing notions of the inevitable extinction of the poorest in society. Instead, they could be relocated – though where, many did not stop to ask – and in picking up the thread in a new place, might be given the opportunity to remake their lives entirely.

'On them will rise large, healthy homes'

The London County Council was established in 1888 in order to bring a sprawling and unruly city under some form of central control. It was packed with high-minded social reformers – and they sought a means of putting flesh on the bones of their philanthropic ideals. Parliament had not at first agreed that any such action with regard to housing was necessary: in the 1880s, a Royal Commission looking into the housing conditions of the poor had concluded – in keeping with the laissez-faire ideology of the day – that little should be done by way of intervention; and even the fretful wonderings of the Prince of Wales had not been enough to alter the views of successive governments.

By the end of the decade, however, attitudes had altered sufficiently to enable the passing of the Housing of the Working Classes Act of 1890 – and at once the LCC took steps to raise money, obtain permission and put into effect its first great example of public works. 'Is it not time,' suggested one administrative do-gooder in clarion terms, 'for this great metropolis to rise in her intelligence and strength and free herself from these dark vestments of the past and enable her children to rejoice in a newfound hope for a healthier and happier life?' The dark vestments the Council had in mind, of course, were those of the Old Nichol and its benighted residents. Within months, the LCC had declared its intention of buying up and razing the slum – and by

1894, 15 acres had been torn down, as the authority set about eliminating the largest area of black and dark blue on Booth's maps. In its place would rise the buildings of the Boundary estate: well ventilated, ordered and orderly, they would be a testament to modernity and to the ambitions of the LCC; and to the reach and potential impact of public housing on society. The estate would stand amid an entirely new street layout: the very streets and alleys of the Old Nichol would vanish.

The question of the destiny of its 5,000 displaced inhabitants was another matter: it became an excellent example of the gap between social theory and its implementation. Booth himself painstakingly traced the social consequences of the clearance of the old slums. He records an interview with one Reverend Loveridge, a clergyman like Jay (he was based in the adjoining parish) but one cut from rather different cloth. Booth describes him in his usual pithy manner as 'a regular old woman in appearance, manners, and I imagine the conduct of his parish'. Loveridge flatly contradicted Jay's descriptions of the local inhabitants: they were, he claimed, essentially the labouring poor, striving to better themselves (a fact equally observed in Booth's own earliest records); and 'whoever told us that Mount Street and Old Nichol St should be black told a malignant lie'. So far, so blunt – and it seems clear from Booth's account that Loveridge and Jay were not friends. Loveridge had taken exception to Jay's rewriting of the history of church activity in the area; and he was an enthusiastic supporter of local charities, while Jay disapproved of charity on principle. Booth seemed at times to be adjudicating between them: as he quizzed Loveridge on the various social and charitable activities funded by his parish, for example, Booth asked: '"Have you any clubs of any kind?" [...] "If you mean pugilistic clubs, no," said Mr L. glancing of course at his neighbour Jay.'

This, however, was not Loveridge's main point. It was that the clearance of the Old Nichol had led to the dispersal of its community – and virtually none of its members had been able to return. Booth noted that this had not been the original intention: the architects of the Boundary had sought a different model, envisaging that the local inhabitants would be moved, as each Boundary building was completed, seamlessly from medieval hovel to modern flat. 'Accommodation was provided,' wrote Booth, 'in the new, imposing buildings of the Boundary Estate, which from time to time were opened as the demolition proceeded; and in designing these buildings trouble was taken to suit them to the special needs of the displaced people, from being provided for costers' barrows and workshops for cabinet-makers and others.'

But this vision did not come to fruition. The original rents were set as low as possible: just enough to cover the basic servicing of the estate. Yet these rents were higher than in the days of the Old Nichol: slightly so, but enough to prevent the previous residents from being able to return. In fact, only 11 Nichol families took up residence in the Boundary – and years later, the errors made by the Council were detailed starkly. 'The Council,' wrote Booth, 'had wanted rents to be within the reach of the Nichol's original inhabitants.' But it made the mistake of calculating rents by room, rather than per family: and families which had crowded into a one- or two-room lodging could not afford the more expensive flats now on offer. 'Thus, although the Council managed the estate efficiently it failed to assist those who needed decent housing the most.' As a result, the dispossessed former inhabitants of the demolished dwellings were forced out into the surrounding area. The intentions of the LCC were good, Booth concluded, but in hindsight perhaps the Council, in its creation of the Boundary estate, had aimed too high. For one thing, the high building costs would have to be recouped: 'Those who cling to the original plan,' concluded Booth, 'may think success could have been won if the ideal had been a little less high and buildings less expensive.' This was a brutal state of affairs; and the consequences were felt in neighbouring parts of London almost immediately.

For where did these dispossessed people go? To other districts of Bethnal Green, Dalston and Shoreditch, bringing with them their fearful reputation for iniquity and criminality and creating new slum areas as they went. Booth noted this developing issue:

As to the character of the people thus removed there is a considerable difference of opinion as to whether they were simply poverty-stricken, degraded and short-lived, or whether criminality was the prevailing characteristic. [...] Whichever view is the more correct, there is no doubt that the displaced belong to the undesirable classes, and we have the recurring note of regret with reference to this or that parish, that deterioration has been hastened by the influx of a contingent from the Nichol.

This was an impression emphasised by further Booth interviewees: by an Inspector Miller, for example, who was able to describe the manner in which Nichol inhabitants ignored first one summons to quit their condemned homes, then a second, until 'finally they had to be turned out'. Even then, Miller noted, 'their first instinct was to get in somewhere else as near as possible. If there is room in any of the neighbouring streets, in they go. They quickly reduce the whole street to their own level. If there is no room, they choose one that is most favourable to their business while if they have no occupation they flock into the nearest area with a similar character to the one they have had to leave. This happened in the Nichol.' One reads such passages with the sensation that migrating birds or instinct-driven animals are being described, and not human beings at all.

Some of these forced relocations – for this in essence was what they were – led to tragedy. In 1896, for example, one of Loveridge's own nieces, Sarah Jarvis, was expelled from the Old Nichol with her husband and children. The story of the family's initial movements likely reflects the experience of many of their former neighbours: they moved from place to place in the locality, eventually settling in a garage building in another corner of Bethnal Green where Jarvis scratched a living as a box-maker. In the following year, however, Jarvis and her nine children died in a fire at the property. The death toll and pathetic quality of the story – the mother and children were discovered huddled together; the father died in hospital from consumption later that same day – set it apart from the conflagrations that were all too common in the East End; and it became a notorious postscript to the tale of the death of the Old Nichol. The national press pored over the story, and poets described the ghastly scene in verses at once prurient, moralising and complacent, as in William McGonagall's *Calamity in London*:

> *Oh, Horrible! Oh, Horrible! what a sight to behold,*
> *The charred and burnt bodies of young and old.*
> *Good people of high and low degree,*
> *Oh! think of this terrible catastrophe,*
> *And pray to God to protect ye from fire,*
> *Every night before to your beds you retire.*

Booth himself gave the tragedy considerable space in his note-
books, including a description of the pitiful property as it was
being cleared by the authorities. 'The whole of the interior[...]
is no longer from floor to roof and front wall to back wall,
than the average suburban drawing room'; and he quoted the
terse newspaper commentary that 'poor folks have to live
where they can, the rich can live where they like'. Later, he
described the funeral, with its respectful crowds, clad in their
Sunday best and washed for the occasion. He quoted an
onlooker: 'There'll be many of them here insisting that they'd
be burnt too, to have such a turn out as this.' The fate of the
Jarvis family disturbed the complacencies of many: ultimately,
however, it had no effect on public policy or the facts on the
ground. The people of the Old Nichol were dispersed, for good
or ill; and a largely new community would come to occupy the
new, handsome red-brick buildings constructed on this patch
of London ground.

The Reverend Jay surveyed the scene in the spring of 1900:

Fifteen acres, covered with utterly insanitary and bad
houses, have been cleared, and on them will rise large,
healthy houses, let out in small flats, with common yards
behind them and faced by broad, well drained streets. The
people of the locality will still have poverty to fight with
and hard work to do, and small chance of comforts, but

they will at least be respectably housed in rooms which will make health and decency possible.

Jay was describing the inauguration of the Boundary estate by the Prince of Wales – who within a matter of months would become Edward VII. The royal visitor explicitly referred to Morrison – and so, by implication, to Jay too. 'Few indeed,' the Prince noted in his speech, 'will forget this site who had read Mr Morrison's *A Child of the Jago*.' The LCC had certainly moved rapidly to implement its first and most cherished public policy: in the course of the 1890s, the slum had been torn down and the first estate buildings erected with startling speed. The sheer scale of the place – a score of large blocks housing over 1,000 flats – was in itself impressive; it was considerably larger than the largest of the private Peabody and other estates scattered across the city. Jay had achieved his goal; and had witnessed an immeasurable improvement in the quality of life in his patch of east London, altering it out of all recognition.

The new inmates of the Boundary estate were artisans, for the most part: people with a trade or livelihood that placed them a crucial notch above the 'vicious and semi-criminal' inhabitants of the East End slums; and approximately half of them were East End Jews, who could afford these new housing units. Among them were Celia and Simon Finklestein, Russian Jews who had recently arrived in the East End – in the company of tens of thousands of other Jews – to escape religious persecution in their Russian homeland. By 1896, they had prospered to such an extent that they could afford the rent of a two-bedroom flat on Calvert Avenue. Such folk were, in other words, the respectable face of the working class – and their installation in these new blocks of flats was celebrated as a concrete example of the amelioration of the working-class experience, of money invested wisely and spent well, for the greater good. Jay's comments – on the cleanliness and hygiene of the Boundary estate and on the virtues of its broad and excellently drained streets – indicated the sense in which the filth and criminality, fear and darkness of the past had been swept away in order to let in the light. It was heady rhetoric, resonating with a fair proportion of the population of a new, Edwardian Britain who wanted a break with a burdensome, difficult past.

And the buildings themselves were a testimony, as the *RIBA Journal* wrote, to 'the great body of skilled artificers who have striven to make this estate a model of good workmanship [...] If any members of this Institute are ever tempted to visit Boundary Street, and find the workmanship worthy of admiration, will they think of the silent unnamed workers by whose patient labour this great structure has been built up?' They were designed with thought and constructed with confidence, lacking the elaboration of the Victorian past and sporting instead a certain reserve; they were pleasingly proportioned and finished practically and well. The workshops located on the fringes of the estate would provide employment; the communal bath house would ensure cleanliness; the local shops on Calvert Avenue would be patronised by Boundary residents; everything necessary would be available on site. They were designed, in other words, to instil a sense of pride and civic confidence. As Owen Fleming, the idealistic 23-year-old chief architect of the scheme, put it: '[B]locks precisely the same? Monotony? Without any architectural feeling? The Eastender deserves better than that.'

Yet these new homes were certainly not luxurious: the dimensions of the rooms were small and they could feel cramped; and most of the units featured, not a bathroom on the premises, but a toilet on the shared landing. They were self-consciously utilitarian, using ordinary materials in ordinary ways. 'An opportunity of designing a working man's dwelling,' noted the *Builder*, 'is not the occasion for experiments which might be tried, in his absence, in the house of a colonial millionaire.' And they were dense, as the Old Nichol had been dense – though in a fundamentally different way: for whereas the slums had been low-slung, consisting of a few storeys at best, the buildings of the Boundary estate rose into the sky in their five uniform levels. And very many inhabitants could be packed into the available space, as in the Nichol – but in distinctive style. It was a new world, a new beginning in this corner of the East End.

The spirit of the Old Nichol was echoed in the Boundary estate in other ways. The LCC had realized belatedly that it was difficult to ensure adequate water supplies in the highest flats – and the result was the creation of communal laundry facilities in the estate. The *Daily Graphic* was impressed, although against its better judgment: the newspaper implied that the new residents were likely to be ungrateful; and that they hardly deserved the modern facilities now being lavished upon them:

> On account of the impossibility of getting water up to the tops of the buildings, the Council has built a large central laundry, forty-two troughs, all numbered, forty-two drying horses, four taps, hot and cold, to each trough [...] The convenience of a laundry can be enjoyed for 11/2d an hour; but those who know the ways of tenants will not be surprised to hear that the sum is begrudged.

Nor might the tenants approve of other aspects of Boundary life either. Each household was issued with a stern rulebook consisting of no less than 14 golden rules, violation of one of which could lead to eviction at a week's notice. Tenants were responsible for sweeping the communal stairwells daily; and washing them once a week; windows must be washed once a week too; laundry could not be displayed to public view. These rules were enforced rigorously by the council's estate superintendent, Henry Webb, who strove tirelessly to make the estate respectable.

The new respectability of the Boundary estate brought issues in its turn – for not all of these new tenants were prepared to put up with the seedier side of life in the East End. The estate was *different* and there was no reason, therefore, why passers-by should urinate against the walls of the buildings; or prostitutes take their clients into its shadowy corners in order to transact business; or robberies take place in broad daylight. 'I have reluctantly decided to withhold my rent,' complained one leaseholder who had taken a shop on the ground floor of one of the new buildings, 'as a protest against the state of affairs which I did not contemplate when I agreed to rent these premises.'

As for the Circus, rising at the end of Calvert Avenue: this was the principal feature of the entire scheme. The rubble of the Nichol was piled into the central space of the Boundary estate and eventually topped with soil and landscaped into a raised garden, complete with a bandstand. This feature demonstrates that the principles which underscored the estate – the coolly utilitarian notions of practical need – were leavened by a touch of romantic pleasure and idealism. Fleming had envisaged 'a central circular garden raised in terraced form so that the eye is refreshed by banks of flowers': his idea was that the tenants, though they could not be compelled to use the gardens, ought at least to have a view of them. And this central raised garden and

A 'central circular garden raised in terraced form so that the eye is refreshed by banks of flowers': Arnold Circus, with its 'wonderful hanging gardens of Virginia Creepers', formed the striking central feature of the Boundary. The raised mound was formed from the debris of the razed Old Nichol – and a bandstand was eventually installed in 1910, setting the seal on a new, self-contained world.

bandstand would indeed be visible from most of the five-storey blocks; it would be the hub of this wheel of buildings and radiating streets, the central element in what – if it was ever to be a success – must be a living community, and not merely an atomized collection of individuals and dwellings.

On summer evenings courting couples might stroll along Calvert Avenue and around the Circus while a band played in the twilight; and already by 1897 – the estate not yet complete – the landscapers had been busily planting 'wonderful hanging gardens of Virginia Creepers'. *British Architect* noted indulgently that 'we believe that the "keep the grass" committee are very pleased with themselves about this piece of artistry'. The band-stand would eventually be installed in 1910. Booth had already described the Circus and its environs as 'another world', and applauded its 'moral atmosphere'. In the face of this all-encompassing respectability, the fearful Nichol and its unfortunate inhabitants were, it seemed, already turfed and landscaped out of existence.

'When people want to live in a ghetto'

In its first four decades, the Boundary estate thrived, with its businesses and workshops prospering as a result of such a density of nearby homes and customers. Raymond's greengrocer and general goods store, for example, opened at 15 Calvert Avenue, sourcing its fruit and vegetables at nearby Spitalfields market; and – with the row of other shops on the street – providing a focus for this new community, and an example of how an estate of public housing could function well and smoothly. And the Jewish character of the estate remained strong: Simon Finklestein's son Harry, for example, operated as a shoeshine man on the estate, and led prayers at the synagogue on nearby Brick Lane. But the Boundary and its hinterland was what the Finklesteins' granddaughter Minnie – now in her eighties – calls 'an island, a precious island', a safe haven or refuge in a sea of virulent anti-Semitism; Oswald Mosley's British Union of Fascists – the Blackshirts – received 8,000 votes in Bethnal Green in the local elections of 1937. On the estate, however, Jew and gentile rubbed along quietly: Joan Rose, whose father – of Huguenot descent – remarks that faith and affiliation 'didn't mean anything; it wasn't important'. But change was coming – and its effect would once more transform the character of this corner of east London.

In the 1930s, the British government built more than a million council homes; more than another million were constructed in the years after the war – and this new availability of modern homes began to change the Boundary community. From the 1930s onward, for example, the Jewish population of London's East End began to dwindle: they were attracted by the modern housing – with private bathrooms, hot and cold running water and all modern conveniences – available in such areas as Stamford Hill, where a sizeable Jewish community had long been settled. The Boundary flats themselves were modernized in the 1960s – Streatley Buildings, one of the earliest and least architecturally distinguished of the buildings on the estate, was pulled down at this time. By this point the Jewish population was largely gone – indeed, the population of the East End as a whole had halved since the 1930s – and a new community was putting down roots in the East End.

The Boundary's inhabitants, it was felt, must be able to work, shop and spend their leisure hours in the tranquil surroundings of the estate. One result was Raymond's handsome grocery at 15, Calvert Avenue: the business sourced its fruit and vegetables at nearby Spitalfields market.

A Bengali population had existed in east London since the nineteenth century, when sailors began arriving in the city's docks from British India. They came predominantly from the Sylhet region of what is now northeastern Bangladesh: and in the course of the twentieth century, this population gradually established itself in Britain. It became commonplace – particularly after the establishment in 1947 of separate states of India and Pakistan – for Sylhetis to come to east London in order to raise sufficient money to buy farms and land in their home place; and the east London textiles industry, relinquished by the Jews, became the preserve of Bengali workers. Many of these increasing numbers of Bengalis settled in and around Shoreditch: in the census of 1971, a quarter of all households in and around Brick Lane were Asian, most of them Bengali; and the Huguenot chapel on Brick Lane that had been converted into a synagogue would in 1976 be converted again, this time into a mosque. Brick Lane and its neighbourhood, just to the east of the Boundary estate, gradually became well known in Bengali circles – in Sylhet as in London itself – as a place where a livelihood might be made in the London rag trade; and as more migrants made the move to Britain, the first Bengali tenants moved into the Boundary itself.

In 1971, civil war exploded in Pakistan: the result, at the end of a nine-month conflict, was the formation of the independent state of Bangladesh. The war triggered a rapid expansion in Bengali immigration to Britain – and the great majority of these new arrivals also came to the East End. There was no shortage of willing workers, then, and no shortage of community support and sustenance – but there *was* a chronic shortage of decent housing for the expanding Bengali community. And this situation existed alongside another, equally difficult social situation – for the changing demographics of East End society were leading to increasing social problems and to increasing levels of racial tension.

The issue of housing proved to be almost intractable. Many Bengali families were being housed in areas and on council estates where nobody else wanted to live; this situation in turn brought them into conflict with elements in the white working class communities who lived nearby, and in particular with the National Front, which was especially active in the mid-1970s. Bengali families were settled on tough East End estates – only to abandon their tenancies in the face of threatened and actual violence. And at the same time, thousands of council properties, empty through neglect or inefficiency, were scattered across the East End, with the Greater London Council (GLC) responsible for approximately 90 per cent of them. Community activist Terry Fitzpatrick, who was in the vanguard of the housing reform movement at this time, remembers 'writing a leaflet saying that in 1974 there were 3,200 people on the waiting list – and that there were sufficient empty properties in Tower Hamlets to clear [the list] overnight'. These were frequently situated in the very areas where the Bengali community already existed in numbers, and where new families would therefore feel secure. Unable to get acceptable homes, more and more Bengalis found themselves living in crowded and unpleasant conditions – even if they were at the same time running successful local businesses. Something would inevitably have to give.

On Easter Saturday, 1976, a small group of Bengali families arrived at Pelham Buildings, a Victorian tenement block near Brick Lane owned by the GLC. The building had been slated for demolition, the council intending to build new accommodation at some unspecified future date – and as a result, Pelham Buildings was standing largely empty, and increasingly unkempt. The Bengali families unsealed the doors and entered the building – and by the end of 1976, some 60 families were squatting inside. The building was neither pleasant nor comfortable (it lacked windows, for example), but it was better than the places the Bengali families had just left. As Fitzpatrick notes: 'Once the thing got rolling, once there was a momentum to it, you could have squatted twenty families a day.'

The situation had been encouraged by a number of local activists, who, while accepting that squatting was illegal, felt it served a practical function in urban ecology: for it involved not merely the occupation but also the renovation and utilization of an otherwise useless and empty space. This was an opinion clearly shared by many in the Bengali community: there was never any difficulty in finding families willing to exchange their living conditions for somewhere potentially better. And regardless of how local councillors viewed the situation, there was no appetite, amid a climate of rising ethnic tension, for television images of Bangladeshi women and children being thrown out onto the street. As a result, no squatters' evictions ever took place at Pelham Buildings; and in January 1977, the Bengali Housing Action Group (BHAG) was formed to help the squatters scattered across the East End.

Around that time, the Conservatives took control of the GLC: it might have been assumed that the new council would hold a rather more dim view of the illegal activity in Tower Hamlets and other boroughs – but in fact, the new administration took steps to formalize these living arrangements. George Tremlett, the Tory leader of the housing policy group for the GLC, had promised in the election campaign that he would be a scourge of the squatters – but once in power, he altered his policy. ('Do you want to fight 60 homeless families living in poverty? I didn't take on the GLC housing job to do that'.) Tremlett, as it happened, was not a typical Tory politician – outside office hours he was a rock music journalist – and his different course was both radical and deeply pragmatic. He held a secret meeting with the then Labour Environment Secretary, Peter Shore, and proposed a deal to solve the housing problem – but in a way that would ensure that the Bengali squatters were not jumping the housing queue. There would be a squatting amnesty: the situation on the streets would be accepted at administrative level; and made official. Shore agreed, and in October 1977 the amnesty was announced.

The new arrangements – which were directly in contravention of Conservative party policy – pivoted on a notion already familiar to residents of the Boundary: the idea of sanctuary or 'safe areas': of estates designated as being secure environments for the Bengali communities. 'It has been explained to all concerned,' wrote local government officer Harry Simpson, 'that at no time do we compel people to go to certain areas, that we are perfectly prepared to make offers of accommodation anywhere if anywhere is acceptable, but that if offers outside the "safe area" are refused on grounds of fear, the refusal is accepted as being reasonable and a further offer within the 'safe area' is made'. Experience showed, Simpson added, that the great majority of Bengalis opted for accommodation within the "safe area". As a result, BHAG was invited to present to the GLC a list of estates in which it would be willing to see its clients housed – and one of these was the Boundary, with its existing community of Bengali families. Shortly afterwards, some of the Bengalis living at Pelham Buildings moved into the Boundary, just around the corner. The estate had begun the next phase in its life.

The policy was leaked by GLC officials who favoured the traditional notion of dispersal – and it received widespread attention in the media, inspiring both fear and praise. The term ghetto was used for the first time: 'A Bangladeshi ghetto,' wrote the *Daily Telegraph*, 'provided one translates that hysteric's catchphrase into the less emotive term "Bangladeshi area" – is not an obviously bad thing.' The *Daily Mail*'s take was: 'Ghetto, E1 – and some frightened families just can't wait to move into it', adding helpfully that white families in the 'safe zone' would be offered alternative accommodation if they feared being 'swamped' by their new Bengali neighbours.

The *Guardian* agreed that such 'ghettoes' were not necessarily a social evil – so long as their inhabitants were there of their own free will. In a piece entitled 'When people want to live in a ghetto', it commented: 'The GLC may allow Bengalis to live together. It must not force – or even encourage – them to do so'; and added that 'the only morally acceptable reason for allowing ghettoes in this generation is to give the next generation the freedom to escape from them'. Tremlett's own view remained wholly practical: '[I]t was,' he said, 'pragmatically trying to deal with problems that had arisen for the first time. [...] You deal with the situation as you find it and you try to find the answer that helps more people than it hurts; it's as simple as that.' The East End witnessed violence in the wake of the policy's implementation – but the deed was done; the movements of people had been accomplished.

The Boundary, then, became predominantly Bengali, and it would remain so into the 1980s and 1990s. The young couples who had arrived on the Boundary started families: and Virginia Road school, having once taught predominantly Yiddish-speaking pupils, became home to their Bengali-speaking successors. Even now the estate's evolution continues apace. The Right to Buy legislation of 1980 affected the Boundary profoundly, and in ways that took time to be perceived clearly. Many of the families who had taken up residence in the estate in the 1970s were now in a position to buy their flats – sometimes for as little as £15,000; eventually, as much as 40% of the estate was privately owned. At the same time some upwardly mobile Bengali families chose to leave the East End, as the Jewish community had done before them – and the social texture of the Boundary began to alter once more.

It now became less and less possible to be housed by the local council in the estate: there were simply fewer properties available for rent; while those for sale on the open market – eagerly trading on their proximity to the City – began to command prices in excess of £400,000. There remains, however, a substantial proportion of residents who have lived for several decades on the estate – with the result that the Boundary is, paradoxically, both a highly sought-after locale *and* a council-owned estate in one of the poorest corners of London. Its social composition is, accordingly, highly complex – and a good example of this lies in the juxtaposition of properties and lives above the grocery at Calvert Avenue. Here, Richard Wallace, who works with a London hedge fund, lives in a second-floor property purchased in 2006, when it was in poor shape. His flat boasts a spare room and a dressing room inserted where the communal rubbish chute once ran. Just below live Rushna Begum and her seven children in a council property, in the flat once occupied by the Huguenot-descended Raymonds; Rushna Begum has no bedroom of her own, but sleeps in the living room.

The Boundary remains distinctive today – for its handsome architecture, its quiet streets, and its central hub of green around which the streets revolve; for its textured history and range and breadth of its population; and for a stability and sense of community that remains perceptible. On a visit to the Begum flat – where her grandparents once lived, minding the shop below – Joan Raymond glances out of the window onto Calvert Avenue: the flat was, she says, '[V]ery cosy; I used to love to come up here [...] I know that technology and everything in life moves on, but I'm sorry that's not still the butcher's, I'm sorry that's not still the delicatessen, I'm sorry that's not still the rent office, I'm sorry that's not still the doctor's – and I wish someone had a photo of it, as was.'

Today the strip of awning-ed shops on Calvert Avenue, though it contains representative examples of fashionable Shoreditch, once again features a cafe, a grocer and greengrocer, and a laundry. The Rochelle School may have morphed into a private arts space, but the playground of Virginia Road still rings with the sound of children's voices. Yet the fabric of the Boundary – its exquisite buildings and generous open spaces – is expensive to maintain: and the response of the local Tower Hamlets council, faced with constant funding cuts, has been to attempt repeatedly to privatize the estate – to the alarm of many of its residents, who perceive their own needs, their own security of tenure, to be under potential threat. For all its longevity and solidity and seeming sturdiness, the future shape of the Boundary seems fluid once more, and the stakes are higher than they have ever been.

The Thoroughfare
CALEDONIAN ROAD

*On the whole there is a general tendency
to betterment in this district, which would be
more pronounced than it is were the houses
better. But even now it is a thieves' resort.*

Charles Booth

Caledonian Road stretches for two miles through north London, climbing steadily uphill north and east, from the congestion of King's Cross to the Nag's Head at Holloway – and it passes on the way a number of worlds, by turns commercial, penal, deprived and gentrified. Yet more worlds cut into and intersect with the 'Cally' beneath its surface: trains on the Piccadilly and Victoria Tube lines cross the line of the road on their runs north and east to Highbury and Holloway; the Regent's Canal, the north London rail line and the high-speed Eurostar trains entering and leaving nearby St Pancras, all cross it from east to west. Today, this sense of endless movement – these continual shifts of scene, rapid entrances of people, goods, and fortunes – is further emphasized by a new front immediately to the west, as the wastelands behind King's Cross station are opened to vast new development.

This impermanence, in fact, has always been one of its defining features. From its – relatively recent – birth, Caledonian

Road has been the location of fortunes shifting, waxing and ebbing; a scene through which strangers pass. It was built in the 1820s – a period when London was setting out on its most frenetic period of expansion – and it is difficult not to sense that the plasticity of these origins help to explain the capriciousness of today's Caledonian Road: its fretful, unaccountable nature, its endlessly unfolding look and architectural character. To walk the length of Caledonian Road is to be shunted repeatedly backwards and forwards through time – an experience as unsettling as it is energizing.

The street that Charles Booth walked at the end of the nineteenth century was also conspicuously mixed in nature: commerce, heavy industry and residential areas all jockeyed for space in one of the most densely populated parts of London. Caledonian Road housed many institutions: prisons and cattle markets, Turkish baths and huge public houses; and was already criss-crossed by an elaborate transport infrastructure. In fact, it seems impossible to chart the evolution of Caledonian Road without telling the story of its railways and canals: their existence, no less than the existence of the street itself, seems to epitomize the Victorian obsession with communication, with transport, with an urgent need to travel, explore, trade, record and seek pleasure. The story of this street, therefore, is also the story of the people whose business it has always been to keep London moving: the bus conductors and

The proximity of St Pancras and King's Cross stations has always profoundly influenced the character of Caledonian Road. In this image of the road's early-nineteenth-century origins, smoking and sooty trains slice through the district: in the shadow of the embankments, meanwhile, life goes on frenetically.

rail workers, coalmen and stokers that made Caledonian Road their home.

The street's existence originated in the need for London to move faster and faster – yet even before it had begun to fulfil this function, it was already perceived as being a strange place and one that was out of bounds: it lay just beyond the city's boundaries, a no-man's-land removed from the reach of the civic authorities, a resort for dissenters, martyrs and criminals. That sharp edge would become a persistent theme in the road's story;

and it remains a distinct part of its identity today. The Cally has always been a place that epitomizes the uncontrollable city – although this does not, of course, mean that the authorities have never sought to control it. As we will see, however, life on Caledonian Road has always been influenced by a marked degree of independence and resilience: qualities that have proved to be its saving grace.

The conditions in which so many of its people lived have been a persistent plague on the commercial life of the area – and this in turn connects to the powerful sense that Caledonian Road has always been a firebreak: a dividing line between a fitful affluence to the east and consistent deprivation to the west. The road itself has never been affluent: not in the early nineteenth century, as it was being driven uphill through Islington's open landscapes to Holloway; not at the turn of the century, when Booth set out to explore the area; and not in the course of the twentieth century either. Only today are signs of a tentative gentrification appearing, as this area of north London experiences unprecedented levels of redevelopment – and now once more, the fortune and destiny of Caledonian Road are being influenced from beyond its boundaries.

* * *

The origins of Caledonian Road lie in a commercial decision taken in 1808 by a landowning family in the parish of Islington.

The Thornhill family hailed originally from Yorkshire: over centuries they had built their wealth through marriage and canny acquisition, until by the eighteenth century the family held extensive states in Yorkshire, Lincolnshire and on the edge of London itself. Now, with the economy booming as a result of the demands of the Napoleonic Wars and London itself on the brink of a population explosion, George Thornhill decided to invest in the new industrial revolution – beginning with a move to let out the southwestern corner of his Islington estate on brickmaking agreements. His great grandson Edmund Thornhill notes that George 'wanted to make sure his land' – on which he had previously gone snipe-shooting – 'was going to be worked [...] Of course [he] was taking a punt because he was expecting people to come and live there and effectively this was a speculative scheme [...] long before the idea of selling off plan. It was a very exciting time – part of an urban revolution.'

Thornhill's decision was a wise one, and eventually provided much of the impetus towards the development of this corner of London. The district was already opening up, and, with the river Fleet (coming down from its sources high on the hill of Hampstead) providing a reliable water supply to a range of industries, intensive industrial development was on the way. The bricks being fired in kilns on Thornhill's Islington land were soon in huge demand; and after the formal opening of the Regent's Canal in 1820, they were being freighted east and west to help build other parts of London. These were auspicious times in which to make a fortune.

The area continued to develop in the following years. In 1826, the builder and developer Thomas Cubitt acquired 24 acres in the area known as Copenhagen Fields, near King's Cross, which had an established reputation as a gathering place for all kinds of political radicals: as recently as 1795, a throng of 40,000 had listened to speeches in favour of the Revolution on the far side of the Channel. Cubitt, however, bought the area with further brickmaking in mind, as a means of supplying the building work down the hill in Bloomsbury. In the same year, a new home for the Royal Caledonian Asylum was established in the area: the institution had been founded in 1814, after much discussion, as a means of 'supporting and educating the children of soldiers, sailors and marines, natives of Scotland, who have died, or been disabled, in the service of their country, and of indigent Scotch parents resident in London, not entitled to parochial relief' – and in particular, as a means of caring for and educating the destitute children of Scots soldiers killed in service during the Napoleonic Wars. The institution had expanded in the post-war years; and its new premises in these green fields above the grime of the city were felt to be healthy and airy.

New residential zones were also beginning to open up in the area and in other outlying parts of London. These differed fundamentally from the earlier developments that had, in the course of the eighteenth century, remade areas of nearby Mayfair and Marylebone: rather than build imposing town residences for the gentry, George Thornhill and others were catering to an expanding middling class of traders and merchants; and rows of modern terraces began snaking across the landscape. The results were transformational, establishing in brick the architectural tone of the neighbourhood. In 1823, for example, Thornhill had released plots of land in the area between the canal and the Pentonville Road, at the southern terminus of what is now Caledonian Road – such speculation being a good example of the ribbon development that was unfolding along all the principal routes into and out of London. Other landowners followed his lead and the area soon began to be built up. And the speculation paid off: a senior official at the Inland Revenue moved into 1 Caledonian Road, a successful merchant into 13, a solicitor into 26 – each household with two servants. And then, in 1826, Thornhill took steps to underpin his new developments, by investing in the creation of a main thoroughfare that would strike north and east into Islington.

This new road was built by the Battle Bridge and Holloway Road Company; and initially it was a toll road linking the Pentonville Road with the Holloway Road, then one of the principal turnpikes into London from the north. Thornhill died in 1827; but in 1831, his son purchased the road and its tolls outright, allowing the family to plan further developments in the area. It was at first named Chalk Road, but the presence of the Asylum at Copenhagen Fields soon had its effect and the name was changed to Caledonian Road. Various plots of land were auctioned off to investors and builders, each of them hoping to take advantage of the burgeoning settlement of the area. One of these was Robert James Stuckey, a property speculator and the son of a Shoreditch bricklayer: he was responsible for building 111 houses in two years, and in the process establishing the form of the southern end of Caledonian Road, including Caledonia Street and the elegant curve of Keystone Crescent.

The Thornhill family continued to influence the area, particularly in the creation of the squares and terraces of Barnsbury, on the east side of Caledonian Road. Before the beginning of construction work, the area had consisted of little more than scrubby fields, the unpromising home of marginal farmers and drifters; and of intermittent scenes of violence. All this was now washed away: work on the large elliptical development of Thornhill Square began around 1847 with the construction of 33 houses on the west side of the area; Thornhill Crescent, completing this elegant oval to the north, was begun two years later. The central gardens were formalized in 1852; and the development topped off with the consecration of St Andrew's church in 1854. Barnsbury soon became a favourite with the well-to-do professional classes, who were attracted by such upmarket developments.

This genteel area represented one aspect of life on the Caledonian Road – but it was not typical of the area's general flavour and character. The burgeoning middle class was presumably undaunted by other fixtures on the scene, striking in their own way, but certainly not picturesque. The noisy and malodorous Metropolitan Cattle Market, with space for 7,000 cattle, 42,000 sheep and 8 abattoirs, was inaugurated by Prince Albert on a large site on the west side of Caledonian Road in 1855. Meanwhile, the new King's Cross railway station, which was designed by Lewis Cubitt – brother of Thomas – formally opened in 1852; the rail lines that served it curving delicately so as to avoid any violation of the boundaries of Barnsbury itself.

On the western side of Caledonian Road, the side containing the cattle market, the sulphurous brick and tile kilns and industrial plants and the basin of the Regent's Canal, different conditions prevailed – and these were perhaps more in keeping with the dominant atmosphere of the Cally. In the slum district of Belle Isle, the drainage was poor, open sewers ran between the shacks and houses, sewage oozed through the cellar walls of recently constructed housing; the houses themselves were filthy, and most of the residents kept pigs. The planning in the district didn't help, either: the sooty, smoky railway lines, though they had avoided Barnsbury, ran straight through this less favoured district.

A knacker's yard adjoined the cattle market; soon, railway passengers were complaining of pieces of dead horses suspended in full view of the slowing trains and of the overpowering odour of boiling horseflesh. Animal carcasses were cooked down in vast copper vats and were eventually used as cat food; shacks and cottages were set amid the nauseating stench. The inhabitants themselves, however, were enterprising, even in their leisure activities: for a game of cricket amid the bones and cauldrons a dusty field could be scratched out between heaps of junk and filth. 'For wickets they had a pile of

The land west of the Cally, with its water resources and good transport links, was home to intensive – and very dirty – industry: the kilns of Belle Isle and King's Cross produced bricks and tiles that would contribute to the construction of Victorian London.

old hats and broken crockery; for bat the stump leg of an old bedstead, and for ball the head of a kitten.'

These less savoury aspects of the west side of the Caledonian Road were now underscored further by a range of private enterprise. Attempts were made to spruce up this area and tone down its raucous atmosphere: for example, modern houses and flats were built – including the privately funded Beaconsfield Buildings overlooking the cattle market, constructed in 1879 in a spirit of optimism to 'provide healthy and comfortable dwellings for the labouring classes'. But it proved almost impossible to

A typically rowdy and chaotic late-century scene set at the vast, noisy and malodorous Cattle Market on Caledonian Road, as an inspection morphs into a riot: farmers and policemen attempt to control unruly cattle, the horses are threatening to bolt – and even the sheepdog looks mutinous.

transform this side of the street into a tolerable quarter of London, much less a fashionable one. Meanwhile, even Barnsbury felt sometimes perilously close to the edge: as a querulous letter to the local newspaper made clear, respectable middle-class residents could only put up with a certain amount of racket and chaos from the lower orders:

> Sir – if any of your readers are unable to imagine what Pandemonium must be, let them take a sleeping apartment in the Barnsbury district, and from the hour of 11 o'clock on Sunday night until the dawn of Monday, they may make up their minds, if at all susceptible of more than ordinary noises, to be thoroughly awoke by the hooting of cattle drovers. It is not simply the vociferation of such men which disturbs the rest of the light sleeper and the invalid, but the positively awful, Godless, filthy language these characters give utterance to, which constitute the fearful annoyance to which the inhabitants are subjected.

By the end of the nineteenth century, Caledonian Road had achieved its shape and character, and its variety of moods. The terraces of speculative houses lining its margins remained, but their tidy front gardens had been built over – in a syndrome typical of the Victorian period – by shop extensions, rows of which stretched up the hill. This led both to the decline of fleetingly fashionable residential areas, and also to a scene of crowded commerce. The Cally featured every form of shop under the sun: butchers, bakers, greengrocers, tobacconists, public houses, coffin-making emporia, lawyers' and land agents' offices, pie-and-mash shops; the streets were thronged with hawkers, barrows and flower and fruit sellers; and at night, the whole scene was lit brilliantly with gas lamps. As one anonymous journalist noted, the industry of the shopkeepers could not be faulted – although this did not mean that the street generated great wealth. 'To be candid, I fear I must describe most of the business places that abound here as mean,' the writer noted. 'The commodities they chiefly deal in may be described as pennyworths, sweets, firewood, pickles, newspaper, tobacco, bloaters, jam, periwinkles, and haberdashery about complete the assortment they keep. The takings daily cannot amount to much, but here you will always find an elderly man or woman in charge, early and late, showing a patience and a perseverance worthy of all praise.' Not one of these shops seemed set fair to stand the test of time. The essentially transient, fitful quality of the place was already well established.

Some commentators gazed with distaste upon this shifting scene: in his novel *Thyrza* (1887), George Gissing described the street in terms that would have mortified any champions it might possess. It was doubtful, noted Gissing, 'whether London can show any thoroughfare of importance more offensive to eye and ear and nostril':

> You stand at the entrance to it, and gaze into a region of supreme ugliness; every house front is marked with mean-ness and inveterate grime; every shop seems breaking forth with mould or dry-rot; the people who walk here appear one and all to be employed in labour that soils body and spirits. [...] You look off into narrow side-channels where unconscious degradation has made its inexpugnable home, and sits veiled with refuse. You pass above lines of railway, which cleave the region with black-breathing fissure. All this northward-bearing tract, between Camden and Islington is the valley of the shadow of vilest servitude.

And in referring thus to servitude, Gissing was presumably also thinking of another great – indeed, unmissable – fixture on the Caledonian scene: the looming grey walls and vast radiating wings of Pentonville Prison, which had been completed on Cubitt's old brick fields in 1842.

Pentonville possessed this same paradoxical quality of tran-sience: vast and solid though it was, it often held prisoners only fleetingly, before they were transferred out of London to serve their sentences elsewhere. The institution was established as a Model Prison: where inmates might, with the help of God (whose chapel was located at the heart of the building), he made to see the error of their ways. But from its very beginning it was a place filled with fear and degradation: it practised, for example, the 'separate system' of keeping prisoners in utter isolation and ensuring they could not communicate one with another; although a popular form of prison management, the separate system was not without its critics. 'The press will aid the public in its truly Christian crusade against cruelty,' cried the *Illustrated London News* in 1843, 'and these new model experiments upon the endurance of nature will cease to degrade the sacred name of justice, to make the law monstrous, and its retribution a disgrace and sin.' Henry Mayhew agreed, noting 'the agonies that must be endured by men in separate confinement'; and condemning those of his contemporaries who dismissed the inmates at Pentonville as 'very dogs, creatures fit only [...] to be shot down and swept into the dust bin'.

Later, Pentonville became associated with the radical politics that played such a visible role in the life of nineteenth-century Islington in general and of Caledonian Road in particular. During the wave of Irish Fenian unrest in London in the 1860s, for example, activists could rely for succour on members of the very large Irish immigrant community, which, after the potato famine of 1845–49, had moved to Britain and settled in and around Caledonian Road. The juxtaposition of Pentonville (where some of the Fenians were held) and

Caledonian Road (where some of them lived) did not go unnoticed: on the floor of the House of Commons, it was suggested that in the interests of security, Englishmen and Englishmen alone should be appointed to guard the 'Model Prison at Pentonville'.

The press, meanwhile, was having a field day: the political cartoons of the early 1860s portrayed the Irish immigrant community as a lower form of the human race, the missing link between ape and Englishman; and following the Clerkenwell bombing of December 1867 (in which 20 people were killed) Sir Richard Mayne, the Commissioner of the Metropolitan Police, told the *Pall Mall Gazette* that there were 10,000 armed Fenians in London. Some 50,000 special constables were sworn in to deal with the perceived threat to gas works and public buildings; sewer workers were drafted to assist four teams of police searching for explosives in the tunnels under government buildings; and government offices had their floors strewn with sand as a precaution in the event of an attack of 'Fenian fire'. It was an indication of the latent anxiety underscoring life in London even in the heyday of Empire. It also indicated that the Caledonian Road – still only 40 years old – remained a locus of particular discomfort: with its economic, social and political instability, it was in many ways a law unto itself.

'A bitter struggle to live'

Several studies were undertaken of Caledonian Road: over a 14-year period from 1889, Booth and his assistants visited on three main occasions, gaining in the process a vivid sense of the fluid nature of life in the area. Some features remained intact in this period: for example, escaped animals – flocks of sheep, squealing pigs – from the cattle market retained the power to cause chaos on the road, even as the market itself declined year by year. ('They had a bull the other day for 36 hours in an area. Another time a flock of sheep got loose into Rackstraws drapery shop, one went in, the rest followed. Loose pigs are about the worst to tackle. They will squeal so to attract a crowd in no time, and make the police ridiculous.') More potent, however, was the sense that the very housing stock had visibly diminished in quality and coherence. A good example is the case of Rufford Street, on the unfashionable west side of Caledonian Road: once the site of detached mid-Victorian villas, the street was rebuilt in the early 1890s as (rather unusually) four-storey terraced homes – the aim being clearly to attract moneyed folk to the area, as to nearby Barnsbury. This speculation was to no avail: by 1897, the terrace was already in freefall, the houses were let out as rooms and flats; and Booth, observing the brave attempts at ornamentation on the front elevation of the terraces, recorded 'a very rough district. Seems worse now than 10 years ago.' In the poverty map that followed, Rufford Street was indisputably 'vicious and semi-criminal'.

Booth was very aware that the Cally had dwindled, even in the period of his visits to the neighbourhood: the streets that in his 1891 poverty map were marked in lighter pinks and lighter blues were ten years later all a degree darker in complexion. His survey of Lyons Street – now demolished but originally in the shadow of the railway viaduct halfway up the road, and one of Booth's door-to-door 'sample streets' – indicated that in some parts of the area, a tentative grip on respectability remained: the residents of the short street scraped together a living from needlework, carpet-beating, jobs at various engineering works and at the fish market at Billingsgate; and some of their children even went to school. But their houses, though maintained, were in poor shape – and nothing could be done to change this state of affairs. There is a sense that the smallest misfortune – an accident, a week's illness – might be enough to sweep away any security such people had managed to accumulate.

The road presented specific challenges to Booth. It was hopelessly unwieldy, for one thing, its very length and its cluster of worlds and diverse experiences making it impossible to survey as he had other London streets. 'The district is cut up by great thoroughfares and by several railway lines, and by the artificial channel of the New River [i.e., the Regent's Canal],' Booth noted, 'but the divisions thus formed carry no social significance.

There is no symmetry or convenience or natural order of any kind in these arrangements. All seem hap-hazard, and it is probable that the account I have to give of the local influences and religious life of this great district will reflect the absence of well-defined sub-divisions, either physical or social.'

He was, however, determined to come to some understanding of this odd corner of London, and he proved equal to the challenge. The presence of so many railway stations in the area – St Pancras having by now joined King's Cross at the road's southern terminus; York Road station nearby – could not help matters, adding to the tides of humanity washing in and out of the area on a daily basis. The presence of the smelting and other noxious industrial plants was also noted: the area had become a centre of lead processing, for example, with raw materials flooding in from as far away as Japan and Australia; boats arrived into the London docks from Spain with oranges at the top of their holds and lead at the bottom; and the latter was despatched at once to Caledonian Road. Booth was, as usual, keenly aware of the conditions in which these labourers worked: he itemized the 52-hour working weeks, the absence of meal breaks, and the trouble the employers were increasingly having over issues such as union membership and pension requirements. The employers did not believe 'in a living wage', and he reported on their terse attitude to such a notion: 'it sounds very well but business must be regulated by supply and demand: who looks

after the mortar if [the employer] does not make a living profit?'
Meanwhile, the blue lead itself, though a little less poisonous
than the white variety, had the potential to cause serious health
problems among the workers. (Short men – so Booth was told –
were apparently less susceptible to lead poisoning than their
taller colleagues.)

Booth remarked on the ills associated with other trades too:
the warehousemen, for example, whose life expectancies were
shortened drastically from lack of light, sleep and proper meals;
and the marginal lives observed by the headmaster of Gifford
Street school in the course of an interview: Bennett Williams
spoke starkly of the lives eked out by those 'who say they can do
anything and who are the first to be thrown out of work in bad
times and the last to be taken on again. In many cases a bitter
struggle to live.' As for the street as a whole, Booth came to the
conclusion that it was in its entirety 'very diminishing': the
movements of people and of industry, of the changing city as a
whole, had not been kind to it or to its future prospects; and the
pockets of prosperity that did exist would remain tentative, until
the world around them changed too. Its population of middle-
and working-class shopkeepers, industrial labourers and
servants had little or no hope of substantial betterment: indeed,
it was all that the people could do to tread water. There was 'a
good deal of poverty and many more tenements'; and such
private homeowners as existed kept themselves to themselves,

A Caledonian street scene, 1904. Booth would have been familiar with the paraphernalia of life on the street: the trader's barrow, the posters, the worn, cracked pavements – but perhaps less familiar with the unexpected sense of silence and tranquillity evoked in this photograph.

behind closed doors. 'There seemed,' he concluded, 'always to be a lack of enterprise [...] and of late years the tradesmen have had a very hard struggle.'

Among these tradesmen were the Cally's cabbies, omnibus drivers and railworkers – given that the street owed its very existence to its ability to quickly and smoothly transfer people from one place to another, their trades were over-represented in the area and Booth devoted a significant amount of time to their stories. One omnibus driver whose regular route ran from Hammersmith to Holloway via Caledonian Road, had been driving buses for over 35 years, and during that time had

> 'noted many changes; always going down. When he started his main load was from the post office. There he was full up each time with a load at 6d each, all dwellers in or near the Caledonian Road; they paid the same price in the morning; it made 1/- a day each for bus fares. Very different now – shops were the same then as now, but doing another class of business altogether. The butcher for instance kept 16 horses to serve his carts, now he does not keep one.'

There were in addition hundreds of cabmen who lived around Caledonian Road, its location close to King's Cross ensuring that there was always a passing trade of businesspeople wanting to flag a transport. Earlier in the century, Mayhew had itemized the class of criminal-minded people who aspired to driving their own cabs: 'costmongers, jewellers, clerks, broken-down gentlemen, footmen, pickpockets, burglars, housebreakers, many ex-policemen and shopkeepers'. By the time Booth was exploring Caledonian Road, however, the profession had risen in the world. Cabbies occupied a desirable part of the social spectrum: theirs was considered a lower-middle-class trade – a fact Booth saw for himself in the course of his visit to Lyons Street. On the second floor of one dwelling, for example, he found Mr and Mrs Lenner: he was a cabbie, while she 'attended to home duties'; they maintained a stable at the rear of the premises for their cab horse and were, he noted, 'well-conditioned persons' – maintaining a tenuous hold on respectability, as indeed did the majority of the inhabitants of the street. The Lenners had attained a position, in other words, that was the envy of some of their less fortunate neighbours.

Booth was absorbed by the professions in the area: he perceived that this was a means of understanding not merely the commercial and economic situation of life on Caledonian Road, but also its social and domestic context. Control over certain shops and businesses, for example, passed from parent to child: outsiders were neither necessary nor welcome; and family businesses could provide insights into the greater society within which they operated. Booth was especially keen to understand the business of the pawnbroker: a trade which was a key bellwether of economic circumstances – and a very significant presence along the entire stretch of Caledonian Road. It was a trade, Booth theorized, that depended on instinct and knowledge of human nature; it could not be taught.

Booth went further, seeing pawnbrokers as akin to social psychologists: to be good at their job, they must be able to see into the heart and soul of the community around them. They must be able to intuit how an array of customers would operate; to assess their needs; and understand how social class and the importance of maintaining appearance were at all times key motivators. Certain customers would travel considerable distances to visit a brokerage unknown to them; local customers would have to be wordlessly assessed on the spot and dealt with accordingly:

> When the poor man has only clothes to dispose of he goes to the shop where he is known because he will get more on them than he would elsewhere. This is where local knowledge is of value. If the broker knows his customer and also knows that he is almost sure to come for his clothes on the Saturday after he also knows they will not be left on his hands and therefore he can afford to advance 6d more on them than he would have otherwise have done.

Booth also understood the ambivalent role played by the pawnbrokers' establishments in the life of Caledonian Road. On the one hand, he could appreciate the critical functions they provided – in the form of financial safety nets that other institutions could or would not offer – all with the added advantage of complete discretion. They raised and loaned money and published no accounts. 'In a sort of way,' he mused, 'they are the modern representations of the old private bank.' On the other, they certainly had links to the criminal underworld: they handled stolen goods on a regular basis, on the understanding that no questions would be asked. It was an unspoken rule that such goods would never originate in their own neighbourhood: instead, they would arrive on Caledonian Road from distant corners of London, essentially untraceable.

Booth interested himself in this seamy side of the business, noting that it was the task of certain police officers explicitly to keep an eye on the local pawnbrokers. Each morning, a list of stolen goods would be distributed to each pawnbroker; and the law permitted the police to access the pawnbrokers' lists at any time in order to check for stolen goods. There was need of such law enforcement activity. In November 1889, for example, a couple named William and Ellen Brown, who lived on Gifford Street on the west side of Caledonian Road, broke into a house in Peckham, and then attempted to sell their stash on the other side of the Thames. The plaintive details submitted to the Court by the householder listed a missing umbrella, shirt, purse and handkerchief, all of which duly turned up in a

pawnbroker's shop on Caledonian Road. The shop owner testified that 'the female prisoner pawned this shawl and petticoat
for 8s., in the name of Mary Wright [...] on 11th November
she pawned a handkerchief, and on December 9th a pin for 2s.
[...] I knew her as a customer, and have no doubt she is the
person.' Ellen Brown received three days' imprisonment for her
crime; her husband a rather more substantial sentence of a
year's hard labour. Booth's sense was that the 'diminishing' of
the Caledonian Road was reflected not merely in the plethora
of such professionals as pawnbrokers, but more generally in
the nature of local crime and vice. The proximity of the railway
stations guaranteed the presence of prostitution, for example,
especially in the street's lower reaches – but the prostitutes that
congregated in the area had come there because they had
reached the end of the line. The oldest profession operated a
strict pecking order – and the women of the Cally were among
the lowest of the low. 'They walk by grades,' a policeman on
Oxford Street explained to Booth. 'The best in Piccadilly and
Regent Street, these same women as they grow older descend
to Oxford Street, then to Tottenham Court Road, after that to
the Euston Road, finally they reach King's Cross and cannot go
much lower.' And another policeman added that the women
to be seen on Caledonian Road took to this profession out of
sheer indolence – because they were too lazy to sustain a
proper job.

Sharper forms of criminality thrived too. A speciality of the area was its gang culture: rival gangs, sometimes from other corners of Islington, would meet in and around the Cally for pitched battles. Booth recorded a death from a gunshot wound during one such encounter; he noted gang members carrying nail-studded belts as weapons. These gangs were responsible for spreading fear among the residents of nearby middle-class districts of Islington, who complained that these battles took place – especially in the tough lower reaches of Caledonian Road – without any police intervention. Pentonville, of course, awaited some of these individuals – and Booth observed the comings and goings from this most dominant of local land-marks. He noted that many of its inmates, once released, tended to be put straight back in again. 'One of the many sights of the Caledonian Road,' he noted, 'is in the morning about 9am. Outside the prison gates short term prisoners put there. Always a crowd to meet them when they come out with coats and hats. Each has a ticket for a free breakfast at the St. Giles Christian Mission house when he comes out, most of them go straight there. [...] Often a man no sooner gets out that he is touched on the back by a policemen and hauled off on another charge.' These men tended to confirm to a stock type: 'flat headed, undersized and bull necked'.

It was presumably with some relief that – given the sheer scale of Caledonian Road and the chaos and violence that characterized much of its everyday life – Booth gravitated once more to the local clergymen as useful sources of information. The tone of their disclosures was rather different and considerably less bracing than those he had encountered elsewhere in London. But the interviews were still instructive – as in the case of the Reverend F. O. White of St Matthias's, which took place in the course of Booth's first visit, early in the spring of 1890. This church was on the unpromising west side of Caledonian Road – on Blundell Street, just to the south of the cattle market – and White's demeanour, manner and clothing were reflective of his environment. Booth described him variously as 'very short, small and insignificant', 'untidy, dirty, smutty' and 'altogether a very pitiable old thing'. He then added, as though in explanation: 'he has been here for 16 years'.

White possessed many mechanisms of a functioning parish – a curate, various members of staff and a full 15 Sunday School teachers. But the local people simply would not attend morning services, though some came to evening prayer. ('It is no use expecting the people to come in the morning,' Booth noted, 'they work hard and late and will stop in bed in the morning. It is of no use telling them to carry the cross.') It seemed that White himself was at least partly to blame: he was an 'acidulated old bachelor' who was more at home amid the dusty ledgers of English history, and had no interest at all in the welfare of his actual parishioners.

As for the typical Sunday service at St Matthias's: the exterior and grounds of the church were dirty; the interior severe and undecorated; White's performance on the pulpit was dreary, and lacking in substance, authority and conviction. The sermon consisted of a call for money to keep 'this very poor specimen of a church' open – but Booth was not convinced: 'I could not help feeling,' he noted tartly, 'that the church would gain in frankly shutting up the place until it can make arrangements to have some life put into the work.'

The work of other churches and missions was more convincing. At the City Mission on Caledonian Road, Booth observed a practical passion at work that was rather missing further up the hill at St Matthias's: the staff was enthusiastically raising funds to pay for food and other necessities for the local people; and by relying on a system of paper tickets, largely avoided bringing money into the relationship. Booth was impressed at this example of grassroots activity: 'a large portion of the population,' he wrote, 'are touched and the church is filled. The key note throughout is sympathy with the people. What they do must certainly brighten the lives of the poor.'

Similarly, the Wesleyans on Caledonian Road were gratifyingly busy, by dint of their practical work with their flock – membership of which seldom embraced the very poorest. The observations about local social changes of a Mr Greeves ('clean shaven, thin, wiry') chime with Booth's own:

Mr G says that the population around his church are descending socially, in Camden Town and Tufnell Park etc., there is a good deal of shifting. The congregation at All Saints seem to have no lack of money and there is no difficulty in raising as much money as is wanted for church purposes which a large amount is given for outside obligations including £180 for foreign missions. Except through meeting and funding schools the church does not touch the poorest but there is a good sprinkling of those below the middle class.

Other churches engaged directly with the very poorest of the Caledonian Road poor: from the missionaries working in the old slum area of Belle Isle, for example, Booth records a population who live by their wits (and drink to relieve a precarious existence); and from the 'rather dull' Methodist minister, a report of efforts made to combat the dreaded 'indifference' of the local people.

The prevailing Caledonian climate was distinctly unpromising. There were the glum attempts at social housing on the west side of the road, where the Beaconsfield scheme – which had been inaugurated with such enthusiasm – had failed rapidly to live up to expectations. Poorly constructed, even more poorly maintained and featuring – among other horrors – plagues of rats living in its rubbish chutes, it was soon renamed 'The Crumbles' by the locals, and it began dragging the west side of the street even further into dilapidation. It was, wrote Booth, a 'badly-lighted grimy place. It contains no less than 480 tenements, and accommodates a population of three thousand souls, and though the name is now an anachronism, one of the blocks is still known as "the thieves' cage"'.

Some of the inhabitants of the Crumbles were employed: as 'outdoor railway men, not porters, known technically as "bank" men, some cabmen, builders, labourers, hangers-on generally. [...] Most would be about 3 months in the year out of work. Women are jam makers, meats makers, confectionery ...'. It was a place of anger and despair: members of the Salvation Army, when they first arrived to do its duty at Beaconsfield, had been pelted with stones and bricks. Booth rapidly categorised the complex as dark blue – yet he concluded, surprisingly, that it was not the worst place in London in which to live: ten years earlier, its residents would probably have been destined for Pentonville – but not any longer; and some of the women still attended Church.

And there were other factors that lifted Beaconsfield from the lists of the semi-criminal. One was provided by a certain Dr Gwyther, a Manchester-born medic who had retired and moved south to London, and whom Booth interviewed in the middle of the estate. All was grimy and dark when he arrived (though, thankfully, nobody seemed eager to pelt Booth with stones) but a 'cheerful' Gwyther soon put him at his ease. The gentleman

had come across the estate quite by chance: he had arrived to
visit a blind patient who lived there, saw the conditions in which
the residents were obliged to manage, and decided to see if he
could do anything to help – and ever since had been running a
club in the estate. The doctor's approach was deliberately down
to earth: with the residents, who suspected him of harbouring a
religious or political agenda, he opted for a bluff approach:
'Thought you might like a room to sit in and hear some music
occasionally but for goodness sake don't come if you don't want
to,' was his answer. That has been his line all along. "Come if
you like but don't if you don't like, it doesn't matter a straw to
me!" He has been there 8 years now.'

The result of Gwyther's music room had eventually been the
establishment of a club for men and boys, featuring singing and
acting classes and gymnasium activities – and with a membership
drawn from the inhabitants of the building, 'most of whom are
"odd" men, labourers and their families and a few thieves'. (The
ladies were permitted entry from time to time.) Gwyther placed
the administration of the club in the hands of the people themselves – and commented that they seldom did anything which
he might have reason to oppose. This was a rather different kind
of patronage from the sort which operated, for example, at the
Albany in Deptford: here on the Cally, the people at least
appeared to have the final say, even if the real power continued
to reside elsewhere.

Booth was impressed – perhaps in spite of himself. The club was the scene of sustained drinking and gambling, to be sure – but at least these drinking and gambling sessions were taking place in a safe, orderly environment; for the club members took it in turns to clean the premises on a daily basis. And drunkenness was not permitted. 'The fact is,' said Booth, 'now they are tremendously proud of the club; every day it is swept out by one of them, everything put in order, they look on it as their own doing.' And the club was not a charity: 'In winter his kitchen makes soup and it is sold for what it is worth. Any real case of destitution, starvation he would refuse and has done so but they are of very rare occurrences.' This was another version of the steel-edged philanthropy of the time – but as far as Booth was concerned, it worked; and one consequence was to help raise the Beaconsfield estate a level above black. But its fundamental problems and afflictions – in common with those along the remainder of Caledonian Road – would remain intact.

'That was just life in King's Cross'

The street map of the borough of Islington portrays several V-shaped areas, formed by the sets of long streets that come down into the south of the borough from Holloway and Highbury. One, at the Angel, is formed by the convergence of

Liverpool Road and Essex Road at the south end of Upper Street, with its froth of designer shops, restaurants and antique emporia. The other V is formed by the meeting of Caledonian Road and York Way at King's Cross – where such designer shops are few and far between. Headline writers have begun to refer to the area caught in this convergence as the 'V': a place where social problems have the deepest of roots; and where incidents of violence remain stubbornly high. These were issues prevalent in the area for over a hundred years; one of the dominant themes in the years that followed Booth's visits was the persistent violent undercurrent in the area. The gang warfare recorded along the road in the nineteenth century, for example, continued into the twentieth: Copenhagen Street now became a favourite hangout, with gangs of boys and young men gathering to inflict grievous bodily harm on each other – for reasons that had little to do with any particular grudge and everything to do with location and local identities. One report, of October 1907, details a scene in the Swan public house on Caledonian Road, in which a group of 'Clerkenwell boys' entered the premises and demanded to know the origins of one of the customers. Bemerton Street, was the reply 'and proud of it': what followed included gunfire, running battles involving some 30 youths, and the ultimate conviction of a 17-year-old to 'three months with hard labour to consider the way life was leading him'. Several days after this first battle, a second act included more of the same – and led to yet more prison sentences.

Other forms of violence also continued to leave their mark. In the course of the twentieth century, the Irish community in Islington continued to grow, and Irish terrorism periodically to operate from safe houses around Caledonian Road – in 1955, for example, a cache of Bren guns and other weapons was discovered in the cellar of 257 Caledonian Road. Sometimes the locales chosen by IRA operatives seemed a little odd – as in the case of the footpath outside Housman's bookshop at the southern end of Caledonian Road. Housman's, a renowned London institution, specialized in radical politics and had been a presence on the road since 1959.* In 1978 an IRA parcel bomb, left in a post box outside the shop, exploded; local lore has it that a post box at nearby King's Cross station had been the intended target. It was a good example of an incident designed not merely to create short-term headlines – but also to contribute to an ongoing sense of threat in the city. The incident at Housman's, though not fatal and certainly less shocking than many subsequent IRA attacks, nevertheless tied Caledonian Road into a wider sense of tension in the British capital: a state of affairs that persisted into the 1990s.

The social problems that afflicted the area had as much to do with the neighbourhood's fragility and its continued sense of

---

* Above the shop today is a warren of small offices out of which operate small anti-war, anti-cuts and anti-globalization publications.

Pentonville Prison has been a Cally landmark since the mid-nineteenth century – and as a potent symbol of the English penal system, a terrorist target too. Here, an IRA car bomb has exploded below the perimeter wall of Pentonville (1973).

transience. Charles Booth, like many other observers, had recognized that nothing on Caledonian Road seemed designed to last – a fact that would become even more evident in the coming century. In part this was due to the shoddy building practices which had almost inevitably accompanied the explosion of speculative building up and down the road in the previous decades: problems with sewage, flooding and damp had not been confined to a house here or a house there, but were persistent features of the entire district. 'In Caledonia Crescent, there is a dense population, and it unfortunately happens that particularly on the north side, the drainage is imperfect,' noted the *Builder* periodical in 1891, referring to the southern terminus of the road. 'There are untrapped sinks at the backs and fronts of the houses, and in some cases the closet drains pass through or before several houses. In one we could name, there is a meeting of these drains, and in it there has been a large amount of sickness if not death; while generally throughout this place, the attendance of medical men is far too much in request and it would be found that the death rate is much higher than it ought to be'.

And there were other signs of transience. In 1901, the Caledonian Asylum – a landmark in the area for the best part of 70 years – was closed and demolished. The oppressive proximity of Pentonville – added to that of nearby Holloway prison, which became a women-only jail in 1903 – was eventually felt to be a bad influence on the school, which once more moved in search of the green fields and fresh air that were no longer to be found on Caledonian Road. And in search of a calmer environment, also not to be had in the locality: if anything, the tenor of life on the road would grow ever more unruly in the years to come, as its very fabric began to disintegrate – a process that would take most of the century to reach a culmination.

Second World War bombing raids took a heavy toll, particularly in the area west of Caledonian Road and north of Copenhagen Street that now forms the heart of the V. At the same time, the site of the former cattle market closed; the last of the abattoirs followed in 1953. Other landmarks lasted a little longer: in 1966, the Greater London Council took over the management of the 'Crumbles' and at once began to rehouse its unfortunate residents; the last families were relocated three years later. The buildings themselves remained a baleful presence on Caledonian Road until 1971, when they were finally demolished and replaced with a small park. In the meantime, much of the slum housing along the western side of the road had been cleared and replaced with flats, houses and maisonettes – and the Bemerton estate, which has become the latest development containing many social ills that continue to afflict the area.

The original Bemerton Street was built in 1852, one of five terraced streets stacked along the west side of Caledonian Road. It had a 'respectable' reputation: in fact, the living conditions there were little better than elsewhere in the neighbourhood, its inhabitants suffering the usual chronic housing ills of overcrowding, lack of ventilation and non-existent levels of hygiene (Booth had categorised it as 'very poor, casual, chronic want'). The street was at length demolished in the widespread post-war clearances; and between 1969 and 1973, the modern Bemerton was built in its stead. The new estate might have been imagined as a panacea: efficient, clean and orderly. 'I was so happy to have a flat there,' remembers one resident. 'It had two bedrooms, it had a little garden; to bring my children up there I thought was wonderful. I thought I'd won the lottery.'

But the Bemerton failed extravagantly to live up to such expectations, witnessing everything from drugs raids to death by strangling and stabbing. At one stage, demolition seemed the only solution – but in the spring of 2011, Islington council opted not to proceed with a wholesale clearance of the estate. The residents were, perhaps, wise as to the repercussions of such a move, knowing that such wholesale clearances have seldom swept away social problems; and that a new clearance might simply introduce gentrification by the back door, pricing them in due course out of the area. Instead, the general opinion was that the Bemerton might yet be improved – and that looking afresh at the security apparatus that surrounds the estate would be a good start. Of the steel doors and iron bars that form one of the estate's most visible features, for example, one former resident notes: 'There's no way in. You go through one door, and then you get up to your landing and go through another door. Would you want to live with these iron bars?' Another says: 'They've put up all these gates and security doors and all the rest of it and they don't work – they just come up the sides of the buildings instead. They've got good imagination [...] I know people who wouldn't ever set foot on this estate'.

As for Caledonian Road at its fitful, doubtful 'best': even Barnsbury was already on a steep decline at the time of Booth's final survey. He had written disparagingly of the Richmond Crescent area: 'not red, pink – city managers. But not so good as Thornhill Square. Very ugly houses, depressing, dark street'; the neighbourhood in general was 'going down'. The entire area was already fraying at the edges, with its squares unkempt, its terraced houses neglected. Matters would not improve after Booth's departure: early in the century, the middle classes were in full flight to the suburbs, abandoning such districts as Barnsbury to the workers; and by the end of the Second World War the area had been turned over to tenements and slum housing – the traditional division between the east and west of the Cally now blurred in a hitherto unprecedented fashion.

Unlike neighbouring districts, however, Barnsbury experienced an urban resurgence that was startling. In 1947, the green centre of Thornhill Square – until that point private, the domain of keyholders only – was opened to the public; and in 1953, the park was redesigned to mark the Queen's coronation. It was a sign of things to come – and by the 1960s, gentrification of the area was underway. This process took time to build momentum: a 1968 pilot survey of Matilda Street, on the southern edge of Barnsbury, reported that of 160 households interviewed, 127 had no access to a bath, 138 shared a toilet, 15 had no kitchen sink and 25 were living in overcrowded conditions. But public policy was shifting: the 1969 Housing Act signalled a change from large-scale redevelopment towards the renewal of existing housing stock – with an emphasis on the private sector bringing about renewal. It enabled local councils, for example, to award housing restoration grants – if the homeowner matched their award pound for pound. Such a scheme inevitably favoured those with financial means – and Barnsbury was one of the first

Thornhill Square, Barnsbury, built in the 1840s to provide homes for London's burgeoning middle classes. The area declined into slums before gentrification got underway in the late 1950s; Tony Blair famously took up residence in Barnsbury before becoming prime minister.

areas to witness a housing renewal, as an influx of young professionals transformed it. Barnsbury became synonymous with spiralling house prices, with a newly fashionable south Islington, and in particular with the Labour Party – a process that attained its apotheosis in 1993 when the future prime minister, Tony Blair, purchased 1 Richmond Crescent. The renewal of Barnsbury, however, also demonstrated the ability of the gentrification process to create social dislocation: a traffic calming scheme introduced into the new Barnsbury Conservation Area had the effect of funnelling traffic through working-class parts of the area instead; and little of Barnsbury's new wealth has made its way south towards Pentonville Road or west onto the far side of Caledonian Road.

In the mid-1980s plans were revealed to run the proposed high-speed rail link from the new Channel Tunnel into King's Cross. This massive engineering project was proposed in tandem with Norman Foster's Office City scheme for the derelict lands behind King's Cross; and would have resulted in the removal of such landmarks as the Great Northern Hotel and the Camley Street wildlife reserve. Moreover, the new line would run in a shallow tunnel across the south end of Caledonian Road: a large number of properties would as a result have to be demolished; and a 'big dig' would cut the road – and a number of its tributary streets – in two for several years. The scale and impact of these proposals, and the sense that they lacked anything approaching a human dimension, ignited widespread local opposition. Certain features brought a degree of notoriety to the scheme – in particular the decision to table it with a minimum of consultation. The plan to demolish the elegant curve of Keystone Crescent – one of Caledonian Road's signature architectural features – ignited bitter protests from conservationists. What the engineers and planners did not know was that among the working-class Keystone residents was one articulate middle-class resident: Randal Keynes, the great-grandson of Charles Darwin and the grandson of John Maynard Keynes. He had come to the

Cally in the early 1980s, seeing the beauty and convenience of life on the Crescent: 'it's so special,' he says, 'so self-contained'. Though certainly not perfect: 'there were [...] kerb crawlers and drug dealers coming into the back streets to do their deals [...] and we'd also have the sex workers coming and serving their clients in our basement area. That was just life on the Crescent, life in the south Cally, life in King's Cross at that time'.

The planners, recalls Keynes, 'just blocked off the whole streetscape as an area to be acquired, demolished and then built up by new big land owners. Nothing about the people or their shops: they just had this idea that they didn't need to consider anyone living or working in premises in their way, because *they* were the rail company – and rail companies were allowed to rule. My first reaction was anger [...] because they had simply missed the point that we were there. They simply felt that no-one could want to live or work in King's Cross [...] that there was no need to bother about who was there now, that everyone would be happy to leave. [...] There was no evil in [the planners' attitude] – just stupidity.' Another resident adds drily that there was a widespread attitude that the King's Cross community consisted only of drug addicts and prostitutes.

After a sustained campaign of opposition ('we petitioned,' says one resident, 'and we petitioned and we petitioned'), the plans were redrawn so as to save Keystone, which was then rapidly listed. But locally, more demolition was planned, of a row of shops from 10–26, Caledonian Road, including a health food store, cafe, chemist, florist, newsagent and confectioner, men's and women's outfitters, greengrocer, barber and deli-catessen: all businesses that formed the heart of a functioning community. There was no guarantee that these units would be restored: instead, the area would remain in the ownership of the railway, making it more likely that an office building would take their place. The domestic scale of this section of the Caledonian Road, in other words, would be destroyed for good.

The scene was set for a bitter battle in parliament, against the backdrop of the property crash and recession of the late 1980s which diminished considerably the appeal of the original proposal. London was littered with empty office space; the numbers ceased to add up – and the scheme was eventually thrown out by the House of Lords. The high-speed link was revised, its line following a less destructive path – and its terminus was now not King's Cross, but the neglected and under-utilised St Pancras, leading to the glorious restoration of that station and its frontispiece Midland Hotel. And there was one significant local by-product: the blight that had affected the lower Cally while this dispute went on, had led to a collapse in local house prices: now some local residents who had rented their homes from the local council could afford to buy these same properties that, before the dispute, would have been out of their reach.

The fight against the King's Cross scheme had considerable local significance. It brought together a united front of residents and interested parties that was not opposed to development in all its forms – but instead that sought to emphasize a new kind of urbanism, one that invested in planning principles based on the notion of community consent. This community had historically been economically and socially challenged – but key to this argument was the fact of its very existence, against considerable odds. The situation was also laced with a degree of irony: after all, Caledonian Road itself had come into being as a result of private investment and a desire to forge transport links between one part of a burgeoning metropolis and another. The difference was that a community had barely existed before the building of the road; today, by contrast, the existence of bodies like the Cally Rail Group – which monitored the planning of the new line into St Pancras and which continues to observe the King's Cross development plan – indicates that a sense of community coherence survives in the area.

The gargantuan King's Cross development is being watched with both interest and apprehension on Caledonian Road. It has the potential to change the area in radical ways: to bring new people, new resources and new jobs into this corner of London; and to banish for good, perhaps, the long history of urban deprivation that has clung to the margins of the neighbourhood. But it also has the potential to cause the sort of social disturbance witnessed in the past by many other London neighbourhoods: for the gentrification being experienced on the southern reaches of the road – along the Regent's Canal, for example, and in the courtyards of the revamped Regent's Quarter of former warehouse space – can ultimately prove to be exclusive. Rents are already spiralling on the lower Caledonian Road: established businesses are already being driven out; and the result is that the social mix that has always set the Cally apart is now threatened. The paradox that underlies the life of the Caledonian Road remains intact: how can such a community – so apparently transient, tentative, fragile and divided amongst itself – nonetheless retain such will and staying power? The answer, perhaps, is simply that it *has* – and this is in itself a cause of considerable satisfaction.

A Street of One's Own

PORTLAND ROAD

The inhabitants are, in fact, rather criminal

than poor, or if not strictly criminal,

a very little removed from criminality.

Charles Booth

When Charles Booth began his initial survey of Portland Road in 1890, he discovered in this part of west London a situation unparalleled elsewhere in the city. A perpendicular line seemed to cut Portland Road into two stark halves: chronic deprivation dominated the northern end of the road; relative affluence the southern. There existed, in other words, not only a familiar disparity of wealth between rich and poor – but also a startling physical proximity between these social groups. The northern half of the street was coded by Booth in an unmistakeable dark blue:

Casual earnings, very poor. The labourers do not get as much as three days work a week, but it is doubtful if many could or would work full time for long together if they had the opportunity. Class B is not one in which men are born and live and die so much as a deposit of those who from mental, moral and physical reasons are incapable of better work.

The southern half, meanwhile, was a distinct pink and red: 'Shopkeepers and small employers, clerks and subordinate professional men. A hardworking sober, energetic class.' Nowhere else in London, in Booth's considerable experience, did two worlds rub shoulders in such jarring fashion.

These layers of social geography were significant enough – but the area was strange in other ways too. The difference between the eastern and western sides of Portland Road was striking: to the east lay the splendid mansions of the Ladbroke estate's mansion houses on Notting Hill, marked on Booth's maps in yellow: 'Upper middle class, servant keeping class. Wealthy'. Immediately to the west – literally adjoining the properties that ran along the western side of Portland Road – stood the remnants of that slum known as the 'Potteries' or 'Notting Dale'. This, in Booth's own words, was a black district, 'as deep and dark a type as anywhere in London [...] the lowest class which consists of some occasional labourers, street sellers, loafers, criminals and semi-criminals. Their life is the life of savages, with vicissitudes of extreme hardship and their only luxury is drink.'

Today, Portland Road lies on the edge of one of London's wealthiest neighbourhoods – and it remains acutely divided.

A gypsy encampment in Notting Dale (1877). The large gypsy encampments of Notting Dale predated the formation of Portland Road. Later, gypsy families occupied homes in the Dale before their descendants moved onto Portland Road itself – thus forming a tangible link to an incongruous past.

The heavy traffic and dappled shade of Holland Park Avenue gives way to the characteristic lines and dimensions of Portland Road – which is rather narrower and less grand than the ostentatious streets of Ladbroke Grove to the east, and the more distinctive for it. Its terraced houses, with their facades painted in shades of white and sweet pastels, speak of boundless wealth; so too does the commercial heart of the street at Clarendon Cross, with its rarefied shops, staggeringly expensive cafes, boutiques and antique stores catering to a rich clientele. On the side streets – on narrow Pottery Lane, for example, branching to the west – lie smaller Victorian mews buildings, these too breathing wealth.

But towards the north end of Portland Street, as it curves east to join Clarendon Road and the well-heeled commercial quarter of Blenheim Crescent and the Portobello Road, the atmosphere changes abruptly. This end of the street contains a precinct of public housing: some of the flats in Winterbourne House and Nottingwood House have been purchased over the years by their occupants – but enough council tenants and enough poverty remain for this section of Portland Road to measure some of the highest levels of social deprivation in London. This is a jarring juxtaposition of worlds – the wealthiest five per cent and poorest five per cent of the city population living at opposite ends of the same street, according to the

Borough of Kensington and Chelsea's own statistics – yet in historical terms, it is not startling in the least.

* * *

The atmosphere of Portland Road has remained remarkably consistent. The street of today and the one recorded by Booth over a century ago seem equally spiked with gentility *and* poverty, with an ugly sense of salubrious and insalubrious worlds grating against each other. This world, however, was many decades in the making, the culture and climate of its surroundings pivotal in shaping this strange streetscape. The years have witnessed the playing out of many human histories in this once outlying corner of London. It had been dominated by the question of housing: by the appearance of layer upon layer of speculative building – some of it highly ambitious, some relatively modest, some positively daring in its assumption of ultimate financial gain. All of it, however, rested on factors ultimately beyond the control of the developers: on the creation of an adequate transport infrastructure, for example, and on the vagaries of a fluctuating economic climate. The result was a story of urban development that seemed at times almost anarchic, with affluence and squalor existing in the very closest proximity. The telling of this story, furthermore, underscores the extent to which the history of Victorian London was one dominated by economic imperatives, against which human needs always played second fiddle.

A century and more before Booth set out to survey Portland Road, the neighbourhood in which it now stands consisted of little more than fields: an area of countryside within London popular with travelling gipsies, with anthropologists, social commentators and tourists who came to gawk at these large encampments of gipsies and their outlandish lives; and – as the nineteenth century opened – with industrialists eager to quarry the fields for bricks to build the capital city that was beginning to spread out across the surrounding landscape.

The history of the area features a range of pungent and colourful characters. Samuel Lake, for example, was a sewage collector, chimney sweep, pig keeper and pimp who around the time of Waterloo abandoned these previous occupations in and around Tottenham Court Road for rather greener pastures a few miles further west. Here, Lake could make money free from the watchful eyes of angry neighbours: once established around Notting Dale, he bought some land – and soon he was joined by other pig-keeping entrepreneurs. On the site of what is now Connaught Square in Bayswater, for example, the self-appointed 'Pigmasters to the West End establishment' had traditionally existed on scraps from Mayfair houses – but in 1820, they were evicted from the area by their landlord, the Bishop of London. They too now migrated west, bought or rented small plots of land and moved their pigs in.

This swelling population of pigs in Notting Hill would play a central part in the economic history that followed. Lake rapidly understood the potential profits that might be made from the business: living quarters for both humans and animals were squeezed into the area, which soon attained an unenviable reputation for filth and odour. Offal was boiled in open vats; and animal and human ordure alike collected as stinking, stagnant lagoons in the deep concavities left by the brickmakers. All of these foul lakes emitted the gaseous stench of hydrogen sulphide; the largest of them lay immediately to the west of today's Portland Road and was known as the 'Ocean'.

The area unsurprisingly was known for its abiding atmosphere of ill health: its inhabitants were marked by their sunken eyes and shrivelled skin, continual sickness and loss of appetite. Influenza, cholera, diarrhoea and dysentery outbreaks were common; and the rate of smallpox infection in Notting Dale – which suffered from decades of neglect, and festered (quite literally) in its own filth – was double that of other districts of North Kensington. Events in the outside world served to aggravate this already hellish situation: following the Irish Famine of 1845–9, for example, large numbers of Irish immigrants fetched up in the Dale, adding to the area's already considerable problems. In the *Builder*, however, one pig keeper hit back, saying '[i]f a pig was a nuisance, why we should have no more pork. It was a nuisance to the pig dealer to have a respectable neighbourhood, and the best thing the complainants could do would be to remove.'

The slum was accessible only via a small, unprepossessing alley known locally as 'Cut Throat Lane': today's quaint Pottery Lane, branching directly off Portland Road. It was an opening into another world: for it passed from the environs of respectable London into the dirty, disease-ridden and criminal underworld of the Dale – what became known locally as the 'Mouth of Hell'. Years later, Booth would note the 'very general rule that groups of poor streets, when cut off from communication with the surrounding district and so lacking the guarantee which through traffic provides, tend to become disreputable'. And indeed, the slums that lurked beyond Pottery Lane proved Booth's rule: until the establishment of the Office of Metropolitan Buildings in 1844, there was no public control whatever over standards of building in London – and given the absence too of any private supervision, shacks and shanties could be erected at the resident's discretion.

As early as 1838, the particularly poor conditions at the Potteries had attracted the gaze of the Poor Law Commissioners, who noted that some of the shacks in the Dale were actually built over these lakes of filth and excrement. Their reports were ghastly. 'In some instances,' they noted, 'the floors have given way, and rest at one end of the room in the stagnant pool, while the other end, being still dry, contains the bed or straw mattress on which the family sleeps.' The result was a blasted, fetid landscape that was apparently incapable of being revived. Lake had been remarkably prescient in his planning: when the Medical Officers attempted to clear the Dale, he 'seems to have foreseen this evil day, and "for the purpose of pig-keeping" had been inserted in the very leases which the people were able to produce; so that nothing but a special Act of Parliament could remedy the existing evil.'

The population of the Dale was highly transient, with some residents remaining in the area only a night, others a week, others again months or even years. From time to time, such transients might be moved on by the authorities: towards central London or Whitechapel, returning in due course to Notting Dale. As other slums were cleared, these populations in their turn would emerge in the Dale – all aspects of a gyratory system moving through London like a vast oceanic current. 'These people are poor,' Booth noted later, 'in many cases distressfully so, but there may be truth in the statement of one of our lay witnesses that "in these bad streets there is generally money going; it is the way if spending it that is amiss." The inhabitants are, in fact, rather criminal than poor, or if not strictly criminal, a very little removed from criminality.' And Booth reflected that such a class of people existed in higher concentrations in Notting Dale than in any other quarter of London.

By the 1820s, however, the area immediately to the east of what would become Portland Road was opening up to systematic development. The Ladbroke estate was built over the course of 50 years from 1821 – though very much in fits and starts, depending on the economic health of the outside world. The estate as originally conceived was highly original, at least in London terms: it consisted of a spectacular estate, focused on a large central circus with radiating streets built around garden squares – the intention being to combine the bucolic pleasures of the countryside with the urban amenities of the city. Classical groves alternated with tiers of leafy crescents; stucco villas alternated with plain brick terraces; and the great spire of St John's loomed over the plane trees like an obelisk in a park. In every direction there were to be gardens: private and semi-private, hidden and half-hidden, with glimpses of knolls and leafy dells – as though the real country began only a few steps beyond the last back door.

Financial crises forced these grandiose plans to be greatly scaled back: the original bold vision would never be fulfilled, but the area of Ladbroke Grove was nevertheless impressive. It threw into sharp relief the form of the neighbouring land: although other builders had floated the idea of developing further housing on the flanks of the Grove, the area of Notting

Hill as a whole was still too remote and too poorly served by public transport to allow for successful speculations. Instead, the land became a racecourse, wedged uncomfortably on the seam between the bosky pleasures of the Grove and the ammoniac fumes of the Dale: the Hippodrome opened in 1837, its track running north–south on the line followed today by Portland Road.

The proximity of the Hippodrome to the poorest part of the capital, however, encouraged an audience far removed from what the designer had envisaged — as detailed in a *Sunday Times* report of 1837:

> A more filthy or disgusting crew than that which entered, we have seldom had the misfortune to encounter. The invaders had not kept to the path, but, relying upon their numbers, they spread themselves over the whole of the ground, defiling the atmosphere as they go, and carrying into the neighbourhood of the stands and carriages, where the ladies are most assembled, a coarseness and obscenity of language as repulsive to every feeling of manhood as to every sense of common decency.

And even the racing was not a success, with the stakes low and the quality of the horses poor; and in 1842, the Hippodrome closed. The shape of the future Portland Road began to form along the former steeplechase track – and within four years, the street had been substantially completed.

Even before it came into existence, then, Portland Road had assumed the character later observed by Booth. It lay on a faultline between two worlds; it formed a vital border, a firm division between the lofty ideals of Ladbroke Grove to the east and the stinking slums of the Dale to the west – and it was quite distinct from either. Significantly, however, the relationship between these worlds was not one of mutual ignorance, but rather of economic symbiosis. Later, George Duckworth, one of Booth's primary assistants, focused on this relationship, this 'parasitic poverty [...] where a race of poor dependents has grown up encouraged by the indiscriminate giving of the well-to-do'.

In fact, this *indiscriminate giving* as observed narrowly by Duckworth was a form of mutuality: a trading of goods and services, a social transaction that fulfilled the needs of both rich and poor. The latter might provide labour, for example, and in return acquire scraps and leftovers that would feed both them and their pigs. And in a rather broader economic context, the swine of Notting Dale were a useful source of protein for the entire city's ever-growing population. It was a system that worked reasonably well most of the time – though by no means always, as noted in this sketch of 'Tucker's Cottage', the oldest house in Kensington Potteries, circa 1855:

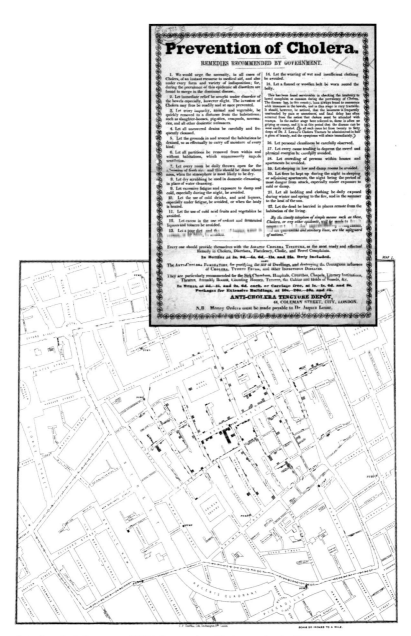

John Snow's cholera map of 1854: Snow painstakingly traced a deadly outbreak of the disease to a single pump dispensing contaminated water on Broad Street, Soho. This map – stark and notorious – was a forerunner of Charles Booth's iconic images of London.

The neat streets of the West estate, Bermondsey, centred on respectable Thorburn Square and its handsome church; Reverdy Road runs north-south immediately to the west. The area's food processing plants and tanneries provided ample working-class employment, but conditions could be marginal and harsh – a fact reflected in the energetic left-wing culture of the district.

The densely packed streets of Deptford, its High Street cut by the railway line from London Bridge to Greenwich. Deptford High Street was red-edged, signifying commercial prosperity – but poverty lurked in the streets on either side. Much of the area's housing was cleared in the 1960s and replaced with high-rise estates, dispersing the local working-class community and fostering long-term social and economic woes.

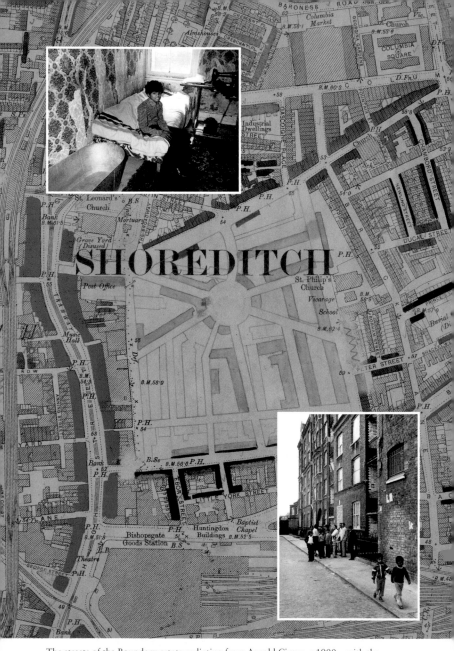

The streets of the Boundary estate radiating from Arnold Circus, *c*.1900 – with the black of poverty pressing against the margins of the new estate. The Boundary was built on the razed rubble of the Old Nichol – until its demolition in the 1890s, one of London's most desperate slums. By the 1970s, the predominantly Jewish population of the Boundary had been replaced by a Bengali community.

Caledonian Road, Islington. Here, the elegant oval of Thornhill Square – built in the 1830s and 1840s to house London's burgeoning middle classes – contrasts with the fearsome void of Pentonville Prison. But at the time of Booth's surveys, Thornhill Square had entered a spiral of decline: the well-to-do of north London did not, perhaps, want to live adjacent to the enormous, rowdy and malodorous Metropolitan Cattle Market.

Portland Road was a borderline between the broad avenues and grand villas of the Ladbroke Estate and the grinding poverty, disease and slums of Notting Dale. Booth's map illustrates the shocking proximity of these two worlds better than a thousand well-intentioned reports. Today, Portland Road has been hyper-gentrified: its wealthy residents no longer live their lives out on the street itself – and its corner shops and groceries have vanished.

The stately line of Camberwell Grove as it climbs steadily uphill from Camberwell village. Note the inconsistencies in Booth's survey: here, the confident red edging of the Grove signifies bourgeois wealth – a far cry from the boisterous commerce and trade of (equally red) Deptford. Today, the graceful houses of the Grove are among the grandest and most impressive in London.

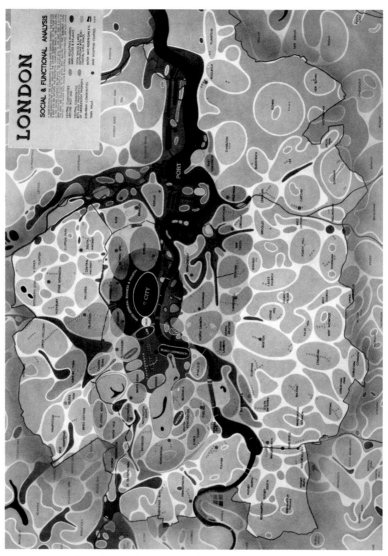

London as a machine: this was the dream of modernist planning as it envisaged the capital city in the aftermath of war. Each district would serve a discrete function – and the impact of such plans would be felt first and most profoundly in working-class east and south London.

We most of us keep a horse, or a donkey and cart, and we go round early in the morning to the gentlefolk's houses and collects the refuses from the kitchens. When we comes home we sorts it out, the best of it we eats ourselves, or gives it to a neighbour, the fat is boiled down, and the rest we give to the pigs [...] When they have lots of company they gets a deal of refuse [...] When the families goes out of town the servants is put on board wages, and they scrimps and saves everything, we ain't wanted to call then 'cause there's not a scrap left for us, oh no, we ain't no use then.

The vagaries of economy and fashion proved to be levellers of sorts, in this corner of west London as elsewhere. The *Building News* observed of Notting Hill in the early 1860s that: 'a large number of houses have been erected. Many of them are now fit for occupation, others are in progress; whilst on other portions many have been abandoned and left as carcasses, apparently for want of funds to complete them.' The piece noted that 'courageous builders have occasionally touched them and lost heart and money by the venture [...] with misfortune came insult, and the opprobrious epithet of 'Coffinrow' was fixed upon the dead street, where the windows had that ghastly form. [...] The whole estate was as a graveyard of buried hopes.' By this point, work had come to a dramatic halt on the Ladbroke estate: the census of 1861 records a half-finished Portland Road ending at

Number 103; and the *Building News* described 'the melancholy vestiges of the wreck [...] crumbling decorations, fractured walls, and slimy cement-work, upon which the summer's heat and winter's rain have left their damaging mark ...'

Many of the street's residents were of a 'working class', including coachmen and painters, with the occasional 'scholar' thrown in to leaven this mixture; and multi-family occupancy was very common. A palpable connection between the street and the long-standing gypsy encampments in the Dale, meanwhile, had been forged: in 1862–3, 50 gypsy families settled in permanent homes in the Dale, promising to abstain from fortune-telling, drunkenness and swearing; these reformed characters sold their horses, ceased speaking Romany and acquired hawkers' licenses. Later, members of this new settled community would migrate a street or two to the east to settle on Portland Road itself, influencing its population profile in the generations to come. Booth would later record the 'gypsy blood [...] very evident among the children, and noticeable in the streets.' One former resident recalls: 'I couldn't believe it when my mum told me my granddad was a gypsy. But it made sense: lots of us on Portland Road came from gipsies; our family lived on Bangor Street in the Dale and then they all started to move to Portland Road'. And another recalls that his grandfather was a gypsy. 'He used to make pegs, and make flowers, and he used to stand with a basket outside Barker's in Kensington High Street and sell them. That was the way he used to earn his living.'

The census returns, meanwhile, reveal decade by decade shifting patterns: households at the lower end of the road boasted a servant or two; and a tentative middle-class colonization was bedding in. The census of 1871 reveals an architect and his family living at 48 Portland Road, in company with two servants. Ten years later, a respectable widow, with private means, has taken up residence with her two children; by 1891, another respectable widow has appeared – although this time her daughter works as a typist, suggesting a decline in social standards. By 1901, the house is in multi-occupancy: a clergyman and his wife live in the basement; while a woman and her carpenter son live upstairs, in company with a troupe of travelling actors who have rented a room. And, as the survey tracked north along the street, so the residents diminished in respectability and the housing stock in quality – ending in poverty. And there were no house numbers at all for narrow Pottery Lane, and limited records of any kind – perhaps suggesting that census material was difficult to access on the fringes of the slum.

'An unexampled concourse of the disreputable classes'

By the time Booth arrived to begin his initial surveys, the reputation of parts of the district was altering. 'Ladbroke Grove and district' were now, Booth concluded, red and yellow in tone, having once more risen in the world; most of the houses kept a servant or two. But other areas, including Notting Dale, were still mired in poverty and 'inhabited by hawkers, tramps, loafers [...] porters, sweeps, laundresses, and charwomen.' Booth went on to note that the Dale was 'a district, which is not only a disgrace; it is large enough to be a danger also. According to the police these are a succession of streets the majority of whom inhabitants are criminals. Every year the area of criminality is extending.' The waves of this criminal environment washed up along the terraced houses of Portland Road – now more than ever, an embankment of sorts, a division between two societies. And most of all, Booth was fascinated by the proximity of these worlds: for they remained divided merely by a wall, a lane, an alley; and all too frequently, they shared the same overpoweringly contaminated air.

However, legislative reforms – and in particular the Housing of the Working Classes Act of 1890 – were soon to bring about changes. The Act (as we have seen in and around Arnold Circus) effectively enabled local authorities in London to build their own housing. It rationalized the existing housing and slum clearance legislation, making it much easier for local authorities to carry out clearance schemes, and – under certain circumstances – to build with the dual purpose of rehousing and increasing the supply of working-class housing. Following the passing of the Act, the LCC almost immediately began to build new tenement blocks in London to rehouse families displaced by clearance or improvement schemes. One consequence was that whole neighbourhoods could be levelled at the whim of the LCC, regardless of the objections of their inhabitants – and it seems that this was what happened in Notting Dale, where the first mayor of Kensington, Henry King, made a personal loan to the council and remodelled 26 dwellings, demolished 17 others, and rented them out at the sum of 3s. 6d. per week. The apparatus of the state, in other words, had finally started taking notice of the Notting Dale problem, albeit in a way that was far from perfect. So pleased were the authorities with their efforts, however, that a few years later, the LCC declared that the area had undergone 'a very marked improvement' – particularly in its moral tone.

Among the losers from such reforms were the landlords of the area, many of whom rented out their rooms in the Dale by the night. These individuals tended to be portrayed as unscrupulous: indeed, many certainly *were* unscrupulous; but others faced a hard choice between accepting unknown tenants, or leaving their properties unoccupied and failing to make a living themselves. Their plight, however, did not soften the heart of Octavia Hill, who since 1899 had been responsible for the management of a number of houses in the Dale. Hill was an upstanding Victorian: rigorous, firm and demanding of her tenants (in Notting Hill as in Deptford and elsewhere in London) in the matter of sexual propriety, temperance and well-scrubbed cleanliness. Writing her manifesto for progress in 1886, Hill enunciated firmly her belief that the urban poor:

> must rouse themselves from the lethargy and indolent habits into which they have fallen, and freed from all that hinders them from doing so. [...] I desired to be in a condition to free a few poor people from the tyranny and influence of a low class of landlords and landladies; from the corrupting effect of continual forced communication with very degraded fellow-lodgers; from the heavy incubus of accumulated dirt: so that the never dying hope which I find characteristic of the poor might have leave to spring, and with it such energy as might help them to help themselves.

Hill perceived that the key to enabling this culture of self-sufficiency was to sever the bonds of dependency between the poor and their often unscrupulous private landlords, who demanded their rent, come what may. The result of such a relationship was that the poor were driven towards criminal activities, including prostitution, in order to raise this rent – with the further consequence that landlords, in Hill's opinion, held greater power than schoolteachers over the future state of society: 'power either of life or death, physical and spiritual.

There are dreadful instances in which sin is really tolerated and shared'.

It was an explicitly moral vision – but Hill perceived rather less clearly that these landlords were not always the epitome of moral degradation: they were themselves frequently poor; and their rental incomes were crucial to making ends meet. Hill's own model of social housing, meanwhile, posited a form of morality resting on strict control over conditions and lives: it was firmly interventionist in tone. Rents could not be missed or delayed. In return for clean, secure lodgings, the poor must submit their activities to moral scrutiny: Hill and her associates thought nothing of letting themselves into rented properties to inspect them and to offer advice and moral and practical guidance to the people who lived there.

Booth's own views were a little less rigorous and had altered over time. He was aware now that the enforced disintegration of such communities as the Dale had substantial repercussions both locally and further afield: problems which had been confined to one spot now radiated, plague-like, into nearby streets – as had happened in the case of the Old Nichol. He further understood that such situations were frequently highly complex. Many of the individuals and families who lived in the Dale, for example, were not there of their own accord; rather they were trapped there as a result of the reluctance of many London landlords to take on 'Dale' families – even if they came with ready money and deposit in hand. They were to be pitied, and it was right to take steps on their behalf. This was a significant moment, meshing as it did the harsh moral certainties of the Victorians with the understanding that intervention could be appropriate, both morally and in practical terms.

Booth himself espoused the idea of slow, incremental change that would eventually mould the world into a new form. 'In spite of the poverty and drunkenness, domestic uncleanliness, ignorance and apathy that still prevail,' he wrote, 'things are surely making for the better [...] it is a process of tinkering. Improvement is not coming structurally from a Haussmann or socially and industrially by the light of master minds, nor is attempted by the dangerous road of revolution.' As for his ultimate vision of a new and better world: it was based on a literal knowledge of the fen-like, toxic land of the Dale; and it consisted of a London 'spreading itself over the Home Counties, not as an escape from the evil left behind, but as a development of energy which will react for good over the whole area as it now exists, even in its blackest and most squalid centres [...] expansion acting like a drainage on stagnant, water-logged land'.

Booth's notion of betterment depended on the positive effects of change – but he was under no illusions as to the chronic and deep-seated problems faced by the neighbourhood. And his usual clerical informants underscored this point. Their analysis of the roots of poverty in the neighbourhood was familiar: deprivation and excessive consumption of alcohol, in their view, went hand in hand – but, in assessing the present situation, they could also take a longer and more nuanced view of history. The interview, in January 1900, with the Reverend Tasker of St Francis of Assisi Catholic church on Pottery Lane, was fairly representative. The priest had a good deal to say on the evolution of the neighbourhood and on its current state. There was little intrinsically amiss with the housing in the area, the priest explained, in terms that would have pleased Miss Hill: the problem instead was economic. 'In time whole houses came to be let on the day system; its profitableness led to it being further adopted, until, as Father Tasker said, it became the local custom.'

Tasker deplored the bright and attractive public houses that proliferated in the neighbourhood: they were, he claimed, the ultimate cause of much of the drunkenness and social ills in and around Portland Road: sweep them away, he theorized, and two-thirds of the deprivation in the neighbourhood would vanish too. Booth could sympathise with that; he had already noted that 'drunken disorderly cases do not diminish' and that the public houses were a good deal too attractive. Worst of all, however, was the fact that 'fashion has favoured women. None now speaks of women in public houses as something shocking though they used to do so'. And Tasker's comments were echoed by other informants: at the local City Mission, for

example, Booth is told of the local 'patch' of 14 streets supporting 14 public houses; and of the 'river of intemperance' reaching
high-water mark on payday. One solution was to open two
'skeleton houses' on Portland Road: these were essentially
public houses minus alcohol, which functioned as de facto
workers' clubs.

There were other, more unexpected aspects of life that
proved disturbing. The social and economic woes of the world
that knocked at the doors of Portland Road generated much
compassion – and there were many concerned parties, associations and charities trying to alleviate the misery of their fellow
Londoners. This impulse sprang from several sources, including
religious conviction and uneasy social conscience – and it caused
a kind of hyper-poverty to spring up, with people habitually
pretending to be even more poor than they were. 'You must not
look comfortable,' the saying went, 'or you won't get anything.'
This particular situation had long been familiar in the neighbourhood. As early as 1851, Henry Mayhew had separated the
poor into three categories: those who would work, those who
could not work, and those who would not work. Of the
tendency to benevolent do-gooding, he noted coolly:

> There is after all but one way to help the Poor, that is to
> teach the Poor to help themselves; and so long as commit-
> tees of noblemen have the conduct of their household

affairs, so long as my Lord this or that is left to say at what time they shall go to bed and when they shall get up, there can be no main improvement in their condition.

By 1870, the case for charity had been further undermined by certain horror stories. The Kensington Charity Society, for example, was reporting incidences of slum-dwelling skulduggery: 'A lady in Kensington', the society reported, 'was applied to some time ago by a woman, apparently in great grief, who said that four of her children were lying ill, and one dead, and she had no means to bury the body, or to buy nourishment for the sick little ones.' The lady donated funds to bury one child, then a second and then a third – before calling to pay her respects to the thrice-bereaved mother. 'Having found the house with much difficulty, she walked into the room to which she was directed, where she discovered the woman, with her husband and five children – for the burial of three of whom she had paid – enjoying a very comfortable and substantial meal.'

Booth discovered that such reports had bred cynicism in onlookers: charity workers and donors had become accustomed to speaking of a hard, brazen caste living in the slums of Notting Hill; of folk who *could* work but chose not to do so; who had learnt that it was probably easier and certainly more profitable to beg and rely on charity than to labour for an honest wage. And he noted the concomitant falling off in philanthropy and a hardening of attitude: 'They find in these bad districts there is generally money, "it's the way of spending it that's wrong".'

For those in genuinely desperate need – however that was judged and by whom – there was always the workhouse; and in December 1901, Booth made a point of visiting the local establishment on Mary Place, on the edge of Portland Road. Life in such places was invariably grim and founded upon a very Victorian conviction that the poor might be 'educated' back into the workforce, in return for food and a bed. The work, meanwhile, was as grim as the buildings, generally consisting of a round of stone-breaking in the workhouse yard, alternating with a little corn-grinding and kitchen work – all of which took place under strict surveillance. Smoking, naturally, was banned. Later reports spoke of this particular workhouse as being especially harsh in its regime and policies: in 1939, the *North Kensington Citizen* remembered the institution as: 'the cruellest in London. To it were sent the difficult cases from all other workhouses and the threat to send inmates to it was an effective method of discipline to others.' Nor did it succeed in its aims: '[T]he cruel prison discipline, with its task work and starvation diet, drove the inmates from its doors almost as soon as they had entered it' – and inevitably, they washed up among the remnants of the Dale's grim lodging houses once again.

Booth's contemporary comments, in sharp contrast, were more measured. 'The meals,' he reported, 'are of a very simple

The workhouses of London provided a refuge of last resort for the destitute and desperate. The workhouse near Portland Road was a byword for harshness and austerity. This image of St Pancras workhouse illustrates both the scale of such establishments and their regimented natures.

character – gruel, cocoa and bread being the most usual fare, and the accommodation generally very bare, the bed being about the only reasonably comfortable thing … the life, in short, is of Spartan simplicity – healthy says the superintendent, and with no waste'. The superintendent in question, a Mr Edgecombe, added that the workhouse system functioned as 'a valuable deterrent to the lazy, and drunken loafer, not only of Kensington but of the Metropolis generally'. The regime also included a stipulation that all inmates must attend what might today be called a 'restart' interview hosted by a 'mental instructor': this offered advice on how to get out of the workhouse and back into the mainstream of economic life.

But private philanthropy, whether bestowed enthusiastically or not, could never patch the holes in the fabric of society as thoroughly as government agency – and the first decades of the twentieth century witnessed the beginnings of a systematic state intervention into the housing sector that would have a direct impact on Portland Road. By the end of the Great War the question of public housing had become so pressing and so respectable an issue that it was raised at Buckingham Palace itself. In April of that year, George V addressed local government representatives in no uncertain terms: the question of the housing of the working classes, the monarch suggested, had never been so urgent a social issue as it was at that moment. The King made his speech not long before return of wartime heroes from the trenches – but it had a broader background too. Indeed, the monarch framed his speech in moral terms. It was not too much to say, he suggested:

> that an adequate solution of the housing question is the foundation of all social progress. [...] The first point at which the attack must be delivered is the unhealthy, ugly, over-crowded house in the mean street, which all of us know too well. If a healthy race is to be reared, it can be reared only in healthy homes; if drink and crime are to be

successfully combated, decent, sanitary houses must be provided; if 'unrest' is to be converted into contentment, the provision of good houses may prove one of the most potent agents in that conversion.

We have already seen in Bermondsey what a *local* council could do by intervening if it had a mind. The Housing Act of 1930, however, represented a sea change in *national* policy: now, councils and housing associations began to buy up large amounts of houses. This was slum clearance by another name: in the eight years following the passing of the Act, Kensington council dealt with 13 clearance areas (including Notting Dale) – and, as a result, over 200 premises occupied by 1,117 people were demolished. In three improvement areas, including Crescent Street in the Dale, unsatisfactory basements were closed, overcrowding addressed and the existing houses thoroughly reconditioned. Standards were further raised by an Act of 1936, when a survey showed that in the whole of Kensington there were over 2,000 families living in overcrowded conditions: by the end of 1938, over 700 of these families had been rehoused, but meanwhile 138 new cases had been discovered. These issues were exacerbated by the area's many attractions: it was centrally located, had good transport connections to all parts of London and could expect many different kinds of people to want to live in the area – all factors which were likely to aggravate the problem of overcrowding.

On Portland Road, the results of these new housing policies could be seen in the construction of two new estates located at – significantly, given the north–south class divide that was already discernible – the northern end of the street. The genesis of the Nottingwood and Winterbourne House developments lies in the 1920s, when the notion of building them was first mooted to deal with the housing shortage in the area. Some pressure came from the most respectable and influential quarters: the North Kensington branch of the British Legion, for example, called upon the council to acquire the derelict site formerly occupied by the Notting Hill Brewery 'and utilize the site thereof for housing purposes'. The council's response was at that time cool: 'The committee were of opinion that the site in question was quite unsuitable for the purpose suggested and it was resolved.'

As late as 1933, the council was still dragging its heels: the Moyne Report of that year shows a marked local reluctance to become engaged with social housing: 'Private enterprise should be given a last opportunity of re-entering the field of working-class housing, but that if private enterprise fails it may become necessary to regard the provision of such housing as a social service.' By October 1936, the council was complaining that a policy of buying up and conserving the dilapidated Victorian terraces that covered Portland Road was a futile gesture: demonstrating a breathtaking lack of prescience, councillors grumbled that: 'To buy large Victorian-era basement terrace houses here and there in North Kensington would involve undertaking the ownership of scattered property for which there is likely to be a diminishing demand in the future [...] the time will come when this type of property will be a "white elephant"'.

Winterbourne House would be built on land occupied by existing slum housing – and its construction therefore moved slowly: compulsory purchase orders had to be issued and existing houses torn down. The compulsory purchases recorded by the council reveal that in the mid-1930s, there were quite a few property moguls in the area: a Miss Mabel Maud Farren of Croydon, for example, owned all the properties from 181–191 Portland Road; and Sidney Franklin Rider and Gerald Bishop Rider of 132 Ladbroke Grove owned every house from 193–223 Portland Road. Neither these landlords nor their tenants were given much choice, once the decision to build was taken – although assistance of a very minor kind ('[T]he Town Clerk reported that the Chairman had authorised the payment of a sum of £2 towards the removal expenses of Mr Russell of Heathfield Street') might be provided to supplicants.

There are many indications, moreover, that the council felt a sense of contempt towards the residents at the northern end of Portland Road – and that this found expression in an unwillingness to tackle seriously its housing problems. The Nottingwood development was built cheaply, for example, the borough opting for the second-lowest tender. One letter of December 1936, penned by E. J. Messent, Borough Engineer and Surveyor, expressed doubt that Nottingwood residents would require the sort of modern resources that were beginning to be standard in newly-built units. Messent thought that electricity connections need not be installed in the new kitchens: after all, it was unlikely that the new tenants would be of the 'very superior type' who could afford a newfangled electric cooker. Nor, with the looming outbreak of war, was the development provided with an air-raid shelter. Strikingly, this was a deliberate omission: the provision of such a shelter was actively considered, only to be thrown out.

The conditions in many houses on Portland Road were at this time appalling. George Andrews's family was one of three occupying a house further south at 157 Portland Road in the 1930s and 1940s. The family was part of a tight network that included grandmothers, uncles and aunts living next-door and just across the street – all of them 'ducking and diving' to earn a living. Andrews describes in vivid terms how many such families lived:

We had one toilet for three families. […] We had two people live on the floor above us, husband and wife, one was blind and one was part-blind. […] And at the top of the house we had an old soldier from the First World War […] and we all shared that same toilet. […] 269No bathroom. A tin bath.

You fetched it in, put it in front of the fire, filled it up with hot water as best you could, put all the saucepans on the gas and kettles and boiled them up. [...] They done no repairs, they done nothing. [...] We had no windows, all. [...] Since the beginning of the war 'til two years after the war, at least two years, our windows were boarded up, 'cos the first bomb that dropped practically blew every window out in the street, so they put sort of like hardboard up at every window, so you had to have a light inside because you had no light coming in. [...] In the basement [...] the area there was condemned [...] half the floorboards were missing, because if my mum was short of a bit of firewood to start the fire, up a floorboard would go ...

The Andrews family was embedded within a highly intricate social network – one, moreover, with its own pecking order. The impermanence and fragility of employment led inevitably to certain positions, certain jobs, carrying a certain sheen:

A driver was – well a higher a driver, working class. There wasn't many motors, there wasn't that many people drove. I mean, I used to drive a horse and cart round Notting Hill and Notting Dale, when I was twelve. My uncle had a horse and cart, I used to go and get it in the morning, harness it up, put it on the horse and cart [...] and I'd drive it to my great-uncle's house, I had my bike on the back, leave it there, go to school, come home, get the horse and cart, drive it back to the stables, bed it down, feed it, water it, and drive my bike home, and for that I got twelve and six a week. Which is 65 pence now. A week.

Other people's parents crucially had a little more money in their pockets:

Don Tyler: his mum was the dinner lady in our school. And his dad had a job, so they were both working. So he was a little bit better than off than me, always had nice clothes, new clothes. Not posh, not posh, but compared to us, they were one step up the ladder. They were working, they had regular jobs. My dad was on the dole or something, or had a lousy job, you know [...] Anything my dad would do for a living, you know? Selling Christmas trees, mistletoe ...

Set against this deprivation, developments such as Winterbourne with its separate bedrooms and hot running water were considered the final word in luxury. In its early days Winterbourne was a vibrant community, though not a place of improbable perfection. The genteel residents of nearby Ladbroke Grove would have looked askance at the horses that were kept in first-floor Winterbourne flats, and – as former resident Allan Tyrell remembers – at the sights and sounds of certain domestic incidents too:

> And then we had another family up there, he was [...] he was a totter and she was a Bible basher, you know, she was always 'Praise the Lord'; and, whether she was in the Salvation Army, I don't know. And we heard a big row going on, oh, they're off again. And suddenly, we're looking over the balcony at the back and, suddenly, bang, straight through the window come a bit of furniture – a television or what, I don't know, I can't remember now, but that went through, followed by the dog. That was it, the dog was dead. He was laying there and, oh dear, all hell [...] We had a few families a bit like that.

A Change of Climate

In the aftermath of the war, the housing situation across Britain became more of a chronic problem than ever – and increasingly an issue driven by ideology and politics. The Rent Act of 1957 – introduced by Harold Macmillan's Conservative government – removed the rental controls that had been in place in Britain since the Great War, without at the same time providing security of tenure to existing tenants. The theory held that private landlords would now have an incentive to invest in the decaying housing stock up and down the country; instead, however, unscrupulous landlords moved to maximize income from these poorly main tained properties by dramatically increasing rents – and intimidating tenants into vacating properties if they refused to pay.

The Act had a dramatic impact on Portland Road. Rents in the area more than doubled in the 12 months following the passing of the legislation – and by 1958, over 200 notices of eviction had been served in this area alone. The Kensington Tenants' Association said that the legislation 'allows much real evil, encourages oppression of the poor and offers tenants bogus rights, no security of tenure, makes enforcement of repair a farce, and will unless repealed surely lead to widespread civil disobedience'. And there were other repercussions. By the 1950s, Notting Dale had – ironically, given its past history of gypsy and Irish migration – settled down as a staunchly white and largely closed community. Now – as with other areas of North Kensington with a lot of poorly maintained properties – new arrivals were coming into the area in large numbers, attracted by a fluid rental market. These were Commonwealth nationals, part of the influx of Caribbean, African and south Asian immigrants to Britain in the post-war years – and these individuals and families, lacking community links or a strong social network, were especially poorly served by the Rent Act.

Portland Road, 1933, before post-war social changes began to alter the face of the street. The air of grimy neglect is palpable – although too is a sense of sturdy pride and neighbourliness: note the smiling face peeping from an upper window. Yet the future in wait for Portland Road – its new life as an uber-exclusive residential enclave – is simply unimaginable.

The first arrivals inevitably attracted attention: 'we had one black bloke move in there when I was a kid,' says Alan Tyrell, 'and [...] we used to sit outside [his house] waiting for him to come out 'cos he was a novelty'. One result was new 'undesirables' on rental signs: '[W]hat was happening was that very few let [rooms] to the blacks. They used to have a notice up: it used to be "no Irish, no dogs". And then, when the blacks come along it was "no Irish, no dogs, no blacks". Well, the few people that took them in felt sorry for them but, also, it was revenue for them. [...] And of course, people that couldn't get housing, they'd say, "oh, they're nicking our houses" – like you say – nicking our jobs. [...] And – and it kicked off.' Another (middle-class) resident recalls, in slightly different tones, that she 'always felt slightly inferior, because their clothes, they wore marvellous clothes, I think they were tribal things they were wearing'.

But the presence of ethnic minorities in the social mix of Notting Hill ultimately proved to be racially explosive. Portland Road was once more a buffer zone – this time between the white-dominated Dale and the neighbourhoods in which the black and West Indian community began to settle. In the face of this influx of immigration, the white working class felt threatened, a powerful resentment building in the minds of the communities who had been living on Portland Road for generations. The result, as George Andrews recalls, was a spiral of race-driven unrest:

> [T]here was a race riot, and I did see a car chasing a black
> man down our street, what he was guilty of, I don't know,
> maybe it's just that he was black. He jumped off – they had
> running boards in those days, cars – and the fella that was
> standing on the running board, hanging in the window,
> jumped off, bash, wallop, crash and drove off again. Only
> bashed him, you know, they never cut him or knifed him or
> anything like that. The fella got up, shocked out of his life
> and went about his business ...

This scene witnessed by Andrews unfolded on Portland Road
itself and, during this period, the street was a witness to history,
during the most turbulent time in race relations for a generation: indeed, the first recorded instance of black resistance was
when petrol bombs were thrown at white rioters from the roof
of Nottingwood House. But Notting Hill had long been a riot
waiting to happen: its history and social DNA made it a natural
location of unrest, with the maligned gypsy influence of the nineteenth century now exchanged neatly for the contemporary
black and West Indian communities. By the 1950s, the area had
become the scene of regular mini-riots, sieges and murder scenes;
and Booth's observations on the vein of violence in the area were
repeated five decades later. Police records spoke of drunkenness,
violence and obscenity stalking the streets; and of white and
black youths existing in a state of continual friction. The Mau

Mau uprising in Kenya against British colonial power caused tensions to rise even higher; and black men and Teddy Boys clashed on the streets of Notting Hill.

This process reached its unpleasant culmination when the White Defense League (WDL) settled into premises at 74 Princedale Road, a short distance from Portland Road. The WDL stemmed from an especially virulent form of racial politics: it was preoccupied with vehemently opposing 'non-white' immigration, with spreading racist propaganda and with generally stirring up racial trouble in parts of London where the white working class felt under threat. In 1960, it merged with other groups to form the British National Party. The leader of the WDL, Colin Jordan, created headlines when he married Françoise Dior, niece of the French fashion designer and a noted Nazi in her own right. Newsreels of the marriage focused on Dior's choice of fashion accessory (a diamond-encrusted swastika necklace), and a commitment ceremony involving drops of the happy couple's mingled blood falling onto a copy of Hitler's *Mein Kampf*. The wedding reception took place at Princedale Road. (The couple split after a month.)

Racial antipathy and social unrest led Oswald Mosley to attempt a political comeback in the 1959 North Kensington by-election. Mosley offered simplistic analysis and instant solutions, scapegoating the black and Irish populations as the cause of the lack of decent housing – and claiming they would take all the jobs too, given the chance. Mosley did not fare especially well, but his mere presence on the political scene – and his inflaming rhetoric – was enough to cause Establishment discomfiture. Alan Tyrell recalls how Mosley would stoke unrest: 'he'd always pick a place where he knew there would be migrants: he opened one of his offices right opposite a synagogue. So, you've got a bloke that's a fascist, and [Colin Jordan] was just coming on the scene, so you had a bloke that was a fascist right opposite a synagogue, stirring trouble.'

The unpleasant political associations swirling around the area found expression in other, often unexpected, ways: in 1966, for example, art imitated life with scenes from Kevin Brownlow's film *It Happened Here*, shot on Portland Road. The film dramatizes a German invasion and occupation of Britain in the months following Dunkirk, with the country's administration handed over to a body not dissimilar to the British Union of Fascists: portraits of Mosley and Hitler hang in a government building; and the film's black-and-white footage is jarringly reminiscent of newsreel images. One scene, in which British Nazis are attacked by a group of resistance fighters, was shot in the Prince of Wales public house on the corner of Portland Road and Pottery Lane – and, lacking the budget to pay actual actors, Brownlow recruited a group of local English fascists to play the roles.

* * *

The consequences of the Rent Act could be measured in other ways – as some landlords began to realize the value of their assets on Portland Road and to sell up to a new class of newcomers. This was the beginning of the gentrification of Portland. The incomers regarded themselves as 'pioneers': it was an unlovely term, but as in Barnsbury, these young professionals both understood the potential of the decrepit housing that lined Portland Road and had the means to do something about it. These new property owners were not rich per se – but they could rely on an income and a degree of family money; and were prepared to take a chance on the area gradually rising into affluence. A change began to move rapidly through the street – and the process would have long-term and radical consequences for the area as the years passed.

A Houseowners' Association survey of the early 1970s offered rather cold-blooded comments on Holland Park as an area ripe for development. It was, 'a clear trendsetter […] a classic case of rapid restoration of social status. Holland Park has come up very quickly in the last 15 years and there's little slummy property now left to renovate.' It added that the presence of council property in the area had the potential to keep prices depressed, but concluded that 'continued middle-class colonization should ensure healthy capital appreciation. […] If you don't mind living with council flats, this could be a good speculation, even spectacular – prices will soar in time. (Only six years ago you could have picked up a property here for as little as £4,000).'

By this point, gentrification was gathering pace across inner London. The changes on Portland Road were profound: repeated attempts to shift or dilute the presence of the poor in the area had essentially failed, but now gentrification and its by-products – stratospheric housing prices combined with persistent estate agents and the slow dismantling of an indigenous working-class population – were at last having the desired effect. The change was first detectable on the southern terminus of the street, with affluence registering on the creamy pink and white facades of houses; in repaired and painted sash windows; and in newly restored and elegant ground-floor drawing rooms. Meanwhile, the northern end of the street – anchored by the social housing in the area – remained dominated by white working-class Londoners; but this new sense of affluence crept steadily north.

The tale related by Tim and Penny Hicks exemplifies many of the themes of this relentless process of gentrification. The family had until 1968 lived in a small house in Chelsea and were eager for more space: and, says Tim Hicks, 'everyone was saying that north of the park (as they used to talk about) in Bayswater, there are so many opportunities. And we wandered down here [...] you come off Holland Park Avenue, which has always been fairly pleasant [...] and then go into grotland, which it was in those days.' Penny Hicks adds: 'It was a sort of fire break, between what was possible and what was impossible. [...] And we took a chance that it was going to go up, because they were all in multiple occupancy. [...] My mother wasn't very pleased. She couldn't understand why we wanted to leave Chelsea, where we had a house which was dinky-sized but, nonetheless, Chelsea and come here into the wilds of W11. She couldn't imagine it: she said, "well, you can't possibly live there".' The house in question was midway along Portland Road – previously it had been home to (among others) the Andrews family.

Some of the vignettes related by the Hicks family suggest parallel but unrelated universes coexisting at this time on Portland Road. The couple, for example, convinced a Chelsea-based friend to join them in the 'wilds of W11': he bought the house next door and began to restore its crumbling facade himself. One day, the exterior restoration virtually complete, 'he was resting with a cigarette, having been painting all day, and he was looking at his house and admiring it, and this lady from the brothel came out and said, "can I help you, dear?" He couldn't believe there was a brothel opposite him.' And later, the Hickses went on to enroll their children in the local primary school, despite the best efforts of its staff to dissuade them: 'One of the teachers, when we were being shown round, said to me: "you do appreciate, Mrs Hicks, that this is not working class, this is criminal class."'

The former residents of these newly repaired and desirable terraced houses, tended to be moved into council-run properties – or out of the area and out of London altogether. And many, attracted by the promise of space and air, gardens and modern facilities, were more than happy to go: '[S]omeone somewhere along the line said, well, hang on, you know, move these people out, give them the chance to go in a place like Hemel Hempstead, High Wycombe, Harlow New Town, you know, Acton, places like that,' noted Allan Tyrrell of the administrative machinery which directed housing policy. 'And people there – hang on, I'm getting a house with a garden, you know, never had that, I'm getting a house all of my own, you know, and a lot of them jumped at it. And of course, they went and people moved in ...'

George Andrews agrees: he and his wife could now strike out independently, and put down roots in their new neighbour-hood at Acton. 'We was going our own way now, the pair of us. And they [the remainder of the family] looked after theirselves, I went up and saw them every week, you know, they were alright'. There was clearly little room for sentiment: 'You move out of one of those dumps and you got a council flat, you got a bathroom, you got hot water, you got central heating: can you imagine that, after living in a dump like that? You know, they couldn't wait to move, some of them, not because they didn't like the area, they didn't like the people, it's just that they were bettering theirselves, they were coming up a step, they were getting a council house. Out of one of those dumps and get a central heating. Can you imagine that? [...] Beautiful flats. They had bathroom, airing cupboard, central heating, everything.'

People were on the move – and historical echoes were audible. Not only had Booth's contemporaries been eager to see London drape its tendrils across the Home Counties, but as early as 1856, the authorities had demonstrated an enthusiasm for the idea of moving people out to the suburbs:

> By a large scheme for migration, overcrowding would be diminished, and with it preventable disease resulting from this, the most perilous of insanitary conditions. The council having come, apparently, to the opinion that migration does afford the most promising solution to difficult questions [...] as it may not unreasonably be expected that an impetus will be given by these arrangements to the erection of houses for the working classes in the suburbs, we can but hope that care will be exercised to prevent the concessions being so misused as to involve the creation of slums outside London.

This early phase of gentrification excluded many – but for a period in the 1960s and early 1970s, prices remained low enough to allow a (relatively) broadly based community to co-exist in the area. Portland Road was never immersed in the radical counter-culture that was eddying around it in the 1960s and 1970s, but it did host elements of that society: members of Pink Floyd moved in, the radical publication *Oz* was founded nearby; and even the post-punk band Killing Joke used Portland Road as an impromptu squat. The glam hippy bar Julie's at 135 Portland Road was founded by Portobello Hotel owners Tim and Cathy Herring: in these years, it was famously frequented by the Beatles, the Rolling Stones and Roxy Music; indeed, Bryan Ferry's *The Bride Stripped Bare* album was reputedly inspired by Jerry Hall leaving him for Mick Jagger, after he introduced them at Julie's.

For a brief period, old and new coexisted smoothly enough: property prices on Portland Road were steadily rising – but remained pegged back by the relatively small scale of the houses and of the street itself; it was possible for someone of modest means to acquire a house on Portland Road, whereas it was rapidly becoming quite impossible to buy one on Clarendon Road, no more than a step away. Fishmongers and street traders continued to ply their trade door to door: there was a sense of social fluidity between the classes. This phase, however, would not last. Julie's had originally supplanted a local builders' merchant – and, as the nature of the local shops acts as a barometer of any neighbourhood, so the changing commercial face of Portland Road spoke eloquently of its changing nature. The local butcher, baker, and grocer vanished to be replaced by antique shops, expensive boutiques and dog-grooming parlours. The pedestrianization of the central section of Portland Road at Clarendon Cross indicated in bollard and flagstone a kind of social engineering, an acceptance and an embracing of the street's schizophrenia: after all, the disappearance of a practical commercial centre and appearance of a zone dedicated instead to the servicing of an expensive lifestyle at a stroke removed any reason for the working-class residents of northern Portland Road to venture south.

In recent years, the gentrification of Portland Road has moved up another gear – into something resembling a mono-culture. This is hyper-gentrification: the pretty terraces of Portland Road are now home to an elite class of financial analysts, bankers and tax exiles with the very deepest of pockets. The early arrivals – actors, playwrights, musicians, even the occasional puppeteer – are forced out; older residents must contend with persistent letters from estate agents, trying to push a sale of lucrative properties. And the echoes of history are tinged now with irony. So dizzyingly expensive has real estate become in this ultra-fashionable section of west London that the descendants of those first pioneers – by any other measure, families still comfortably off – are unable to afford to live on the street they now call home.

The le Touzel family, for example, moved to Portland Road in 1960, when some people perceived there to be a feeling of animosity between the rich and the poor. Jane le Touzel remembers that 'the poor would worry that we'd put up the rates, I think they just saw us as a bit of an oddity. [...] I remember screaming at my father, who was very sceptical about me moving to North Kensington. He said, "if you want to move into a bloody slum then go ahead". That's what people thought of it back then, a slum. [...] I couldn't care less, because we had a house, we had a garden. I didn't see a garden with bedsteads in it. There were bedsteads there and bits of iron that people had chucked, but I didn't see it like that; I saw it with trees and flowers and things, and it was lovely.'

This image of the terraces of today's Portland Road sums up the attractive, well-heeled face the street presents to the world. Ironically, these expensive houses are essentially modest in scale – and are certainly a far cry from the vast villas of nearby Ladbroke Grove.

Jane le Touzel also recalls the colourful street life on what today is a quiet and super-gentrified street. The Portland Arms nearby, for example, was a regular source of violence and street disturbance – but 'if we went up to the top [of the house] and looked down, we could see them all going "Knees Up Mother Brown" and all sorts of things like that in the pub. My daughter Sylvestra was absolutely enthralled.' Today the children of the original 'pioneers' cannot afford to aspire to Portland Road: Sylvestra le Touzel can remember the animosity which the children of working-class residents of the street felt for her, a seemingly rich little girl – and today, she herself sometimes feels animosity, or at least ambivalence, towards 'the rich bankers who have priced me out of the market. I have to live miles away and drive for over an hour to see my parents.'

But this handsome street still represents a vision of perfection for many – and residency here the achievement of a cherished personal goal. It can come at a hefty price – in dizzyingly high rents – and a lack of a sense of cohesive community; imperfections tolerated in order to achieve a dream of living here. One resident sees this absence of cohesion as a direct result of super-gentrification – especially in its collision with the poverty rooted in the north end of Portland Road: 'It definitely causes friction. I mean imagine being a 15-year-old boy growing up just down the street in a 2-bed council flat and your mum or your dad is a single parent – and then you walk out to school and you're

walking down a road with million pound houses and Ferraris.'
Of the newly-arrived super-rich, she says: 'They're quite suspi-
cious, and that's why there's all the security now, you can't go
and knock on your neighbour's door at nine o'clock at night if
you need help because they'll think you're .... People are suspi-
cious. And that comes with immense wealth: you immediately
think people might be there to rip you off'. Another resident,
Henry Mayhew – the descendant of the eponymous Victorian
social researcher – describes the consequences of this giddying
gentrification in the starkest terms possible. Of the glittering
prize of a multimillion-pound house on Portland Road, he
comments witheringly that 'it's only a tenement building – it's
not particularly exciting'; and of the street in general notes:

> [L]ike all the trendy areas of London it's just lived in by
> investment bankers now, so it just becomes very, very
> boring. I mean you don't know how boring it is until you
> actually experience it. If L. S. Lowry was painting today, he
> would be painting this area, not Manchester, because this
> area is the dormitory for the biggest factory in this country
> – the factory of finance. And Hugh Grant would be making
> his film 'Notting Hill' in Hackney. He's moved on. It's all
> sloped shoulders, factory workers getting up at 6 o'clock in
> the morning. The guy next door gets up at 4:30 in the morn-
> ing, his taxi arrives at 5:15 every flipping morning with its

engine running outside. He jumps in it and he goes and –
well, I was gonna say diddles pensioners and stuff, but he
helps pensioners invest their cash half asleep, and then he
comes home, sloped shoulders, slop, slop, slop, back from
the Tube, slam the telly on, that's it.

And the sense of social dislocation has become increasingly acute.
The working class remains in situ on Portland Road – if only
because they have security of tenure on the estates that continue
to anchor the northern end of the street. Statistics gathered by
the Borough of Kensington and Chelsea itself demonstrate the
stark divisions that continue to characterize life on Portland
Road, where poverty rates in households at the 'wrong' end of
the street are among the worst in the country. Here, social deprivation is accentuated by the failure of the authorities to invest in
and commit to the principle of public housing: as the district
becomes wealthier and wealthier, so it becomes easier to disre-
gard and marginalize the poorest members of society.

This, more than anything, connects today's Portland Road to
a phenomenon across inner London. The process of gentrification is beginning to reach its conclusion: gentrified areas are
joining up; and the remaining available properties are now few
and far between, a process that is slowly but relentlessly expelling
a population of working-class Londoners from the centre of the
city. Public housing no longer exists in anything like the form it

once did – and there is nowhere else for these people to go but further and further from the heart of London. Portland Road is merely one more neighbourhood where this process of population transfer has taken place – but it represents the apotheosis of this syndrome. What happens to a neighbourhood that becomes a social monoculture, hidden behind security gates and protected by security systems? What form does its future take? – and how do such examples affect the London of the future? What of the lives that are lived there? And what of the futures of the communities that have been removed from its environs?

Paradise Regained

CAMBERWELL GROVE

This area well illustrates the tendency
for what may be called the inner ring
of suburban London to be occupied by
a less wealthy class than formerly.

Charles Booth

When Charles Booth first arrived on Camberwell Grove in 1889, he had no doubts as to its position in his colour-coded system of classification. The Grove ran steadily uphill from its northern end in Camberwell village: this end of the street was zoned as fragmented pink and red; but its southern reaches at the summit of the hill were predominantly red and yellow. And no wonder: many of the properties that lined the top of Camberwell Grove were large and stately – indeed, some of them were dazzlingly elegant. Their inhabitants were prosperous householders, well able to keep servants in numbers; and the houses themselves seemed to be weathering well. Most of all, this was an agreeably green and leafy area: its hilly topography, combined with the dimensions of the Grove and its spectacular homes provided a sense of space and – although only a few miles south of the Thames – crucial distance from the metropolis that was pressing all around.

A mere decade later, Booth visited again – and now he discovered a subtle change. The Grove, like Camberwell as a whole, was losing its place on the survey's pecking order: the confident yellows on the hill were slipping, giving way to reds, the reds to pinks; virtually every property was recording a decline in position:

> Broad; leafy; declining; many large houses nearly all in rows. Lodgers coming in to many of the smaller houses, especially on the west side. From red or map to pink-barred, west side, from Aldover Place to Chapel, and from Chatham Place to the end. On the east side from red of map to pink-barred between Edgecombe road and Lettsom Street and the two last blocks at North End. All the rest of the Grove, from red and yellow of map to red.

Elsewhere along the Grove, smaller houses were springing up between the original short terraces of dramatic Georgian properties: these new homes were still prosperous in their own way – but of an altogether lesser order than the wealth and the architecture that had gone before.

Such decline was of course relative: red and yellow rankings were – regardless of what one thought of Booth's maps and elaborate scales – not to be disdained; and Booth himself admired the prosperity and elegance clinging on along Camberwell Grove and its 'exceedingly pleasant' environs. Yet it was striking that the Grove had fallen so detectably in the course of a mere ten years – and the language used by Booth seems not only to refer to a suddenly sullied present, but also to glance into a bright prelapsarian past that was now under assault. His language speaks of a sense of crisis, of a severing of safety and security: the comfortable yellows of his previous surveys were, he wrote, being 'driven back' to the other side of the railway line running into Denmark Hill railway station; the pink spreading along the Grove may have signified a still-comfortable enough stratum of Camberwell life – but it also spoke of the threat of incipient disintegration. And the reasons were self-evident: the flood of metropolitan London had arrived and was washing over Camberwell Grove; and nothing could stem or roll back the growth and flow of such a city. The area was caught now in a spin of decline: and Booth had arrived just in time to record this process for posterity.

* * *

This striking sense of Camberwell as a paradise lost, had long been a motif of life in this hilly district of south London. As late as 1800, Camberwell was emphatically a rural district – and indeed, this can be tracked all the way back to Domesday, when the district was recorded as raising corn, with cows grazing in its sloping green fields and pigs rooting in its woods – all for the benefit of relations of William the Conqueror, who bestowed prosperity enough for the parish to maintain its own church. As London spread and expanded north of the Thames, Camberwell to its south kept its distance: it was crucially far enough from London Bridge to maintain a precious separate identity as a prosperous rural neighbourhood. Camberwell had a name for virtue and purity: the church was dedicated to St Giles, the patron saint of the cripples, who came to the district to take the waters from the well in the centre of the village that reputedly possessed healing powers. Vines, suggestive of warmth and sunshine, were grown on the slopes of the hill of Camberwell; charmingly, the Camberwell Beauty butterfly was identified and named in the area in 1748 – and even the dairy cattle in the district were remarkably munificent, supplying 'not only [...]

This splendid 1776 view of Camberwell village from the Grove captures the famously pastoral world of this corner of Surrey – just a few miles from London Bridge. The first of Camberwell Grove's great houses went up shortly afterwards.

the inhabitants of this place with milk but furnish a good deal for London.'

The village of Camberwell even boasted agreeable royal associations: one of the principal streets in the area was named Denmark Hill in honour of Prince George of Denmark, the husband of Queen Anne, who maintained a residence in the area. The village also featured a traditional village green which for over 600 years from 1279 was home to Camberwell Fair. The ghost of Camberwell Grove itself first appears early in the eighteenth century as the quaintly-named Walnut Tree Grove: its origins not as a through road but simply a tree-lined avenue leading in stately fashion to the summit of the hill. At the foot of the slope stood Court House, the residence of the dukes of Buckingham, holders of the manor of Camberwell until the last duke was executed on the orders of Henry VIII for 'treasonable thoughts'; at this point, the property passed to the Scott and then the Cook families. The tree-lined avenue was formed most likely as a picturesque feature in the landscape; and to enable the residents of Court House to stroll easily to the top of the hill, in order to take in the views over London and the surrounding green fields of Surrey.

The era of this bosky hideaway began to fade early in the eighteenth century. The last of the Cooks lost her family fortune in the South Sea Bubble of 1720; and the estate passed into the hands of a London banker, who occupied part of it and built the

Grove Tavern and Assembly Rooms at the north end of the Grove as a place of entertainment. By the middle of the century, the Rooms was home to the Camberwell Club ('snug dinners, stray balls, and quarterly feasts were the principal duties which the members were called upon to perform; and right well did they acquit themselves, if report be true'), which was patronized by well-off local families. Attached to it was Camberwell Hall, the scene of fashionable balls; the adjacent tea gardens, meanwhile, became a noted resort for visiting Londoners.

Camberwell Grove, its tavern and Camberwell Hall featured in George Lillo's *The London Merchant* (1731) – which measures the changing atmosphere and associations of this corner of Surrey. It was based on a ballad about a murder which had taken place in Shropshire: the producers, however, felt it needed a London setting – and, significantly, Camberwell was selected. The play was a morality tale, concerning the young apprentice George Barnwell who arrives in London, only to fall in with the wrong crowd: eventually he meets a Shoreditch prostitute who convinces him to kill his uncle – the wealthy benefactor in his life – who lived in health-giving Camberwell:

> *A pistol he got from his love,*
> *'Twas loaded with powder and bullet;*
> *He trudged off to Camberwell Grove,*
> *But wanted the courage to pull it.*

In the end, the unfortunate uncle is murdered and his corpse taken to the Tavern – thus securing both Camberwell's foul role in the farcical tale, and the theme of a rural idyll corrupted by the proximity of a deviant and dangerous metropolis.

By the mid-eighteenth century, this theme of creeping urban encroachment had come to dominate the life of the district. Large tracts of south London were opening up to sustained development – and Camberwell was no exception. The two or so miles between the village and London was no distance at all as roads were improved and bridges built across the Thames: Westminster (1750), Blackfriars (1769), Vauxhall (1816) and Southwark (1819) all enabled ready access to wider and wider areas of the city's hinterland. Camberwell's reputation as a healthy locale now laid it open to change: the tree-lined Grove in particular became a desirable place to live, as it was possible to enjoy both an agreeable rural lifestyle in Camberwell and an easy commute to work in London: in her *Perambulations* of 1809, indeed, Priscilla Wakefield summed up the area as a 'pleasant retreat for those citizens who have a taste for the country whilst their avocations daily call them to town'. And this was the essential *raison d'être* of the Grove: these great houses existed not for the aristocracy – as was the case in Mayfair, Belgravia and other districts of central London – but for professional, well-to-do upper-middle-class families.

Modern Camberwell Grove took its shape in the years after 1776 when the estate lands were sold and the old manor house demolished: the earliest houses on today's Grove (Numbers 33–45 and 79–85) date from approximately the same period – at which point, the terraces of Camberwell Grove would have stood out starkly, a geometric cityscape imposed upon the surrounding fields. The tree-lined avenue now became a public road leading from the centre of the village to the top of the hill and on south to Dulwich: the last of the former manor buildings was finally removed in 1798, with the old stables adjoining the road now the only surviving reminder of what had once stood there. Connections to the area's past can be found in the very fabric of these homes: recent renovations on one house midway along the Grove, for example, uncovered a section of limestone dating from Tudor times – a penny-pinching eighteenth-century builder, intent on cutting costs, had incorporated this piece of the former manor house into an exterior wall in order to save on the cost of building materials. Indeed, the terraces, for all their grandeur, were not especially well built: subsidence has always been an issue on the Grove.

Notable residents began to migrate to Camberwell. In 1779, the influential doctor, Quaker and abolitionist John Lettsom established an estate at the top – the airy and desirable southern end – of the Grove: he lived there until 1810. The house is

In 1779, the influential doctor, Quaker and abolitionist John Lettsom established an estate at the socially desirable southern end of Camberwell Grove. He lived there until 1810: among his guests to tea was the Prince Regent.

described in Manning and Bray's *History of Surrey* as 'standing on a considerable eminence, rising gradually for about three-quarters of a mile from the village of Camberwell, and passing through an avenue of elms retaining the name of Camberwell Grove'. Lettsom was notable not only for entertaining here such luminaries as Dr Johnson – but also for having established the first general dispensary in London for the sick and needy. A local ditty is still remembered:

> *When any sick to me apply,*
> *I physics, bleeds and sweats em;*
> *If after that they choose to die,*
> *Why verily – I Lettsom.*

Lettsom might have owned his own estate – but he was nonethe-less the epitome of the new professional resident of the district, for he continued to practise in London, while availing himself of Camberwell's healthy waters and southern breezes in his free time. His tenure, however, was short-lived: beginning in 1810, his estate was progressively built over, with Grove Crescent established in the years after Waterloo.

Only one piece of Lettsom's estate remains intact in the environs of the Grove: a house now designated 'The Hermitage', but originally a kind of rustic cottage of the sort installed by 'improvers' to accentuate the picturesque element in the land-scape. Residents and their guests might gather in this pretty building to take tea – the entire tableau a useful means of improving the appeal of the surrounding area. The records in this case speak of a garden party thrown in 1804 for the Prince Regent – the future George IV – and 500 guests, in which the Hermitage had a starring role: refreshments were served from this pretty nook, and an orchestra created beguiling airs from a concealed position:

> *Such are the soft enchanting scenes displayed*
> *In all the blended charms of light and shade*
> *At Camberwell's fair grove and verdant brow,*
> *The loveliest Surrey's lofty hills can show.*

Other newcomers had more than enchantments on their minds. The Chamberlains – many of whose members would be leading lights of nineteenth- and twentieth-century English Liberalism – were one of the first families to move into the imposing terraced houses of Camberwell Grove; the future Colonial Secretary and Liberal statesman Joseph Chamberlain was born here in 1836. The philosopher John Ruskin and poet Robert Browning were also born in the area: Ruskin designed the stained glass in the new church of St Giles, which was built to plans drawn up by Sir George Gilbert Scott and consecrated in 1844. Ruskin's autobiography *Praeterita* contains many evocations of the green and serene character of the area, surviving in the face of the sustained development and steadily increasing population. Ruskin remembered the Grove of the 1830s and 1840s in moving and evocative terms:

> A real grove in those days, and a grand one, some 3/4 of a mile long, sloping steeply down hill – beautiful in perspective as an unprecedently 'long-drawn aisle', trees: elm, wych elm, sycamore and aspen, the branches meeting at the top; the houses on each side with trim stone pathways up to them through small plots of well-mown grass, three- or four-storied, mostly in grouped terraces – built of sober-coloured brick, with high and steep slated roof – not gabled, but polygonal, all well to do, well kept, well-broomed,

dignifiedly and pleasantly vulgar and their own Grove-
world all in all to them.

Camberwell – and especially the Grove – was striving to retain its
essential character, despite its proximity to the city. In an article
for the American publication *The Ladies' Magazine* in 1823, the
writer described a walk up Camberwell Grove in terms which
suggest an epiphany: 'The place is calculated to call the sinner to
repentance. The trees on each side seemed to me as I walked
along like the buttresses of the long-drawn aisle of some magnificent cathedral.' The author then juxtaposed the grandeur of the
Grove with the development that had begun to press on its limits
– mourning the sight of a rash of houses 'so numerous that they
seem to have sprung up like mushrooms on a summer's night.'

By the time Victoria came to the throne in 1837, Camberwell
was morphing decisively from village into metropolitan suburb.
A new street plan for the greater Camberwell area was laid out
and many of the area's existing buildings first constructed.
Camberwell could not – in spite of its particular characteristics
and sense of splendid isolation fostered by the Grove – hope to
hold out in the face of Victorian London's hyper-development:
the city's exploding population led inevitably to a permanent
alteration in the character of the area. These changes were accel-
erated with the unrolling of the railways across the city and its
hinterland: in 1801, a mere 7,000 people were recorded as being

resident in Camberwell – but by 1841, with the arrival of the railway, this had risen to almost 40,000; and by 1901 to almost 250,000; and Camberwell Road had become one of busiest shopping thoroughfares in London. Far from exulting in its trees and tranquillity, now the Grove was hemmed in by working- and lower-middle-class housing; and by the poor of London – for rather than consign the destitute to the local workhouse, the parish of Camberwell maintained the poor law. 'The poor squeezed out of other parts of London come here', said one local Church official. 'And Camberwell suffers.'

The existing social demographics now began to change. The very properties – health-giving waters and air – that had attracted the original upper-middle-class community to the area were under threat from the fires and smoke, sewage, congestion and pollution brought by waves of additional settlement – and a well-heeled community observed this evolution with dismay. 'Fifty years ago,' sighed the *Saturday Review*, 'Camberwell was in the country. But a child born here last week could assuredly be a Cockney.' One indicator of this decline was the abolition of the ancient fair on Camberwell Green. It had begun to attract trippers from the city – and as standards began to decline and levels of violence and drunkenness to rise, the event drew the gaze of anxious Victorian moralists. It was abolished in 1855 – just one of many such fairs and ancient institutions that vanished in these years, for identical reasons. Scrapping the fair, however, would not persuade the wealthy to remain in Camberwell: as the area continued its evolution, so the wealthy abandoned it, migrating further south into the fringes of London. The new homes built for an anticipated middle-class influx began instead to be subdivided or rented to the less economically fortunate; and key families such as the Chamberlains, having settled into Camberwell life, now quietly pulled up their local roots and moved on.

The 1891 census provided an indication of these social changes and of the complexion of the Grove, as the most frenetic period of Victorian expansion came to a close. The area's rural past was still in evidence, for example, in the form of cow-keeping: two dairymen were listed in the returns as living at numbers 47 and 161. Retailers had appeared at the lower – that is, the northern or 'city' – end of the Grove: a beer shop at number 1, a china shop at number 2, a bootmaker at number 6, a baker at number 8 and a confectioner at number 12, along with a sprinkling of plumbers, painters and bricklayers. A distinct change in profession appeared a little further up the hill: a land merchant at number 34, a timber merchant at number 39, an auctioneer and house agent at number 71, a tea broker at number 80 and a stockbroker at number 90.

Households of independent means clustered higher on the hill; a number of what might be termed 'creative' professions were in evidence too, in the form of singers, artists, professors of

music and art dealers; together with a substantial community of
German nationals. Servants were in short supply at the bottom
of the street – but a good deal more numerous higher up; all in
all, half the households on the Grove could boast servants in
their census returns – although this number would decline
dramatically. The 1891 census captures a time in the history of
the Grove in which life was in extreme flux: there was prosperity enough – but only in clusters and only for the moment.

'Common-place'

In the autumn of 1900, as part of his largest (and as it turned
out, final) survey of London, Charles Booth set out to explore
Camberwell Grove and its immediate environs. The population
of the district was at this point peaking – indeed, these were the
highest levels Camberwell would ever sustain; and these numbers
would fall back steadily in the following years. Booth's inves-
tigative terrain was delineated carefully: an area 'bounded on the
North by Church Street and Peckham Road, on the East by
Vestry Road and Grove Park, on the South by Champion Hill
Terrace and Grove Hill Road, and on the West by Denmark Hill,
forming parts of the parishes of St. Giles and St. Matthew'. The
social breadth and character of the area was noted at once: Grove
Lane, running immediately parallel to Camberwell Grove on the

west, was home to an array of houses and residents, from small artisan cottages to its signature 'rows of large four-storeyed houses' – zoned yellow and red with touches of pink here and there. Declining Camberwell Grove itself housed 'lodgers coming in to many of the smaller houses'; and the shops and smaller dwellings clustered at the bottom of the street confirmed this theme of disintegration pushing in from London and the north.

But this decline was relative: Booth had seen much worse in his exploration of the metropolis; and the future he foresaw for Camberwell, though probably not glittering, was at least not filled with despair:

> [T]he smaller ones [that is, houses] are not small and for many years it is probably that the greater part of this area will be occupied by a well-to-do middle class, of the type occupying the new houses put up on the Grove Park estate. Thus, south of the railway, red will be the dominant colour, just as pink will be north of it.

Such slums as persisted, meanwhile, would be found close to the centre of Camberwell village, 'a fact probably not unconnected with the fact that every point where traffic congests, buses stop, and crowds pass tends to attract and provide for a considerable amount of casual labour – the smaller fry of the hangers-on of the community.'

In this 1880 view, the houses are *in situ* – but their pleasant rural surroundings are emphasized in the spacious gardens and waving trees. The impression Is conveyed that the houses on the Grove have managed to accentuate, rather than destroy, the rural delights of the district.

Booth's relative confidence in the future of Camberwell was bolstered by his police companion, a Mr Walsh, who was based in Camberwell and Peckham, and 'who has had a considerable experience of other parts of London'. The area and its population were fundamentally decent and respectable – a fact signalled in the comparative absence of prostitution from the area. 'Very few prostitutes live in the district,' Booth noted; brothels were rare; and public tolerance of overt solicitation was low. In addition to these virtues, the area boasted a respectable municipal life: public baths and wash houses highlighted the Victorian mania for cleanliness; while the presence of art gallery, theatre, library and 'Technical Institute' signified the improving influences of education, employment and culture. And there were further neighbourhood virtues: nearby Peckham provided a gratifying bustle of commercial activity to add to that of Camberwell village itself: a department store and a proud new clock tower indicated a willingness to invest in the area, combined with a civic pride that was not to be scorned.

All the ingredients were present, in other words, for a reasonably decent and respectable society to function – a sense that was only slightly undercut by Booth's comment that Camberwell was, when all was said and done, little more than 'common-place'. And apparent indications of decline couldn't all be taken at face value: strategy and cunning could equally be at play – as one of his police informants explained:

> [H]e reminded me that the occasional broken window in a decent-looking street, need not mean either indifference or poverty. In reply to my query as to what it was likely to indicate, he said that windows were not infrequently left un-mended in the hope of getting payment from those who broke them, or, in the case of children, from their parents. In some cases the broken window indicated a dispute between landlord and tenant as to who was liable ...

Booth's interview of the incumbent at St Giles demonstrated that the parish and neighbourhood may have been subject to social 'decline' – but that they were still a good deal better relative to other districts of London he had visited. The St Giles living encapsulated this insight: it was, Booth noted, 'one of the plums of the English Church. It is what most are not: a real and substantial "living" with an income of £1600 a year, and a quite palatial vicarage'. The fortunate incumbent, a Reverend F. F. Kelly, was no better and no worse than other clergymen Booth had met in the course of his surveys: for he was 'as may be supposed [...] a worldly-minded man and he shows a strong taint of snobbery: but he is not a fool, he appears to have a kindly heart and the working of his parish seems to reach the general average of sufficiency.'

Booth's records reveal the delicately calibrated nature of Camberwell society at this moment. He learned from his informant that all social classes seemed to be evenly represented in the parish: the population was 'about 14,000 of whom roughly one-third are servant keeping, one-third middle-class people without servants and one-third working class.' But Kelly was well aware of the sands running in the time glass: the wealthy (the 'servant-keeping') class in the parish was decreasing, with a tendency for the vast houses on Camberwell Grove upon vacation to become tenanted – and as the 1891 census had already indicated, as like as not on a commercial rather than residential basis. Several of the houses were already practically factories for the timber merchants and other tradesmen. Equally, however, it was a sign of the state of affairs in the district that 'among the working classes there is no great poverty: nearly all are in work'.

Everywhere there were indicators of change. Whereas the well-heeled class inclined towards the Church of England and public worship, newcomers to Camberwell were rather less malleable. 'It has always been Mr Kelly's practice', noted Booth, 'on the arrival of a new tenant to find and ask whether a call from the vicar would be valued: in the past a refusal was almost unknown, now it is not uncommon.' As a result, the parish itself was no longer in rude health: a state of affairs that Kelly blamed in part on the prevalence of the bicycle in daily life: being too pleasurable to ride, it tended to lead people away from the paths of righteousness; and the clergyman reported that his own sons 'do not go to church at all, and his daughter not always'.

Religious observance in Camberwell, then, was not all it might have been – but education in the district was in excellent shape, featuring a grammar school for boys and (on the Grove itself) the Mary Datchelor Girls' School; while the church offered a primary education for a small fee. Kelly himself took a close interest in the local schools and was in no doubt as to the efficacy of his methods: 'he […] aims in his own teaching and that of the masters to foster intelligence with the result that the Inspector has declared the school to be "one mass of intelligence"; while his 'Sunday school Mr Kelly thinks is "quite unique" […] The result of this system is an increasing number of confirmations.' But Kelly was well aware of the limits of his knowledge and his mission – as he told Booth: '"You must not think the clergy know much about our parishes: we don't." In his case at all events I think this is true.' Camberwell was changing, then – but enough visible signs of its rural past had survived to draw Booth's attention. Along Camberwell Grove itself the houses tended now to attract prosperous 'servant-keeping' farmer tenants who were settling in the area ('they like to get a big house at a small rent') in numbers large enough to sustain their own church – though services, for many, were mostly excuses for a social occasion. Many of these farmers were 'dairymen': the remnants of the city's once-thriving business in milk provision. The arrival of the railways had decimated this local industry: milk could now be transported rapidly and hygienically over considerable distances

– meaning that suddenly 'town-fed cows provide but a drop in the great ocean of milk which is daily consumed by Londoners'.

As a result, those dairy businesses seeking to survive in London itself had to fight for business, work 'abnormally long hours' and operate 'the most perfect business model', if they wished to remain competitive. Such operations tended to be over-represented in areas like Camberwell: Booth's survey, for example, recorded one 'dairyman' resident at 161 Camberwell Grove: Richard Gillham employed five men in total, indicating the continuing economic relevance of dairying in this now-suburban neighbourhood – and Booth's display of more than a passing anthropological interest in this community, its origins and continuing relevance, indicates his awareness of the fact.

The presence of this indigenous agricultural business would be sustained well into the twentieth century: a dairy survived at 73 Camberwell Grove until 1978; and an advertisement from 1915 for Marshall's dairy at number 47 makes much of the fact that their resident cows were 'kept on premises at Camberwell Grove', adding that 'we deliver twice daily in Camberwell, Peckham, Dulwich, Herne Hill, Brixton and Kennington'. The dairymen of Camberwell Grove might have occupied an ambiguous position amid the great houses of the Grove – yet they signified a kind of virtuous industry that, in the eyes of many, continued to set the area apart from the now encompassing mass of London.

But this cherished sense of distinctiveness remained under pressure: Camberwell Grove was continuing its social slide and London its relentless encroachment. The census returns of 1901 and 1911 tracked what previous surveys had uncovered: the lower slopes of the Grove had become even more the preserve of trade and retailers; with middle-class professionals and residents of independent means pushed further up the hill than before. The homes on the heights continued to boast servants – but in diminishing numbers: the census of 1901 recorded 79 households (in general, those at the top of the Grove) with servants – a decrease from ten years previously; that of 1911 noted only 42 such households – a dramatic fall in the course of another decade – and a virtual disappearance of servants from those houses mid-way along the Grove.

A glance at the residents of one property highlights the changes that swept along the street. Number 70 was listed as a boarding house and home to 11 residents: they were predominantly youthful and of lower-middle-class backgrounds, with clerks and students featuring prominently. Strikingly, their places of birth varied wildly: they included Burma, New South Wales, Brazil and France. There was no mention of servants. Had Booth still been in the neighbourhood, he would doubtless have dressed the Grove once again in a mixture of yellow, red and pink – but with yellow now in evidence only at the very top of the street, and the pink much more dominant than before.

This sense of disintegration continued in the following decades: by the 1920s and 1930s, more of the vast Georgian houses on Camberwell Grove had been abandoned by the families that had once lived there, and functioned instead as boarding houses. One vivid piece of evidence of this perceived decline came courtesy of Hubert Llewellyn Smith's *New Survey of London* (1928–33): Llewellyn Smith had been an assistant of Booth, his survey conceived as a deliberate attempt to bring Booth's original conclusions up to date – and his maps reveal a Camberwell Grove now uniformly pink. This new diminished status would be yet further undermined by the poverty and social want brought by the Great Depression. Further evidence appeared in an article in a 1938 edition of the *South London Press*, focusing on the closure of a china shop that was one of the longest established businesses on the Grove. In the piece (which ran under the headline 'Little Old Lady Wants to Close her Shop'), Miss Chaston – the little old lady in question – explained that her parents had run the business before her, but now she wanted out – not merely because she had recently turned 80 years old, but also because the district was 'dropping'.

In the same period, steps were finally taken to check the growth of London: the Green Belt Act of 1938 enabled (though did not require) local authorities to acquire land as a buttress against excessive development – essentially, to throw a cordon of land around the outer limits of the metropolis; while the Town

and Country Planning Act of 1947 regularised for the first time
the concept of planning permission as a fundamental aspect of
the construction process. But by this point, Camberwell was
deep within the mass of London; and the trends and alterations
in the life of the city were rapidly registered here too. Crime, for
example, became more prominent: a series of reports in the
Times in the 1960s fingered residents on the Grove (including
Ronnie Biggs' escape driver) with links to organised crime and
cannabis smuggling gangs.

At the same time, the sub-division of the street's houses into
multiple units and boarding houses continued to gather pace –
not least as a result of stress caused by London's post-war
housing shortage and population increase. A certain variety of
family life – taking the form of large, tightly-knit units living
cheek by jowl as tenants in the imposing houses on the Grove
– became a prominent feature of the local landscape. The bene-
fits were clear: a family safety net mitigated need; and tight
family units helped to offset rising crime levels.

But the Rent Act of 1957 changed Camberwell Grove, as it
had Portland Road: the relaxation of rental controls made it
easier for landlords to rid their properties of such tenants; and
many properties, inhabited if run-down, were now vacated and
abandoned. Commercial interests also began making more
significant inroads into the fabric of the street: Kelly's Directory
– the Yellow Pages of the day – for 1951 lists a jostle of busi-

nesses, including a cleaner, a quantity surveyor, an electrical insulation establishment, a 'Rag, Metal and General Merchant', a chemist, a 'Bead representative' and a 'lubricating oil manufacturer'. The face of the street began to seem dishevelled and run-down: in many ways, these years were the nadir of the Grove's fortunes.

'A loftier view of life'

This was a pivotal point in the history of Camberwell Grove. Gentrification was underway: new arrivals – as in Barnsbury, predominantly youthful, professional and mildly left-leaning – were tempted here by the social mix, bohemian atmosphere and fine housing at bargain prices. They also appreciated the existing social mix ('you have to put up occasionally with your wheels going missing on the cars, but it's a small price to pay') although there were limits: 'having found a lot of people congenial to myself', says one long-standing resident, 'I don't think "well, I wish there were more coal miners or something".' In addition, appreciation of the architectural heritage of the Grove and its hinterland now began to cohere, as if for the first time. This was, of course, only one part of a greater wave of interest in the conservation of Georgian and Victorian architecture across the country in these years: the notorious demolition in

1962 of the splendid ceremonial arch that had greeted travellers at Euston station symbolized the extent to which this aspect of British cultural history was under threat – and one result was the passing, five years later, of the Civil Amenities Act, which provided for the establishment of conservation areas in districts of particular architectural significance.

Soon, the *Dulwich Villager* was remarking that 'like an enchanted Cinderella stepping from the rags of her former self, Camberwell Grove is being reborn'. These young newcomers were tackling daunting restoration projects: many of the houses were now in extreme dilapidation, afflicted by rising damp, wet and dry rot, leaking roofs, gutters and downpipes and shattered windows. 'I think,' recalls Jim Tanner, who with his wife Shirley moved into Camberwell Grove in the early winter of 1959, 'we thought: "it's a fine house, but my God, look at its state, it's in a shocking condition; we can't manage that".' In addition, their friends at the Architectural Press were horrified that they would consider moving south of the river: '"Nobody, nobody lives south of the river, you must be stark" […] you didn't go south of the river, you could never get a black cab over the bridges; they would drop you on the bridge and then you'd have to walk.' This was also an experience familiar to New Zealand novelist Janet Frame, who lived just off the Grove for three years from June 1959. Describing a visit to her London publisher, she noted his disdain for her address: '"Where are you living?" he asked, adding that he didn't care for his authors living in a waste land like Camberwell.'*

And the encounters between these newcomers and the existing residents not infrequently passed through a mutually mortifying prism of changing taste: one resident, the barrister, and novelist Campaspe Lloyd-Jacob, remembers leafleting the houses up and down the Grove and neighbouring Grove Lane in an attempt to acquire a property. She wanted a Georgian house with its light and harmonious proportions, she wanted its period detail intact – and at length she found a family who had lived on the street for 40 years, and who were now willing to sell.

> We wrote a note, I think it was about three or four lines long, I should have kept it, but I think essentially it said that we were looking for a house to buy in Camberwell, we'd had a house sale which had just fallen through, we had a buyer on our current house, we could move instantly and might you be interested in selling your house to us? If so, please phone this number. And we walked all the way up Camberwell Grove and down Grove Lane and around the area and put these notes through people's doors and a couple of people phoned me, but usually to say that somebody that they knew was selling their house, rather than that they wanted to sell their

---

* Janet Frame, *An Angel at My Table: An Autobiography* (London: Virago [1985], 2010), 480

house, but the owners of this house actually called me as I was going out of the garden gate and ushered me in and gave me tea and said that they would be very keen to sell this house to us. [...] That's how it happened. [...] I discovered later that it caused a certain amount of amusement and/or irritation, that we were spotted by the owners of these houses walking up and down Camberwell Grove staring at the windows and chatting and talking and shaking our heads or nodding our heads and walking up some, but not all garden paths. And I think that the people who didn't get a note through their doors felt a little bit irritated by the whole thing

Some of these early gentrifiers fulfilled the modern image of a tribe of deep-pocketed urban professionals. But not all: in 1961, artists David and Janet Hepher bought their house on Camberwell Grove for £2,600: the property had two sitting tenants, one of whom left at once and the other a couple of years later. Other newcomers followed, all attracted by the beauty of the houses on display – and prepared to invest a portion of their lives in restoring their own property; by now, indeed, there seemed to be a skip outside half the houses on the Grove. It was the beginning of an idea that would later become familiar: a grassroots organisation finding a voice and putting it to good use.

At the same time, many of the residents placed great emphasis upon the notion of the Grove as a place of great civility, an oasis in a rough, tough urban world. The QC Conrad Dehn moved into Camberwell Grove in 1978 – and remembers that 'when we bought the house, the vendors, while they were still the owners, gave a dinner party for us and our neighbours, so that we would get to know our neighbours before we moved in, which was an extraordinarily civilized thing to do. It made an enormous difference to feel when you get in a place [...] you've met the neighbours and can say "excuse me, where is this and how do I": you know, all that. [...] I think it doesn't happen often, but I do think it's a very civilized thing to do, and it happened here'. (It certainly wouldn't, Dehn adds, have happened in his previous street in Kensington.)

The presence of this new, youthful and middle-class community of residents now helped to propel the conservation debate forward; and a form of advocacy that would soon become familiar across Britain's cities – articulate, organised, educated – established itself in Camberwell. In 1970, the Camberwell Society was formed, its purpose to protect and conserve Camberwell's built environment against the kind of development that had lately taken place on the Grove. The families settling on the Grove represented in miniature the newly articulated vision of the Camberwell Society as a whole: the impetus – to restore and improve one's property and by implication the society within which one lived – was identical. Camberwell Grove became a conservation area in the same year – one of a growing number of such zones across London; and the direct result of application of this coherent form of pressure. The listing of individual houses on the Grove began shortly afterwards; and the original conservation area was extended in the 1980s.

The protection of Camberwell Grove's architectural heritage had been spurred by a local version of the Euston Arch debacle. At the end of the 1960s, development was planned that would alter fundamentally the face of the Grove, particularly on its eastern side. The local council – by this stage Southwark council, which had been formed in the 1965 reorganization of local government – proposed the development of a council estate on the eastern side of the Grove. The design of the Lettsom estate was similar to other developments across London in this period: it was set out as a series of 19 concrete blocks – and its construction was pushed through in the teeth of opposition from local residents. In Camberwell Grove opposition rallied around a useful symbol: for the construction of the Lettsom to proceed, terraces of (neglected) Victorian houses running from the Grove east towards Peckham would have to be torn down – a small number of the more than 70,000 houses demolished in London in the course of the 1960s and early 1970s.

The houses *were* torn down, and the Lettsom went ahead – although altered in form by the force of local opposition. Indeed, the relatively modest scale of the Lettsom buildings – none of them were more than four storeys in height, a very different proposition from the massive towers going up elsewhere in south London – points to the opposition that rallied at this point in Camberwell; and to its success in influencing the planning debate. In 1970, the planning brief for the development of the estate stated that:

> [T]he design for the development area should seek to maintain a residential facade to Camberwell Grove and the new dwellings should be in keeping with the height, scale and building lines of the existing buildings. Throughout the development area a medium-rise solution is preferred but if higher blocks are unavoidable they should not impinge on the skyline of Camberwell Grove.

The document noted – a little defensively, perhaps – that the scheme, and in particular its street's frontage on the Grove itself, 'has been designed to blend with the Georgian and Regency buildings nearby, and that the appearance will be much more in keeping with the general architectural pattern of Camberwell Grove than the old houses which it replaces. The facing bricks to be used will be chosen to harmonize with the stock brickwork of many of the existing buildings.' For all this ostensible sensitivity, however, the creation of the estate managed to crystallize opposition to further demolitions of existing buildings – and the Grove stands as an exemplar of a new emphasis on conservation.

The local newspaper cuttings of the period measure a local upsurge in interest: 'A Georgian Terrace may be Restored'; 'Georgian Houses Disappearing in Development Schemes'; 'Rescue Repaint Planned for Camberwell's Regency Terrace' and others, all charting the process now underway in parts of Camberwell.

The Lettsom estate itself reversed the residents' relationship with the street. Unlike the original Victorian houses, where the doors opened onto the street, the council house doors open onto the estate; the component buildings present only garden walls to Camberwell Grove itself. And so the Lettsom buildings share a Grove address with the imposing houses to the north and south – but its residents understandably interpret their relationship with the Grove rather differently. Social interaction has never been common; and the children of the Grove tend to enrol in public schools, while those of the Lettsom remain in the state sector. One Lettsom resident speculates about a possible alternate future, had the estate been built in the way first intended:

> If the doors had opened [onto the Grove] you would have had more people walking up and down Camberwell Grove [...] and it might have broken that cycle, that we thought the people that lived on Camberwell Grove were upper class – whereas if we had seen them more walking up and down and spoke to them in the mornings, it might have broken that cycle until we got older. Because it was only when you

started to grow up a little bit more that you realised they're just people like us ...

As the years passed, the restoration of houses on Camberwell Grove proceeded – but it was a long, drawn-out process. Not every property could be pounced on in the course of the 1960s and 1970s and lined up for gentrification (and some of them were so large as to be an impractical purchase in any case) – and by the 1980s, the prevailing dilapidation had become chronic. This was especially the case with the terrace of properties which anchored the southern end of the road, which had passed into the ownership of Southwark council. These properties, with

By the 1970s, the gentrification of the fraying Georgian and Regency houses on Camberwell Grove was well advanced. Skips became common sights outside recently purchased properties, as their new owners began the long process of restoration.

Today, the gentrification of Camberwell Grove is largely complete: the street is one of the most impressive residential areas in London – a fact reflected in spiralling property prices.

their grand staircases and period features had been listed, ensuring that they could not simply be bulldozed and replaced with
modern buildings. The council faced a dilemma.

This southern-end terrace had been constructed in 1841 –
and from that point had always hosted professional families:
lawyers, merchants and architects. The returns from the 1881
census captured an agreeable world along the terrace: 210
Camberwell Grove was home to Edward and Eleanor Margret-
son and their two children; he was an export merchant – and
the household included three servants. Up at 216, lived mother
and daughter Julia and Grace Hastie, who could also afford
three servants. Eight years later, Booth – unsurprisingly – zoned
the terrace as yellow.

By 1899, however, the terrace had slipped to red; servants
began to vanish and lodgers to appear – and by Llewellyn Smith's
map of 1926, the houses had slipped again, this time to pink. By
the 1930s, these substantial properties had been subdivided into
flats – and would stay this way in the decades to come. In the
course of 1956 and 1957, the houses were acquired under
compulsory purchase by the local authority, which intended to
increase its housing stock to provide homes for its tenants. The
terrace would likely have been demolished in due course – but the
listing of many of the properties on Camberwell Grove put paid
to that idea; and until the end of the 1970s, the houses remained
in council ownership – and in a state of chronic decay.

In 1981, Southwark decided to get rid of these listed properties: they had become albatrosses around the authority's neck, horrendously expensive to maintain, and impossible to adapt or modernise in their subdivided state. The council tenants were moved on – and rapidly the empty flats on the terrace were occupied by squatters. By 1983, a community had evolved which ran along communal and collective lines, with vegetable allotments and animal pens established in the overgrown back gardens. Conditions were not pleasant – but the system ran well enough for some years. Wires ran from house to house supplying electricity – one resident notes drily that 'the music was so loud it was vibrating the windows down at Number 19' – and other unorthodox methods were employed too, as a former squatter recalls:

I lived for a couple of grim years in a gigantic pile on Camberwell Grove, just round the corner from the top secret government listening station (easily identified by the large graffiti we used to place on local road signs reading 'This way to Top Secret Government Listening Station'). I became adept at tapping neighbours' gas and water supplies. At one point a resident eight houses down was supplying 40 squatters with power from the spur that ran the train layout in his garden shed. I think he had half a dozen Hornby Dublo models that, for the six months before they caught us, were drawing more power than the British Rail London to Manchester line.

In 1984 Southwark council – displaying the pragmatic reasoning that a decade before had guided events in Shoreditch – tried to resolve this situation by offering the squatters a deal: short-term tenancies of between 18 months and five years through the Hyde Housing Association. This offer generated a furious debate: many squatters, especially those influenced by anarchism and similar ideas, refused any form of cooperation with state authority. A leaflet circulated urging people to reject all deals and a meeting convened at 207 Camberwell Grove in November 1984 also urged the squatters' community to adopt this position.

In the end, though, the majority voted to accept the deal with Hyde; and in February 1985, people at numbers 201–218 Camberwell Grove were 'shortlifed' – that is, given indeterminate licences to remain, with no guarantee of rehousing, but free from immediate eviction. Unsurprisingly, the residents promptly formed a housing cooperative. In July 1985, other houses were taken to the High Court for eviction proceedings and by 1989–1990 many were evicted. Finally, in 1992, the council moved to divest itself of its holdings: four years later, the houses had been cleared – the last remaining council tenant was given £9,000 to move on – and sold to a private developer, with the stipulation that the houses would be restored and sold as private family dwellings. The wheel had turned full circle: the houses once classed as yellow by Booth had become yellow once more.

The character of Camberwell Grove as a whole continues to evolve – and to be tested and challenged. And in the process, the energy and ideals of the Camberwell Society and of the local community continue to be probed. The Society scored a victory in the mid-1980s, when it prevented the demolition of the Victorian railway station buildings at Denmark Hill – but a rather more grave challenge lay ahead, with a British Rail proposal to build a high-speed rail link through the area to the Channel Tunnel. The connections with the experience of Caledonian Road, of course, are clear – even if the Grove and the Cally share few other points of similarity.

In this case, British Rail had originally proposed running its link through south London and into Waterloo: 'the initial proposal,' remarks Conrad Dehn with masterful understatement, 'was that the line should go underneath Camberwell Grove, underneath all these houses, which needless to say the residents were not at all keen on'. A special pressure group was formed in the area – including members of the Society – and when a public meeting was at length convened, the local residents swept away the arguments of British Rail and its representatives. 'They did a very good job,' recalls Dehn, 'and argued sensibly and asked the right questions and so on; and they dropped the scheme, which was just as well. Because really, the idea of having a train going underneath your house was not attractive.' It was an example of energetic and articulate advocacy that that had become second-nature to many middle-class pressure groups.

The 1990s and the new century have seen Camberwell Grove, with its now extremely smart Georgian houses, continue its ascendancy. New development continues to be monitored by the Society, which – far from being a marginalized gaggle of disaffected local residents – is recognised by the authorities as a central feature of the local landscape and invited to contribute to planning discussions. One result of its influence is the second large-scale development on the Grove in the course of the last half-century: that of the former Mary Datchelor school on land sandwiched between the Grove and Grove Lane. The Datchelor school represented high Victorian confidence, its handsome red-brick main building an imposing fixture on the school since 1876, when it was opened by the charitable Datchelor Trust. The school itself closed in 1981, rather than go either private or comprehensive: the main school building was used by a charity, then snapped up by a developer and recreated as modern town-houses and apartments in 2010.

The redevelopment of the Datchelor site was overlaid with echoes of the past. The first plans for the site were drawn up in 2001: they envisaged a thoroughly modern development – and came up against considerable opposition. 'No-one was saying, "we don't want anything to happen",' recalls one member of the Camberwell Society. 'An empty, falling-apart ex-school

The Mary Datchelor grammar school, which opened its doors on the Grove in 1886 It closed in 1981, rather than go either public or comprehensive; latterly, the handsome building and schools grounds have been developed – after much delay and planning objections – as a large housing scheme.

building was of absolutely no use. [...] We wanted it to happen in a way that preserved what was good about the site'. The Society went on to block seven proposals in six years – for the most part on grounds of poor design and excessive density – before finally consenting to a much revised plan. Conrad Dehn was on the Society's committee at the time, and he notes: 'I think probably everybody benefitted. I think the council was quite good in listening to what we had to say, and I think in the end the builders realized that it was in their interests to build things that the residents were happy about. So it all worked out reasonably amicably.'

The land has since been transformed into a large-scale estate of approximately 60 new homes – including a terrace of pastiche-Georgian townhouses and several dozen apartments within the original structure of the main school building. 'Modern houses,' says one resident, 'with a slightly sort of ancient appearance, you know, so rather British' – although another resident, who would have preferred a modern design, refers to their 'Queen Anne front and Mary Anne behind [...] a sort of stage-set approach to life'. A bespoke bathroom now perches where the secretarial staff was once quartered; a master bedroom occupies the headmistress's office. This is an extremely prominent development – although it is questionable whether the mock-period facades of the Datchelor townhouses add much to the architectural quality of the Grove.

The development of the Datchelor site owes much of its final shape to the opinions and tastes of some of the local residents – and is certainly far removed from the Lettsom estate in form and social profile. Yet the two estates share certain characteristics. For one thing, both were designed to 'blend' with and be sensitive to the surrounding environment, though whether either development has been successful in these aims is a matter of personal opinion. Secondly, they represent aspects of the theme of re-use and re-imagining of space that runs through the entire history of Camberwell Grove. This theme of change has never been welcomed by all observers – and this too is a consistent note in the tale of the Grove – but it represents a reflection of an area in a state of perpetual flux.

The future shape of Camberwell Grove is more difficult to predict. The economic profile of the area is wealthy now – wealthier than it has been since its Georgian heyday, 200 years ago. The local population includes, as one resident notes, 'a large number of lawyers [...] artists, literary agents, architects and teachers of Byzantine art history [...] antique dealers, historians, poets and consultants on mysterious European matters, especially Bulgarian ones [...] it's quite a good mix'. But property on the Grove is now extremely expensive, with the great eighteenth-century houses fetching premium prices. Jim Tanner remarks that 'there's no way we could afford to live in the street now, we couldn't afford a flat in this street, let alone a house. We're a marooned little island of human beings, where most of the houses now are owned by people who could just take out the necessary million-pound mortgage or whatever and buy the house and just rip out everything and start again.'

And as the older generation of gentrifiers departs the scene, its properties are being occupied by a new caste of occupants with little in common with the liberal and vaguely leftish aristocracy of the past. In the past, says Tanner, the street was 'dominated by people who had a loftier view of life, and there was a sense of excitement, that there were so many fine old buildings around; we should recognize this and help to protect them; we wanted to do all sorts of things. [...] We were a sort of informal group. We all knew each other, we all had children of about the same age. The children played in the street ...' Nostalgia can be powerful and heady – yet it is difficult to imagine a hedge fund manager doing what a member of the Camberwell Society does on a regular basis: scrubbing off graffiti manually as it appears around the district.

The pleasures and atmosphere of Camberwell continue, in the eyes of many, to be distinctive. One member of the Camberwell Society puts it in singular terms: 'It has a feeling of tolerance and it's a place where you can feel that you can really wear whatever you like as you walk along the street [...] You can walk along the street wearing a really extraordinary hat and no-one is going to frown at you or think the worse of you.

And they may think you're an outpatient from the Maudsley [the nearby psychiatric hospital]. And there are a number of outpatients from the Maudsley who walk along the street wearing remarkable things, and we like that too.'

And in the meantime, the fight to preserve the Grove's texture (its architectural texture in particular) brings its own dangers – for the process of local and national advocacy in conserving and listing such areas as the Grove carries the risk of petrification. After all, the experience of the Grove has been of continual change and alteration decade by decade – now slumping into decay and fragmentation, now restored to within an inch of its life. This is a street that has seen off the agents of destruction in their myriad guises – the wrecking balls and the bulldozers, the ministrations of local and of central authority, of railway companies and of planners. It has emerged with its gracious lines and its spectacular urban setting not only intact, but enhanced as a result of these layers of dramatic experiences. It would be ironic and dismaying if the great houses of Camberwell Grove began, two centuries into their dramatic history, to fossilize into a form that pays no heed to a sharp-edged and remarkable past.

Perhaps the texture of life and diversity of views on this splendid street will ensure its continuing evolution. One resident, living in one of the grandest houses on the mid-section of the street, mourns the fact that few members of the next generation will have the opportunity afforded him to buy a house and restore it with love: '[T]here's no longer any area of London where someone starting out on their career, artistic or otherwise, can walk into a street and take their pick of any empty house needing tender, loving care, buy reasonably and live there for many years to come. I don't think that's life now.'

But for a neighbour living near the top of the hill, the houses have separate lives, a separate existence of their own: they were there before their present custodians arrived – and they will still be there when these present custodians are gone. It is a bracing attitude, and one that sets the future of Camberwell Grove in a spacious context:

> I'm conscious of the fact that it is a very special house and that we are kind of here temporarily – that in a way, the house will continue. There will be people who live here after us. There were people who lived here before us. It's quite interesting that we're quite often defined as being the people who live in this house – so that the house is almost kind of bigger than we are. [...] We become the irrelevance; the house is actually what people are really interested in.

INDEX

Note: page numbers in **bold** refer to illustrations.

ACKNOWLEDGEMENTS

Joseph Bullman wishes to thank the following: Assistant Producers Tom Swingler and Simon Smith. Jaime Taylor, Assistant Producer and Research Co-ordinator for the book, George Andrews, Henry Mayhew and Tim and Penny Hicks on Portland Road. Nicholas Taylor, John Price and John and Pauline Churchill in Deptford. Emma Willis, Executive Producer at the BBC. Executive Producer Simon Ford. Sue Donnelly at the Booth Archive at the London School of Economics. Jane Nicholson, Katie Bailiff and Sue Collins and at Century Films.

Neil Hegarty wishes to thank the following: "Thanks to my family; to Marie Gethins and Catherine Toal; and to Albert DePetrillo, Joe Cottington and Caroline McArthur at BBC Books. Thanks also to the team at Century: in particular to Brian Hill, Tom Swingler and Simon Smith for conducted tours of Bermondsey, Islington and Shoreditch; and Sue Collins for invaluable assistance throughout."

Brian Hill wishes to thank the following: Simon Smith, Conor Maloney Hill and the residents of Reverdy Road.

PICTURE CREDITS

BBC Books would like to thank the following individuals and organisations for providing photographs and for permission to reproduce copyright material. While every effort has been made to trace and acknowledge copyright holders, we would like to apologise should there be any errors or omissions.

SSPL via Getty Images 27, 201; Getty Images 62, 89, 193; Popperfoto/Getty Images 63; Brian Hill 47; Southwark Local History Library and Archive 54; City of London, London Metropolitan Archives 78, 175, 211, 326; Wesleyan Mission Annual 108; Architectural Press Archive/RIBA Library Photographs Collection 127, 273; Geoffrey Taunton/Alamy 133; World History Archive/Alamy 148; Andrew Holt/Alamy 231; Pictorial Press/Alamy 263; Mike Booth/Alamy 285; Mary Evans Picture Library/Alamy 296; Alan King engraving/Alamy 309; Caruthers Fine Pictures 327; Greg Balfour Evans/Alamy 333; London Collection, courtesy of Bishopsgate Institute 154; Joan Rose 178 (top and bottom); Museum of London 200; Geoffrey White/Associated Newspapers/Rex Features 226; Mary Evans Picture Library 301

PLATE SECTIONS
Section 1: Getty Time & Life Pictures/Getty 1; Southwark local history library and archive 2 (top); City of London, London Metropolitan Archives 2 (bottom); Wellbeloved family 3 (top); Lady Lever Art Gallery, National Museums Liverpool/The Bridgeman Art Library 3 (bottom); Minnie Finklestein 4 (top); Julian Stapleton 4 (bottom); Islington Local History Centre 5 (top and bottom); Mary Evans Picture Library/Roger Mayne 6, 7 (top); Southwark Local History Library and Archive 7 (bottom); Amoret Tanner/Alamy 8. Section 2: Mary Evans Picture Library/The National Archives, London 1 (top); Getty 2 (top and bottom); City of London, London Metropolitan Archives 3 (left); Tony Ray-Jones/RIBA Library Photographs Collection 3 (right); SUNSET/Rex Features 4 (top); Clive Dixon/Rex Features 4 (bottom); Hulton-Deutsch Collection/Corbis 5 (top); Getty 5 (bottom); Jessop family 6 (top); Mary Evans Picture Library/Roger Mayne 6 (bottom); Jeremy Selwyn/Associated Newspapers/Rex Features 7 (top); Londonstills.com/Alamy 7 (bottom).